LEGENDARY LOCALS

OF

LAKE FOREST

ILLINOIS

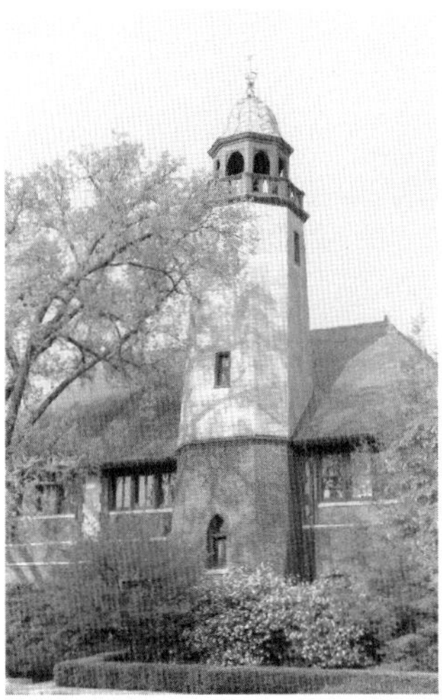

I0805747

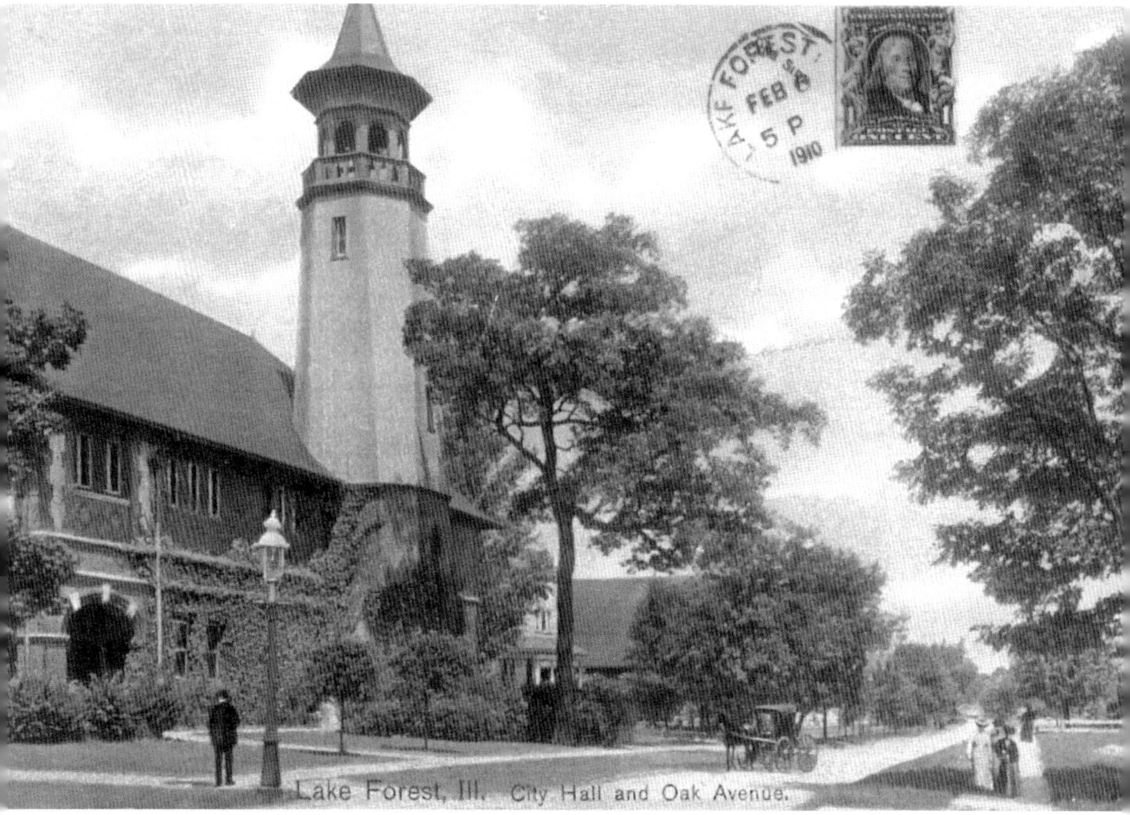

City Hall, Early 1900s
Seen from the southeast is the original tower roof on city hall, which was designed by Frost & Granger and opened in 1899. The architects are profiled in this book. The building's style is English Arts and Crafts as applied in town planning in the period. (Courtesy of City of Lake Forest.)

Page 1: City Hall, Current Structure
Pictured from the east is the current city hall structure, housing city offices and the city council chambers. The building includes the second, 20th-century tower roof. (Courtesy of Kerri Sherman.)

LEGENDARY LOCALS

OF

LAKE FOREST

ILLINOIS

SUSAN L. KELSEY AND ARTHUR H. MILLER

LEGENDARY LOCALS

ISBN 978-1-4671-0214-8

Legendary Locals is an imprint of Arcadia Publishing
Charleston, South Carolina

Printed in the United States of America

Library of Congress Control Number: 2015933478

For all general information, please contact Arcadia Publishing:
Telephone 843-853-2070
Fax 843-853-0044
E-mail sales@arcadiapublishing.com
For customer service and orders:
Toll-Free 1-888-313-2665

Visit us on the Internet at www.arcadiapublishing.com

Dedication

Dedicated to lifelong Lake Forest resident and local historian Shirley MacDonald Paddock in recognition of her outstanding contributions to local history through her collecting, promoting, displaying, researching, writing, and unselfish sharing.

On the Front Cover: Clockwise from top left:
Lake Forest College women, with Anna Farwell (standing, second from right) (Courtesy of Lake Forest–Lake Bluff Historical Society; see page 100), Lake Forest College trustee Francis C. Farwell II with two daughters of Calvin Durand (Courtesy of Lake Forest College Donnelley and Lee Library Archives and Special Collections; see page 89), Sylvia Shaw Judson Haskins, sculptor (Courtesy of Lake Forest College Donnelley and Lee Library Archives and Special Collections; see page 108), Lake Forest Garden Club friends at Triangle Park (Courtesy of Lake Forest Garden Club Archives, Lake Forest College Donnelley and Lee Library Archives and Special Collections; see page 32), a reverend and his daughter (Courtesy of Lake Forest College Donnelley and Lee Library Archives and Special Collections; see page 60), an architect (Courtesy of Lake Forest College Donnelley and Lee Library Archives and Special Collections; see page 37), Capt. James Lovell, astronaut (Courtesy of Lake Forest College; see page 71), Corinne Wood, lieutenant governor (Courtesy of Corrine Wood; see page 95), Lolita Armour Mitchell and John Mitchell Jr. (Courtesy of Lake Forest College Donnelley and Lee Library Archives and Special Collections).

On the Back Cover: From left to right:
R. Douglas Stuart (standing), executive and ambassador, and Dr. Ernest Johnson (far left), college president (Courtesy of Louis E. Laflin Jr. Collection, Lake Forest College Donnelley and Lee Library Archives and Special Collections, see page 89), livery driver Samuel Dent (center) at the train station. (Courtesy of Lake Forest–Lake Bluff Historical Society; see page 67).

CONTENTS

and accustomed to hard work for long hours. Others who had worked in gardens in cold and windy conditions, such as Scotland, Cornwall, Scandinavia, and Switzerland, breathed life into the narrow plant palette in the region, which saw extremes of cold winters and hot, dry summers. By the 20th century, a second wave of specialists was needed to staff new seasonal estates around the Onwentsia Club. The first wave had been centered on schools, the college, and year-round residents. After 1930, staffs shrank with the general economic downturn. Old retainers became experts in many fields, people who could drive, be handy, and garden—or, in the case of women, cook, launder, and clean. This only made the work more demanding and more valued by their grateful employers. Many of the descendants of these support-community specialists stay in touch with Lake Foresters, and a few still live in or near Lake Forest.

This book's thumbnail portraits aim to tell the story of these diverse and specialized individuals, who have lived together here at one time or another, at least for the first century or so of the town's history. Today, many who support these residential establishments live elsewhere, and former townspeople's neighborhoods have been gentrified for professional and managerial families—including families of East and South Asian origins.

Lake Forest stands as a distinct culture, given its atypical local heritage and the larger-than-life stories of notable financial and industrial leaders, scholars, artists, philanthropists, media pioneers, and even an Olympic swimmer. This culture has been nurtured by over a century and a half of midcontinental innovation in many areas, from business to the arts, from social betterment to individual and team achievement. Its early-20th-century story was epitomized in F. Scott Fitzgerald's *The Great Gatsby*, set on the East Coast but derived from personalities and situations found on the upper North Shore of Chicago. Local architecture and garden design have set the pace for over a century in the United States and beyond, making waves as well at London's Chelsea Flower Show. In education, Lake Forest has nurtured achievement, its alumni helping to mold Chicago as did Lake Forest Academy graduate Clyde Carr, who, with Charles D. Norton, Edward H. Bennett, T.E. Donnelley, and Evanston's Daniel Burnham, conceived, created, and implemented the 1909 *Plan of Chicago*.

Lake Forest remains unique, and the stories of those who have been notable deserve to be known better locally, within the larger Chicago area, and beyond. Its leaders in so many fields continue to shape the world around them and to maintain their town as a singularly special place.

CHAPTER ONE

Chicago Business Leaders

The first chapter of this book offers profiles of Chicago train-commuting business leaders who have lived in Lake Forest. In the early years, these men of affairs made their homes year-round in Presbyterian Church–centered, dry Lake Forest, and their children attended local schools, away from the dangers and temptations of the city. The early Presbyterian businessmen had been pioneers, most notably D.R. Holt (*LFEPC*), a New Englander who began in the fur trade at Mackinac and then scouted out and secured a lumber concession at Oconto, Wisconsin, on Green Bay. Based in Chicago, his lumberyard had the first boatload shipped on the Illinois & Michigan Canal, in 1848. By 1860, a family man and strict Presbyterian, Holt wanted his children raised away from the already lurid and menacing city. His wife, Ellen Hubbard, was a sister-in-law of Gurdon Saltonstall Hubbard, also in the fur trade and, in the 1820s and 1830s, a pioneer Chicago businessman. By the late 1860s and early 1870s, the Farwell brothers, John V. and Charles B., of New England descent, had built houses for their young families near each other on East Deerpath Road. In the 1880s, these entrepreneurs traded with the cash-starved state of Texas, giving it a new capitol building in Austin, completed in Vermont marble and with ink in the ink wells, in exchange for three million acres of surplus land in the panhandle of Texas—the legendary XIT Ranch.

In the mid-1890s, a new generation of city businessmen began commuting seasonally, especially on weekends between April and late October. Their Chicago offices closed on Saturday afternoons so that they could get outside and exercise in the fresh air for a half day, playing sports like golf, tennis, and polo. Temperance prevailed, and Sundays continued to be dedicated to quiet Sabbath pursuits, at least until the World War I era. By the 1920s and 1930s, the sporty set was joining the 19th-century families with new homes, often for living in Lake Forest year-round, and lifestyles veered toward the post-Puritan.

After World War II especially, businessmen who moved to Lake Forest built smaller homes, scaled closer to those of the support community neighborhoods, but in new areas—Northmoor, between Sheridan Road and South Park, south of Westleigh Road, and east of the Skokie River; on the Lasker estate in west Lake Forest; and west of Waukegan Road on the north side of the extended Deerpath Road. Also, many more tended to work for Lake County and North Shore corporations—on the south, Allstate and Kraft in the Northbrook area, and on the north, Abbott, Outboard Marine, Motorola, and Johns Manville in the North Chicago and Waukegan area. These middle managers and professionals (the latter especially at Abbott) now drove to work, and the one-car garages of the prewar railroad commuters were replaced by two-car garages; one car was used for commuting to work, the other for driving around town during the day.

What each of these generations of business managers and leaders and their families had in common was extraordinary vision for the possibilities of the Chicago area for growth and prosperity. These visionaries included John V. Farwell, who, in the mid-1850s, built a huge warehouse. He was ridiculed by his commercial peers for taking such a big risk. But only his firm would gather and stage great quantities of uniforms to service the needs of Civil War troops. Marvin Hughitt by the 1870s could project on the Northwest a vast rail network, the Chicago & North Western Railway, which he oversaw until his death in 1928. Banker's son Byron Laflin Smith could see the help needed by successful first-generation Chicagoans who wanted to assure the stable fortunes of their heirs, and so in 1889 he founded his Northern Trust Company.

Many Lake Forest–linked Chicago businessmen were innovators in communications and media. The telegraph was the first electronic technology, and a couple of generations of Chicagoans exploited this hard-wired transmission capability. William Henry Smith, living in Lake Forest by 1875, was the head of the Western Associated Press, a news service. It merged into the Associated Press, which he then ran. *Chicago Tribune* publisher Joseph Medill's grandsons Robert R. McCormick and Joseph Medill Patterson were part of the local Onwentsia set, McCormick playing polo in the early 1910s before moving to Wheaton and Joseph owning an estate in what is now Vernon Hills. In 1919, Joseph founded the *New York Daily News* for the Tribune Company. It would be the 20th century's top circulating newspaper and the first US tabloid. The cousins shared news by wire, then innovatively added photographs. They had their own news syndicate in the 1920s.

A couple of 20th-century chemists come to mind as scientifically trained technologists whose discoveries made them rainmakers for their companies. The first—one of the Chicago Onwentsia members—was William Burton (1865–1954), who earned his doctorate of philosophy from Johns Hopkins in 1889. At the turn of the last century, he was working for Standard Oil and invented at Whiting, Indiana, the first thermal cracking method for refining gasoline, doubling the usable fuel yield from crude oil. By 1918, he was president of Standard Oil of Indiana, a member of Onwentsia, and had built a summer place at 100 North Sheridan Road. This became the home, in 1946, of the Gardner Browns, Elizabeth Brown being a granddaughter of Byron L. Smith. The Browns' sons William and Malcolm donated the house in 1998 to Lake Forest College to be its president's house.

The other game-changing chemist was Ernest Volwiler (1893–1992), hired by Wallace Abbott after earning his doctorate of philosophy from the University of Illinois in 1917. Volwiler helped develop the anesthesia medications Nembutal and Pentothal. By 1933, he was vice president for research; in World War II, he helped Abbott bring penicillin to market. He served as Abbott's president (1950–1958) and chair (1958–1959). He served as board chair at Lake Forest College, and he and his wife built a Jerome Cerny–designed home on Lake Road, near the beach entrance. In his 90s, he was still active locally and served communion at the Presbyterian church.

Many such builders and risk takers, nevertheless, crashed and burned financially; some disappeared along the way, beyond our purview. The earliest example was Sylvester Lind (*LFEPC*), whose booming lumber business was lost in the 1857 panic, soon after he had pledged $100,000 for starting up Lake Forest's umbrella educational institution. By 1863, he finally lost it all; the college-level program closed, and the Chicago-based medical school was left on its own—though, by the 1880s, it was Northwestern's. He rebuilt his fortune, only to lose it again in the 1871 Chicago Fire. Through it all, he was four times mayor and a solid rock in the community and the Presbyterian church, helping to bring to Lake Forest Dr. James G.K. McClure (*LFEPC*) in 1881—a major step in the town's advancement during the next half-century.

A second unlucky risk taker was meatpacker J. Ogden Armour. The second-wealthiest man in the nation in the 1910s, he became functionally penniless by 1923 and died alone abroad in 1927. His is truly an epic, legendary tale of great reward (his Mellody Farm in Lake Forest), gargantuan risk, and a negative result.

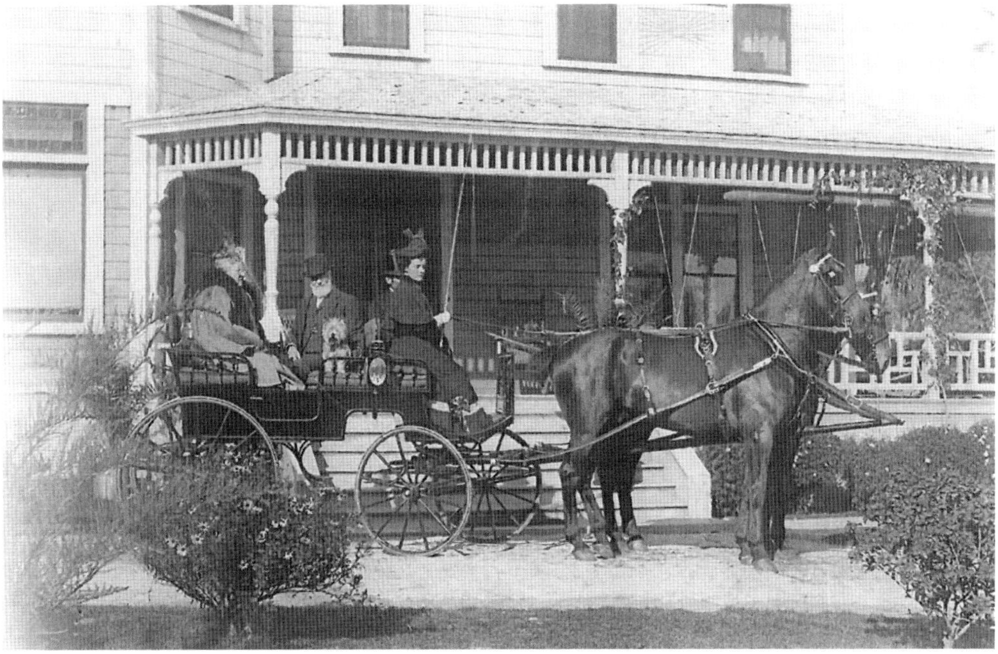

Henry Clay Durand (1827–1901)

Henry Durand, shown here center, with his wife Emma Burdsall Durand, left, and his daughter, Daisy, right, came to Chicago from Upstate New York and Milwaukee in 1851 and entered the wholesale grocery trade there. He and his family moved to town in 1875 with siblings Joseph and Calvin (page 89, bottom), both of who served as mayor (1886–1888 and 1891–1895, respectively). Henry chaired the Presbyterian church building committee in 1886–1887 and donated Lake Forest College's Durand Institute (1892) and Lois Hall (1899). (LFCLASC.)

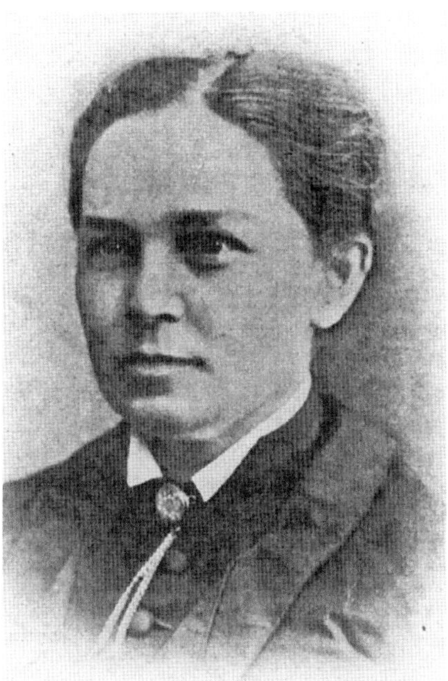

Helen Culver (1832–1925)

In 1900, Culver developed the first great estate west of Waukegan Road, Rookwood. Her house is now located on Ashlawn Drive. She had taken over the operations of her aging uncle Charles Hull's real estate empire—becoming probably Chicago's first great businesswoman. In 1889, she rented the 1850s Hull mansion on Halsted Street to Jane Addams for Hull House, the social settlement that became epic and had a national impact. (University of Chicago.)

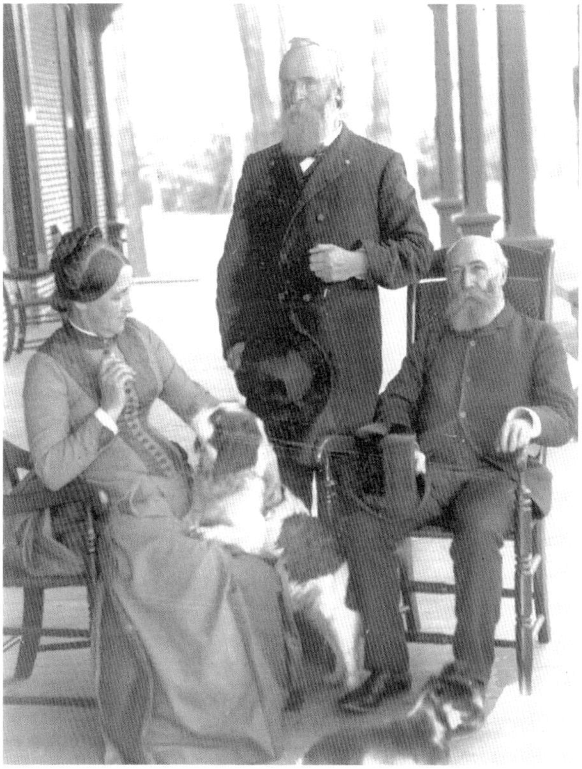

William Henry Smith (1833–1896)

Pioneer electronic journalist, historian, and politician W.H. Smith built two homes in Lake Forest, one in 1875 on Lake Road and Spring Lane (since demolished) and Lost Rock in 1894 on Green Bay Road, now Pembroke Lane. With C.B. Farwell, he played a key role in the 1876 election of R.B. Hayes as president; he is pictured, right, with Lucy and Rutherford B. Hayes. (SMP and Hayes Library.)

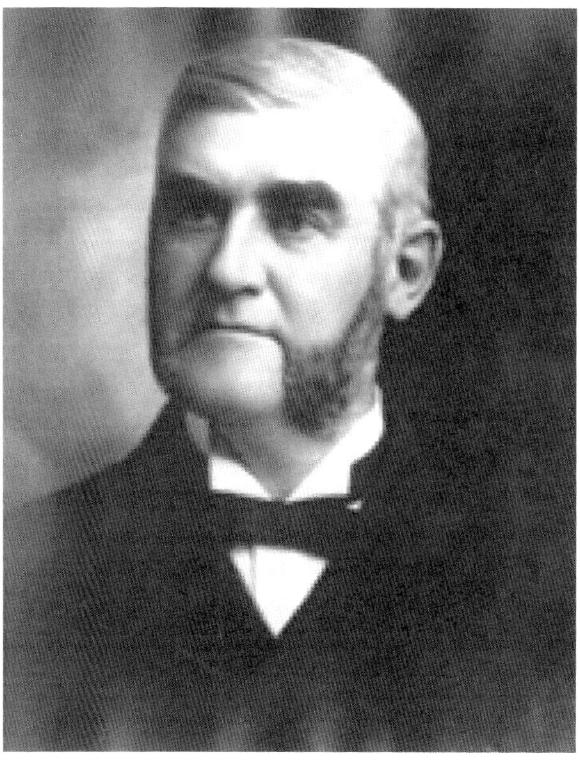

Marvin Hughitt (1837–1938)

A seasonal resident by the 1880s, Marvin Hughitt built the Chicago & North Western Railway (C&NW), now part of the Union Pacific. Born in Upstate New York, Hughitt began as a telegrapher, soon joining the Illinois Central to organize supplies going south in the Civil War. By 1872, he was with the C&NW, and by 1887, he was its president, serving until his death. (LFCLASC.)

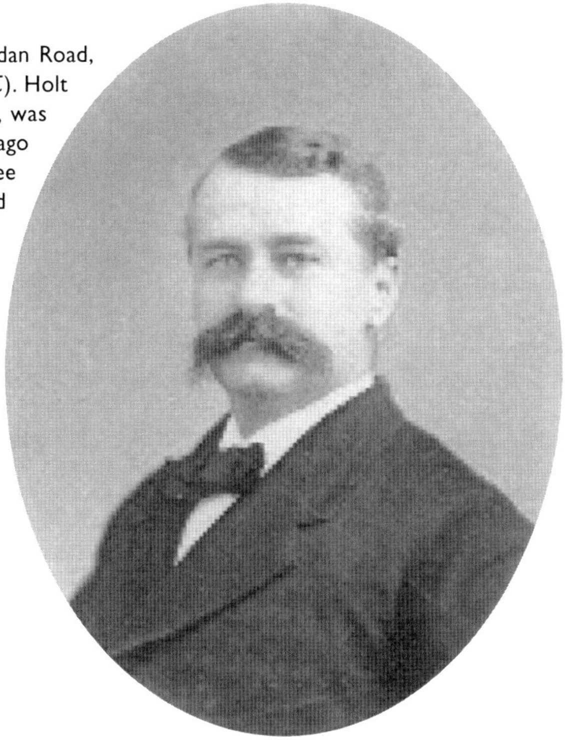

Charles S. Holt (1855–1918)
Holt grew up in town, at 570 North Sheridan Road, the home built by his parents in 1860 (*LFEPC*). Holt went into a Chicago law firm that, by 1918, was Holt, Cutting & Sidley—still a leading Chicago firm. He and Camilla McPherson had three children; a son, McPherson Holt, later lived in Lake Forest, as well. Charles Holt was an active Presbyterian leader and church organist. (LFCLASC.)

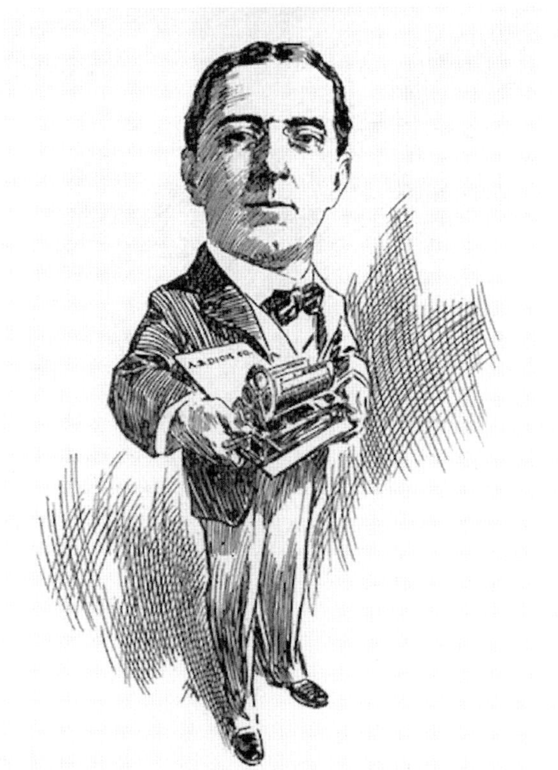

Albert Blake Dick (1856–1934)
The A.B. Dick Company developed and marketed the Mimeograph machine and dominated small-scale printing through the middle of the 20th century. By the early 20th century, Albert Dick was founding a dynasty in Lake Forest from his Westmoreland estate on West Deerpath Road. His son A.B. Dick Jr. led in starting Lake Forest Hospital on family-donated land in 1942 and also served as mayor (1928–1931). Descendants include locals John Dick and Madeleine B. Dugan. (Arthur Miller.)

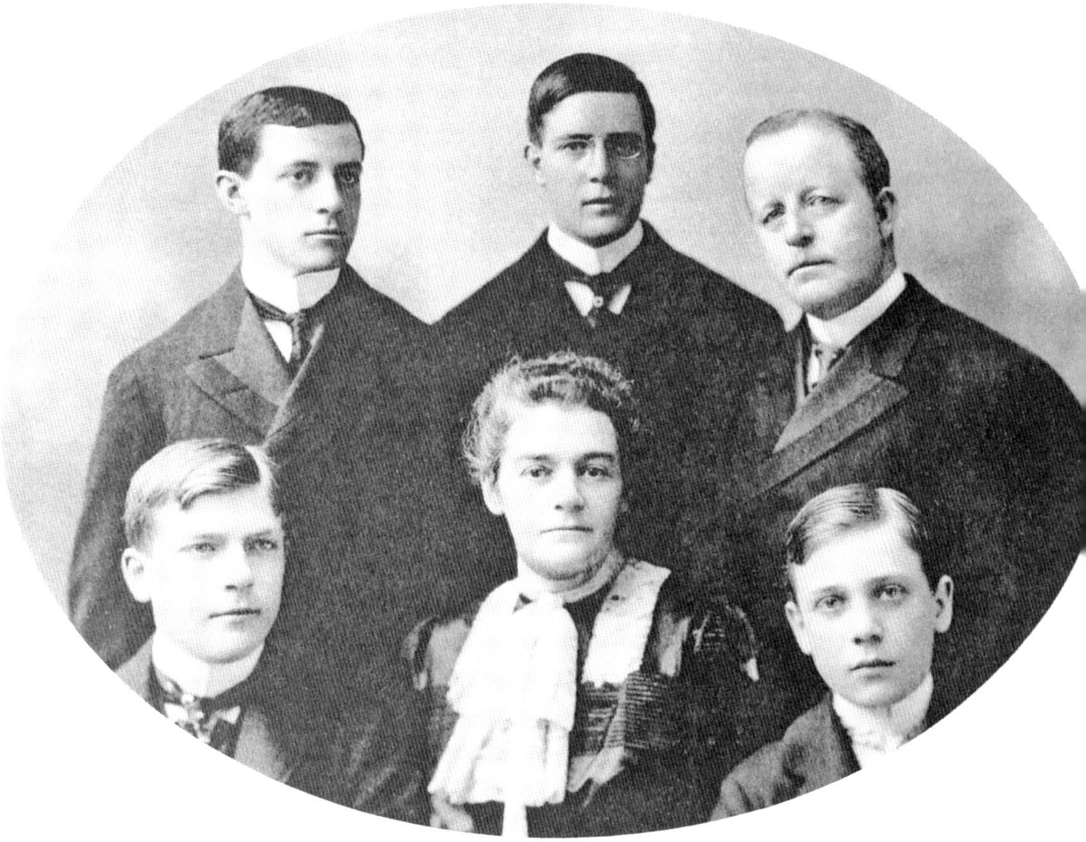

Byron Laflin Smith (1853–1914)

Northern Trust's 1889 founder, Smith was a second-generation Chicagoan whose 1880s estate in Lake Forest reached from the lake to Sheridan Road. It was focused at the point where the otherwise straight Lake Road bows westward, just south of its intersection with Woodland Road. This bump in the line allowed for less crowding of the mid-1890s Briar Hall estate house and immediate grounds, designed by architects Holabird & Roche and demolished in the middle of the 20th century. Byron Smith married Carrie Stone in 1876, and the couple had four boys, Solomon A. II, Walter, Harold C., and Bruce. Byron had founded Northern Trust to safeguard the substantial estates of descendants of successful early Chicagoans, like his own father, gunpowder maker turned banker Solomon A. Smith (1815–1879). After Byron's death in 1914, his estate left eldest son Solomon as president of Northern Trust, Walter the manager of the estate's complexities, and Harold the manager of fledgling Illinois Tool Works. (Bruce had moved away from Chicago and was not close to the family.)

Solomon A. Smith II and his wife, notable children's author Fredrika Shumway Smith, had sons Solomon B. and Edward B. Smith. Both became president and chairman of Northern Trust. They lived in Lake Forest, as does Edward's son in 2015, E.B. Smith Jr. Byron's son Harold C. married Emily Birnie, and they were the parents of Harold B. and three daughters, Elizabeth (Brown), Anne (Waud), and Joan (Hamill). Anne's descendants, David Waud and Reeve Waud, have been active residents in town, and her husband, Morrison Waud (pages 78 and 80), and son Cornelius "Ron" Waud both served as mayor (1957–1960 and 1996–1999, respectively). Elizabeth's son William Brown is a part-time local resident and a trustee of Lake Forest College, a position Byron held a century earlier (1896–1902).

Byron L. Smith is pictured here with his family. They are, from left to right, (seated) Harold (third son), Carrie Stone Smith, and Bruce (fourth); (standing) Solomon A. (eldest), Walter (second), and Byron L. Smith. (Briar Hall, LLC.)

Louis Franklin Swift (1861–1937)

Louis F. Swift, successful son of the brilliant meatpacker Gustavus Swift, built his estate house, Westleigh (since demolished), in Lake Forest in 1899 and its surviving 1916 masonry wing, designed by architect Howard Shaw's firm. He established a Swift beachhead that continues today with many Swift descendants and relations. The future British king Edward VIII (center) visited in 1924. His host, Swift, is on the left. (LF-LBHS.)

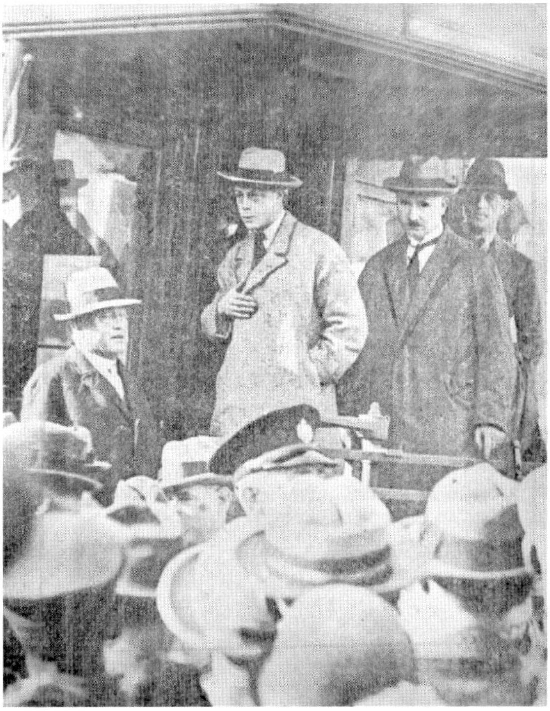

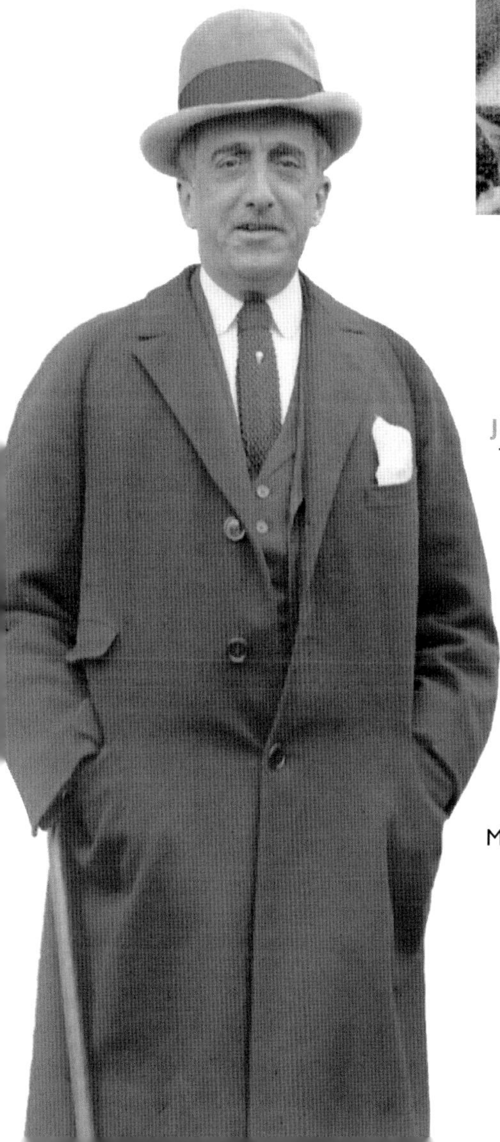

J. Ogden Armour (1863–1927)

The son of meatpacker Philip Danforth Armour, young Jonathan attended Yale and took over the business in 1901, having married Lola "Lolita" Sheldon in 1892. The couple's Mellody Farm, a 1,000-acre estate in west Lake Forest, was created between 1904 and 1910. The business grew from $200 million to $1 billion annually in sales but declined sharply after World War I, with J. Ogden Armour losing his fortune and estate by 1923. His family, though, regained their wealth by 1930, cashing in a penny stock he had bought in the 1910s. Armour's daughter, Lolita Armour Mitchell, appears in a wedding photograph on the front cover, along with her husband, John Mitchell Jr. (DF.)

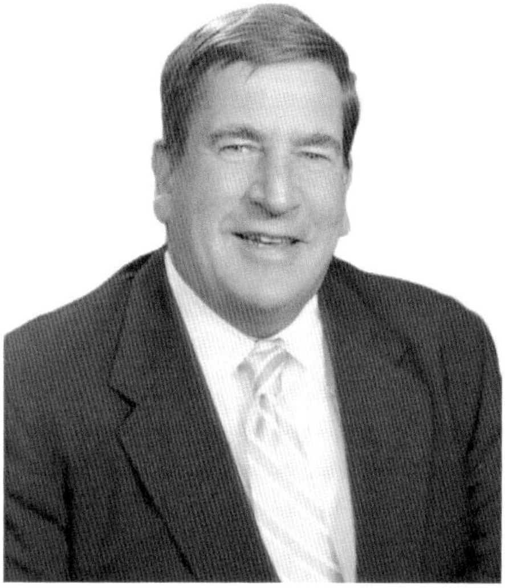

Edward Joseph Wehmer

Ed Wehmer served as founding president of Lake Forest Bank & Trust Co. from 1991 to 1998, launched the Wintrust holding company for local banks in suburbs in 1996, and is now its chief executive officer. Wintrust, headquartered in a northwest suburb, is Chicago's second-largest area-owned banking institution, after Northern Trust. Born in Kenilworth, Wehmer attended Loyola Academy and Georgetown, then worked in accounting at Ernst & Young before going into banking. (Wintrust.)

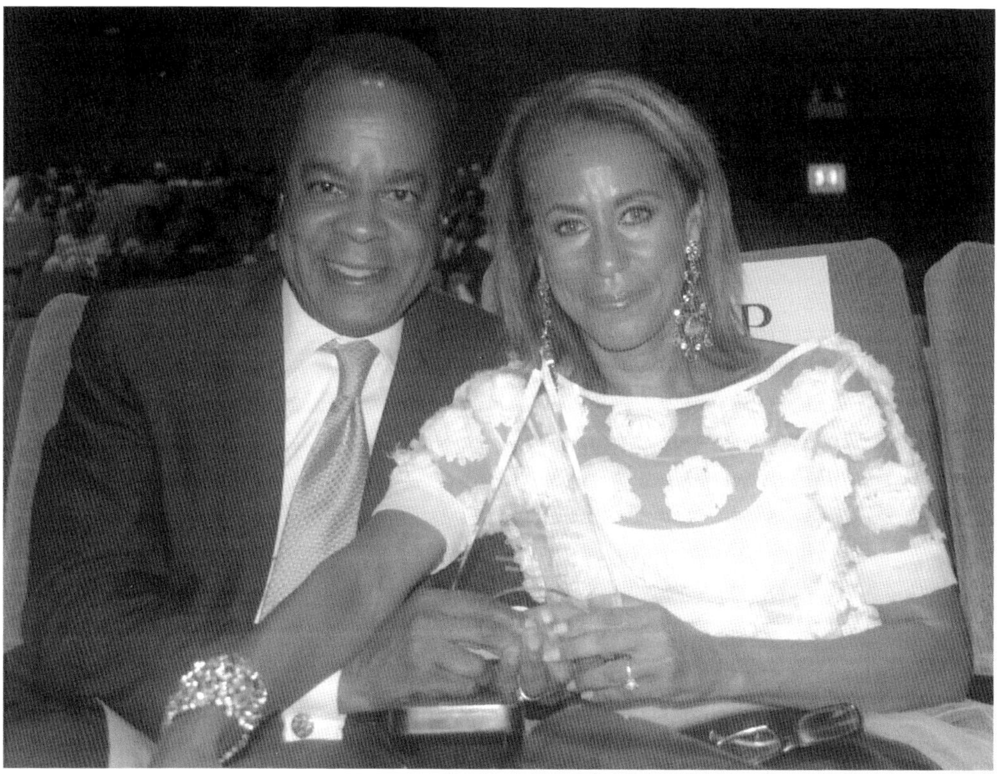

Quintin E. Primo III and Diane Primo

For a decade, Quintin and Diane Primo, both Harvard MBAs, have owned the historic McLaughlin house on Laurel Avenue. Quintin Primo leads Capri Capital Partners, LLC, a real estate investment management firm with over $4 billion in assets. Diane Primo, a Smith graduate, runs her own boutique marketing consulting firm. They were honored in 2012 for their community leadership, epitomized by the Primo Center for Women and Children. (*Social Life Chicago*.)

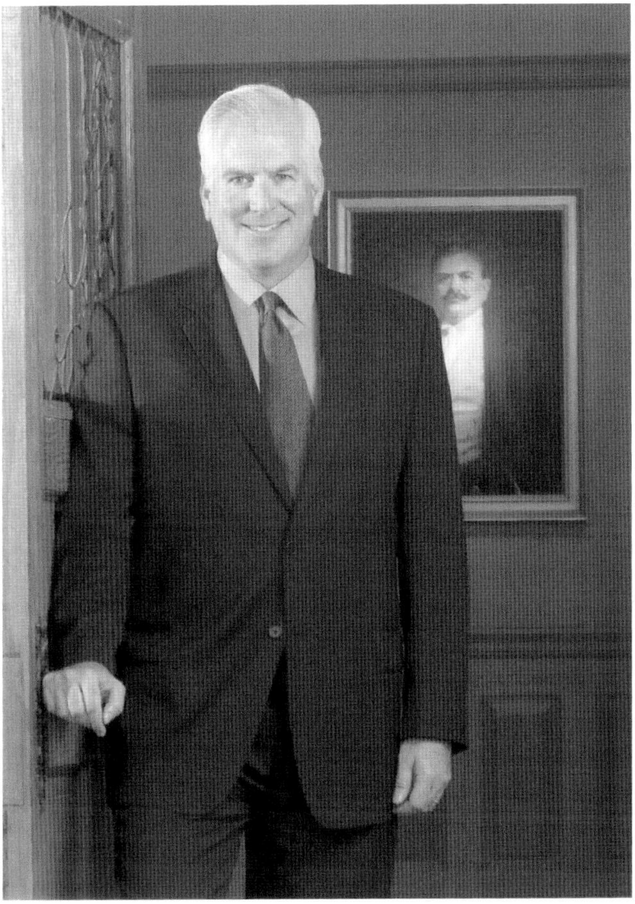

Miles D. White

Nearby Abbott Laboratories was one of the builders of Lake Forest, with generations of Abbott executives among its residents and leaders, such as chemist and chief executive Ernest Volwiler (1893–1992). In this generation, Miles White has been a key builder of both the company and the city.

White joined Abbott in 1984 after earning bachelor's and master's degrees from Stanford University and launching his career with the powerhouse consulting firm McKinsey & Co. He and his wife, Kim, settled in Lake Forest when he became head of Abbott's global diagnostics business in 1994. He became the company's chairman and chief executive officer five years later. In this role, White has transformed Abbott, while creating two of the Chicago area's largest companies, AbbVie and Hospira, from legacy Abbott businesses. As of 2015, the value of the three Abbott-based companies after White took over in 1999 has increased almost sixfold, with combined market capitalization of more than $190 billion.

White focused on increasing Abbott's innovation, accelerating its growth, adding new businesses, creating others, and expanding around the world. In the process, Abbott has thrice been voted the most admired company in its industry by *Fortune* magazine, has been named a leading global citizen on the Dow Jones Sustainability Index for 10 consecutive years, and has repeatedly been named among the world's best dealmakers and leading employers. These achievements have led *Barron's* magazine to name White one of the world's 30 best chief executive officers for seven consecutive years as of 2015.

A builder of institutions, White has chaired or served on the boards of dozens of business, civic, cultural, and academic organizations. Dedicated to the communities of which he is a part, particularly his longtime hometown, White engineered Abbott's purchase of the historic Deerpath Inn, restoring this 1928 Lake Forest landmark as a cornerstone of the community for years to come. (Abbott Laboratories.)

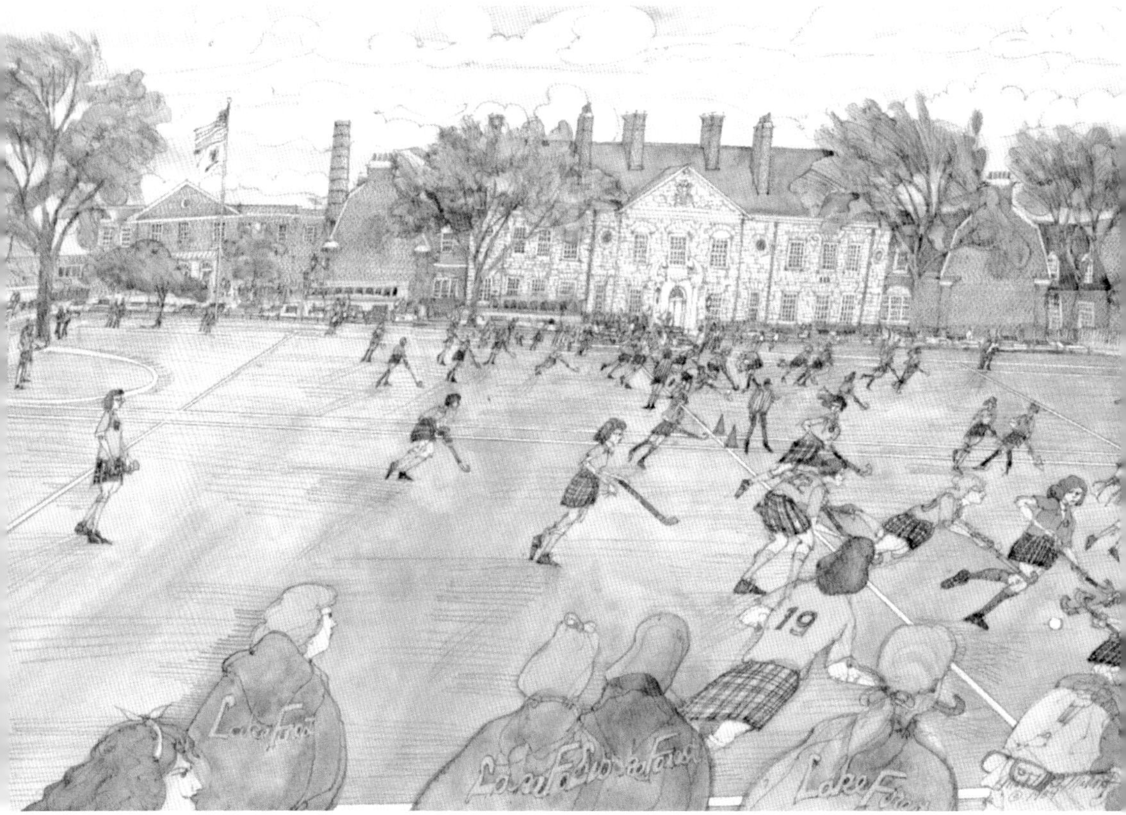

High School Painting by Mark McMahon

Female students play field hockey on the lawn in front of Lake Forest High School, designed by Anderson & Ticknor and built in 1935. The artwork is by resident and alumnus Mark McMahon, a notable second-generation Lake Forest artist. He earned his bachelor of arts degree from Loyola University in 1973.

Mark's murals, paintings, giclée prints, posters, and cards depict a wide range of subjects—places and events in the Chicago region and especially Lake Forest and Lake Bluff, but with many images of favorite vacation destinations in Michigan, Wisconsin, Colorado, and on the East Coast and in Europe. His recent commissions have ranged from Baxter Corporation to the Field Museum to Northwestern University's Department of Athletics and Recreation. This is one of several mostly athletic-themed Lake Forest High School subjects available at mcmahonartgallery.com. A mural by Mark also is mounted in the high school library, formerly both a gymnasium and cafeteria.

In October 2015, Mark and his late artist-father Franklin McMahon (1921–2012) were honored as the Lake Forest Local Legends for the year by the Lake Forest–Lake Bluff Historical Society. Mark was interviewed for the occasion by Bill Kurtis, Mettawa resident and last year's honoree with Donna LaPietra (page 114). This took place in the Lake Forest High School auditorium, partially shown on the far right, above. Mark, Franklin, and their family are pictured and Franklin's career is discussed on pages 112 and 113. (Mark McMahon.)

CHAPTER TWO

Educators and Researchers

Chicago business leaders who have lived in Lake Forest made up the first chapter, and their accomplishments made the community possible. It was under the leadership of Chicago Presbyterians, specifically more conservative, wealthy Second Church members, that the impulse began to launch a suburban town, Lake Forest, far from the temptations and dangers of the metropolis. But the founding had a dual purpose: to start schools for their young people and to create a hospitable town for them and for their families. This second chapter highlights educators, scholars, and researchers. The careers of many developed out of these Presbyterian institutions.

Lind University (1857–1865, afterwards Lake Forest University), which was cofounded with the town of Lake Forest, included Lake Forest Academy, the Collegiate Department, and Ferry Hall. Classes began at Lake Forest Academy in 1858, and instruction began at the Collegiate Department on a tutorial basis in 1859. Women's classes began at Ferry Hall in 1869 and continued to 1974, when this girls' prep school merged with Lake Forest Academy. Ferry Hall was preceded by the Dickinson Seminary for Young Ladies (1859–1867), a proprietary program, and its leaders are covered in *LFEPC*, as is Ferry Hall. The academy has been discussed in that 2000 volume and in *WLF*, in 2012. Also included in this volume are higher-education leaders associated with Barat College (1920–2005), a Catholic women's college until the 1980s. It was then coed for a couple of decades, offering a master's degree in education. Also highlighted are leaders associated with the Lake Forest Graduate School of Management, founded in 1946 as the Industrial Management Institute of Lake Forest College. It has been independent since 1965.

The public schools, too, were featured in *LFEPC*. John E. Baggett, an early-20th-century superintendent of the K-8 program, is highlighted there. Featured in this book is the Lake Forest High School, created in the mid-1930s to resemble a private school perhaps in a former David Adler–designed estate mansion. It was the creation of Anderson & Ticknor, local architects. The spacious front lawn has been preserved and serves as a playing field. The public schools began with the ancestor of today's District 67 (K-8). After a feeble attempt to support a high school in this system around 1900, Lake Forest students of high school age could take the interurban train south to Deerfield-Shields High School. Lake Forest High School finally opened in the mid-1930s.

Other independent and even proprietary schools reflected distinctive leadership. In 1866, an African American Sunday school was begun in the Washington Road neighborhood. Presumably, the school's biblical instruction was supplemented with reading and writing lessons to the young and old, as they were not yet literate, having recently left bondage in the South. One can only surmise that this paralleled freedmen education elsewhere. By 1870, there was a church building on the southeast corner of Washington and Maplewood Roads. In the 1920s, Thorp Academy, a military school for boys, operated on Sheridan Road, opposite today's Sheridan School (K-3), from Crab Tree Road north to Spruce Avenue. The academy used the former Grace Garrett Durand Crab Tree Farm property and was housed in an 1896 W.C. Zimmerman–designed shingle-style structure. Grace Durand's dairy farm moved north beyond the village of Lake Bluff to the former Blodgett farm on the lake in 1905. Today, it is still Crab Tree Farm.

Independent primary schools had flourished from the start, with a boarding school on Washington Road run by Elihu Barber until 1869. It served boys not old enough for the academy (*LFEPC*). By 1888, the Alcott School operated in a cottage on the university campus; by around 1900, it was in a Frost & Granger building north of the Presbyterian church on Sheridan Road. This became the Bell School in the first half of the 20th century. A new Bertrand Weber–designed building on the northeast corner of Westminster Avenue and Woodbine Place was being considered in the mid-1950s, when it was agreed to merge this institution into the Lake Forest Country Day School. The photograph of Clarice Hamill and her daughter on page 58 came from the Bell School's 50th anniversary celebration, held at Lilace Barnes's Glen Rowan, designed by Howard Shaw in 1908–1909. The photograph was saved with many others by Ellsworth Laflin and given by June Laflin to Special Collections, Lake Forest College, in the 1970s. The Lake Forest Country Day School, a progressive school founded in the 1920s, had moved to Green Bay Road, south of Onwentsia Road, and the combined program there thrived and grew.

The first public school, originally on the northwest corner of Walnut and Washington Roads, began in 1860. The school is first documented to be integrated in 1864 city minutes, after emancipation. But it had very likely been integrated from the start, led by the area's first public-school teacher, Roxana Beecher, who served there from 1860 to 1863. Alas, the authors do not know of a photograph of her. She was the niece of Harriet Beecher Stowe, author of the antislavery novel *Uncle Tom's Cabin*, and Roxana was the daughter of Harriet's more rabidly abolitionist brother, William, according to Milton Rugoff in his exhaustive 1981 study, *The Beechers: An American Family in the Nineteenth Century*. Roxana left Lake Forest after emancipation made teaching African Americans less risky and went to nurse soldiers near the battlefields, a growing need after Gettysburg in July 1863. She married a soldier—perhaps one she nursed, Friedrich Preuzner, a private in the 2nd Regiment, Missouri Light Artillery—and lived in Kansas City. She apparently was later divorced. Rugoff writes that "by 1889 she was living with her father, Rev. William H. Beecher (son of Rev. Lyman Beecher and brother of Harriet Beecher Stowe). In Chicago . . . [Roxana Preuzner] lived with her father and sisters Mary and Grace at 118 Honore St. on the city's far north side." Shirley Paddock went to the Rogers Park address and learned that the house had just been demolished. The query for more information was posted on the *Genealogy Today* website in 1998, when Arthur Miller and Shirley Paddock were researching for the Lake Forest College history, *30 Miles North*.

After a century, Lake Forest College and the independent secondary schools brought back racial diversity to the city. Jim Crowe conventions eased in the 1950s, creating broader opportunities for local African Americans. As the civil rights movement made gains in the early 1960s, Lake Forest College and, later, other institutions began to recruit African American students and faculty. By 1962, Pres. William Graham Cole's Lake Forest College was leading in this effort, a half-decade ahead of East Coast institutions.

The history of schooling for younger children has gone under the radar. Joytime, a nursery school at South Park with origins dating to 1950, is featured here as a representative of this important aspect. A Lake Forest Montessori belongs to this preschool/prekindergarten group of programs. By the 1970s, childcare and preschools were flourishing. Women, previously stay-at-home moms, were pursuing their own educations—as at Barat's returning-learner program—or continuing their careers. In that decade, Paula Lillard ran a fine prekindergarten program at the Lake Forest Country Day School, and she went on to found the Lake Bluff Montessori School.

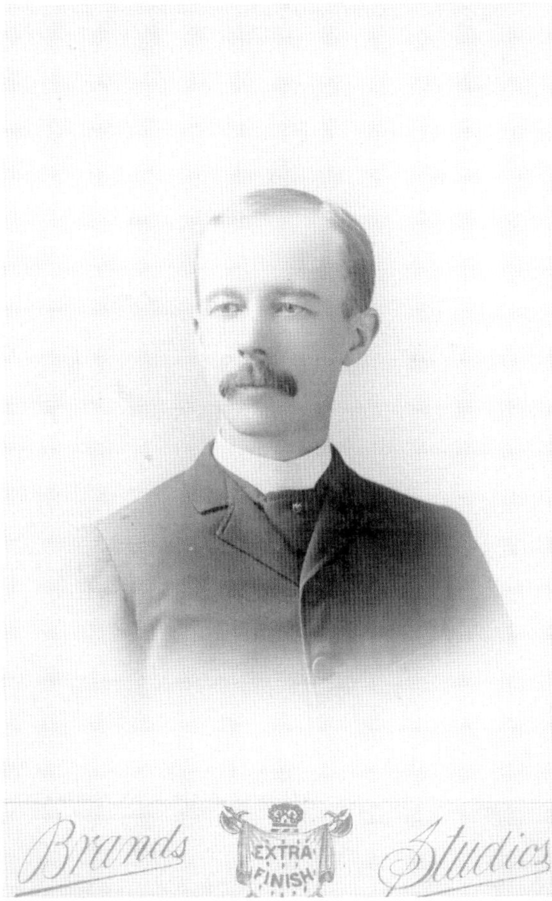

John J. Halsey (1848–1919)
Halsey was an 1870 graduate of the old Chicago University and received an honorary doctor of laws degree from Centre College in Kentucky in 1897. He was the first career faculty member of Lake Forest College, serving from 1878 to 1919, and twice was acting president (1896–1897 and 1906–1907). His father, Rev. Julius Halsey, was a professor at McCormick Theological Seminary in Chicago. John Halsey taught political and social science and wrote, most notably, *History of Lake County, Illinois*, considered the best Illinois county history.

This 1912 county history includes some of the best information about early local residents, persons Halsey knew or had known and very likely interviewed. His chapter on Lake Forest University was the first to be published for an external audience and was the best information available until the college's history, *30 Miles North*, appeared in 2000. Halsey's book had a short article about Lake County's "Landed Estates," and his 1916 firsthand account of the timeline of local estates in *Lake Forest:* Art and History Edition has been an invaluable resource for dating local country places, their owners' identities, and their houses. It was an early attempt to write a systematic town history.

Halsey was a book collector with taste, and his books were bought for the college library after his death, including an 1851 first edition of *Moby-Dick*. He served on the city council (1893–1896), was founding president of the library board (1898–1901), was chair of the District 67 School Board (1903–1907), and later was president of the Deerfield-Shields Township High School board. Halsey School, formerly sited just west of city hall (*LFEPC*, page 45), was named for him. Seven Gables, a Queen Anne–style home built by Halsey and his wife, Elizabeth, in 1895, still stands on Sheridan Road, one door north of today's parking lot for the Presbyterian church, where he was an elder by the 1880s. (LFCLASC.)

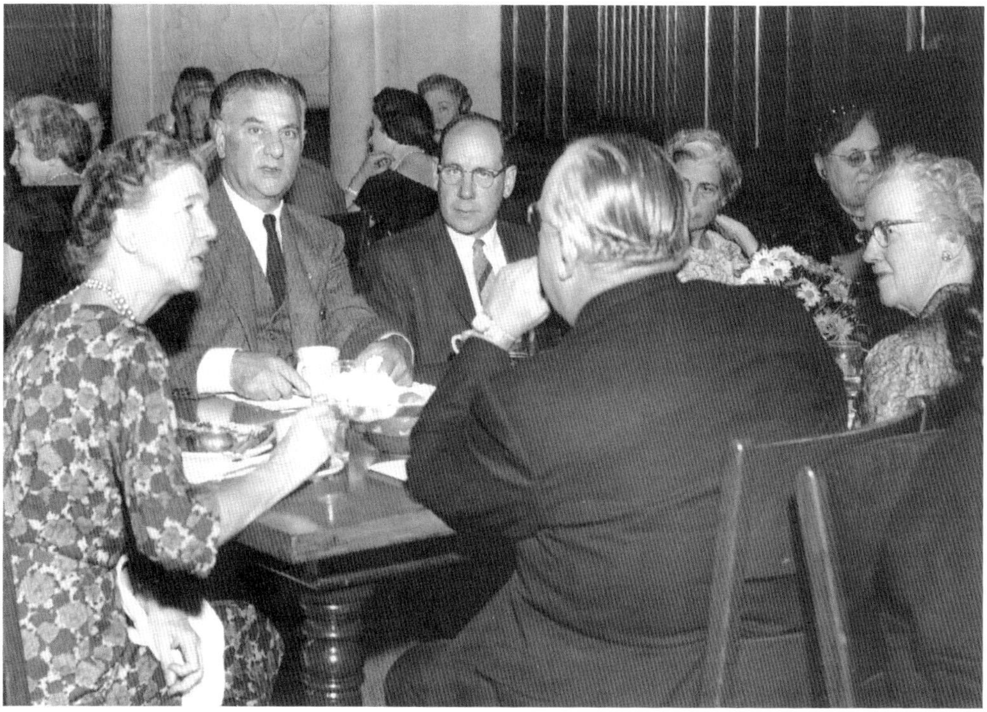

Edward Arpee (1899–1979)

Armenian immigrant Edward Arpee, second from left, husband of Katherine Trowbridge Arpee, far left, was a history master at Lake Forest Academy for over 35 years, beginning around 1929. A graduate of Princeton University, he wrote notable books, including *History of Lake Forest Academy* (1944); *From Frigates to Flat Tops* (1953), about Adm. William Moffett of Naval Station Great Lakes; and *Lake Forest, Illinois: History and Reminiscences, 1861–1961* (1964). (Louis E. Laflin Jr. Collection, LFCLASC.)

Nathan Irvin Huggins (1927–1989)

Early in his distinguished career as a professor of African American history, Chicago-born historian Nate Huggins served on the Lake Forest College faculty from 1964 to 1966. He was the college's first African American professor. Huggins soon was attracted away to Berkeley and Columbia before being invited back to Harvard, where he had earned his doctorate in 1962, as W.E.B. Du Bois Professor. (LFCASC.)

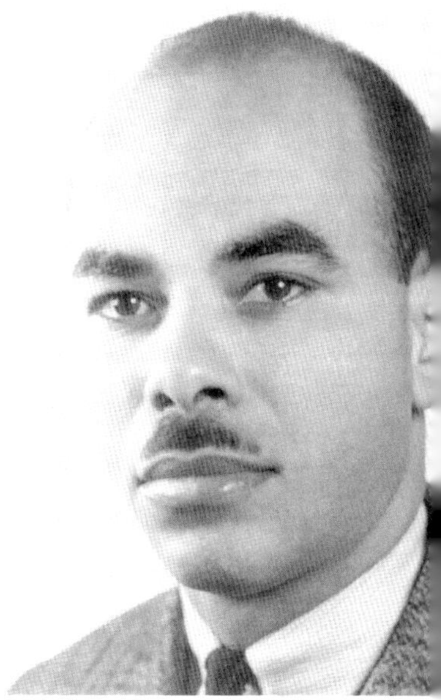

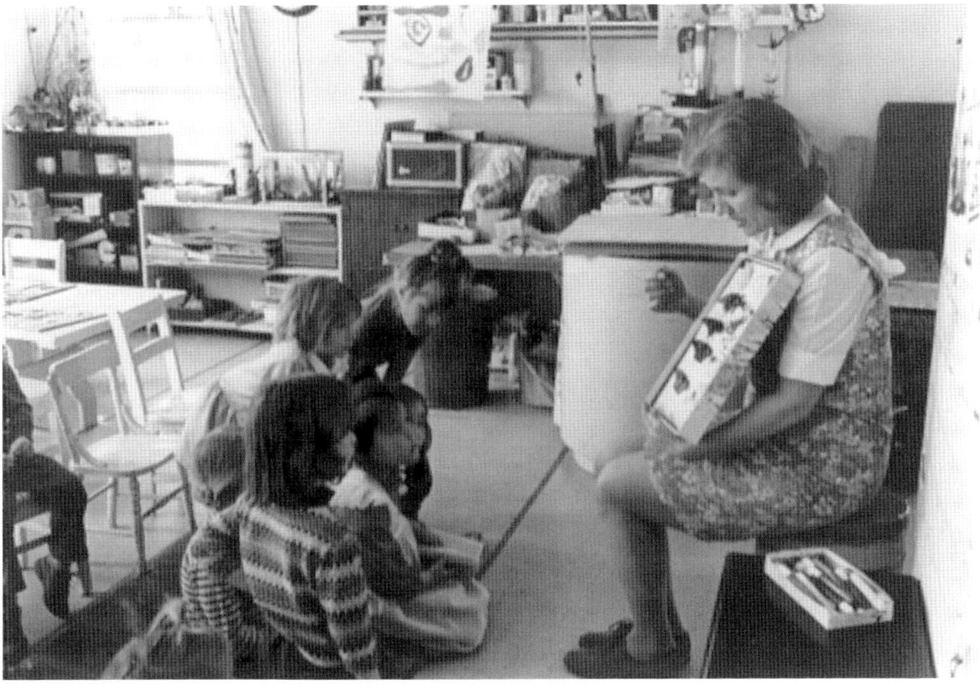

Joy Hodgen (1928–1999)

Joy Hodgen and her husband, Earle, built a day care center on Maywood Road, next to South Park. By 1962, this was a nursery school attended by hundreds of local youngsters. Its nurturing atmosphere was its trademark, a haven for preschoolers whose parents were put off by other programs. After Joy retired, her daughter, Kathleen, continued the school in Joy's style until 2013, assisted ably by Mary Redmond. (*Daily North Shore.*)

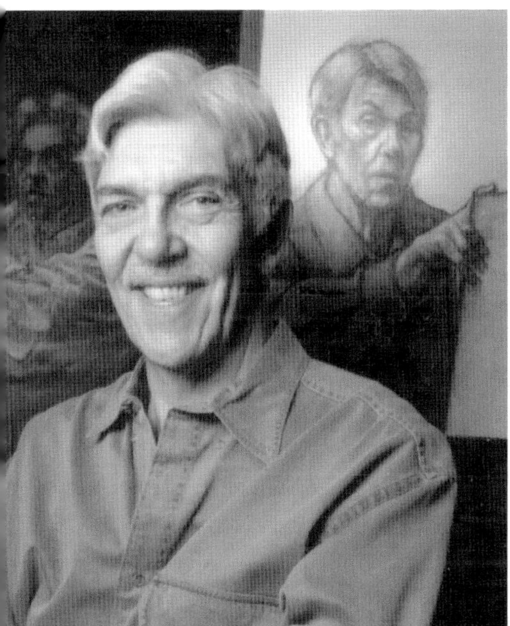

Franz Schulze

Illinois-raised Franz Schulze joined the Lake Forest College art department faculty in 1952, having earned his bachelor of philosophy degree from the University of Chicago and his master of fine arts degree from the School of the Art Institute of Chicago. He took emeritus status in 1991 but is still active on campus and locally after 60 years. A noted national critic since the 1950s, his books include *Fantastic Images* (1973) and his high-profile biographies of architects Mies van der Rohe (1985, revised and expanded with Ed Windhorst, 2012) and Philip Johnson (1994). (LFCLASC.)

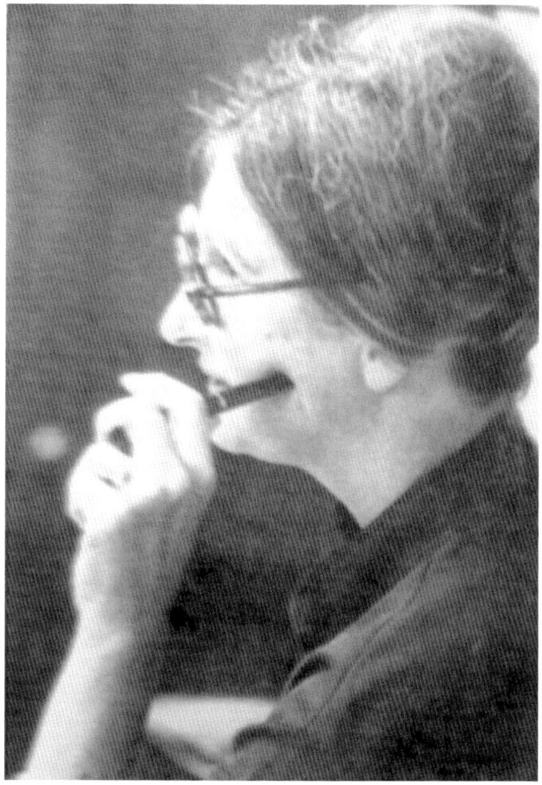

Joan Reardon

Reardon was longtime Barat College English department chair and a scholar of modern American women's poetry. She later became an author of culinary books and of significant books on women culinary luminaries, including M.F.K. Fisher and Julia Child. According to Martha Curry's essential 2012 Barat history, Joan Reardon ably tailored programs in the 1970s and 1980s for women returning to their studies. (Martha Curry, RSCJ.)

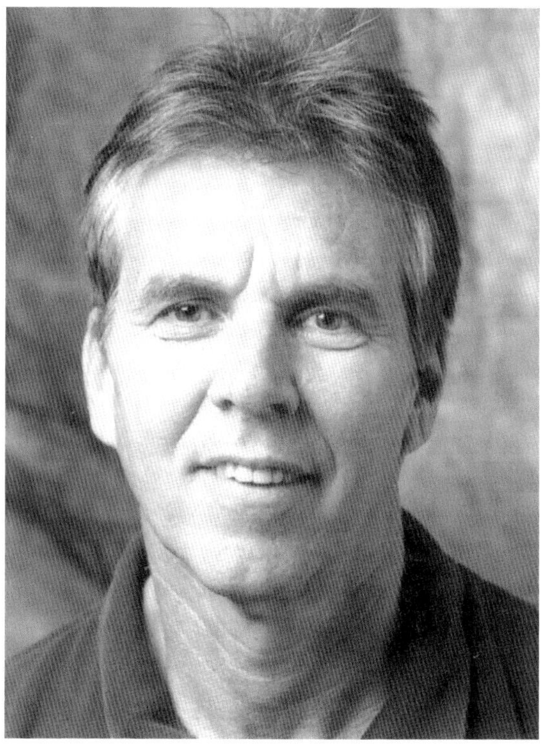

Robert A. Baade

Rob Baade is Lake Forest College's A.B. Dick Professor of Economics and Business. He arrived in 1973 and twice served three-year terms as chair of the department, most recently from 2004 to 2007. He has been interviewed by many media outlets, and he has earned a national reputation from his study of sports economics and the perils for cities of building large, expensive stadiums. (LFC.)

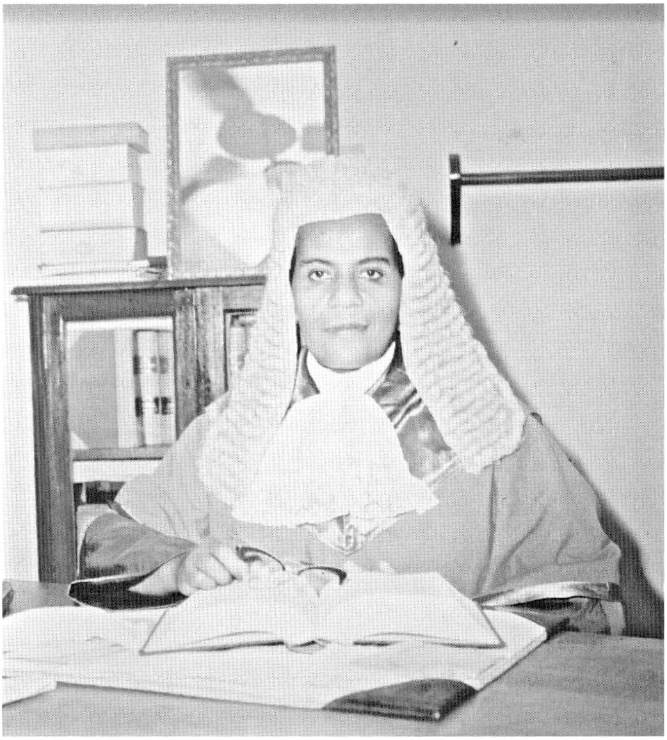

Christopher Mojekwu (1920–1982)

Lawyer, scholar, and educator Chris Mojekwu was born in Nigeria and educated there, at Gray's Inn, London, and at Northwestern University School of Law. At Lake Forest College from 1972 to 1982, his fields of instruction were political science and Africa. An Igbo, he was a key figure in the ethnic Biafran War with Nigeria (1967–1970). According to writer John de St. Jorre, he was "Biafra's powerful home minister and chief emissary in Europe." (LFCLASC.)

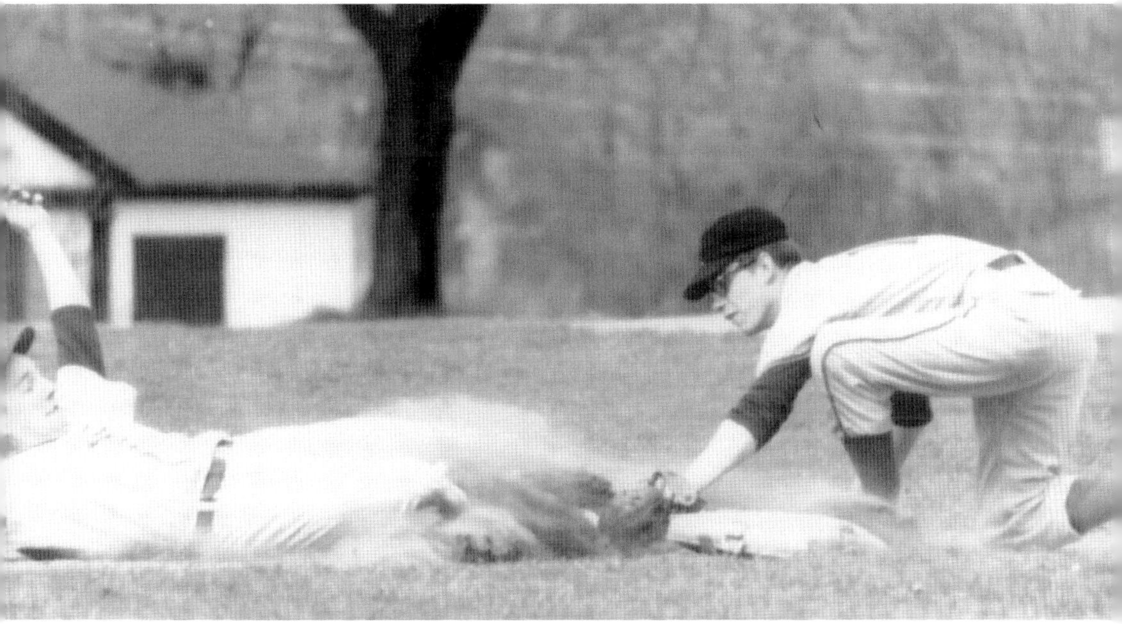

Robert Bullard

A 1968 Lake Forest College graduate, Bob Bullard, who played college baseball as shown at left, spent his career teaching and sharing administrative duties at Lake Forest Country Day School. That independent K-8 program celebrated its 125th anniversary in 2014. Bob and his wife, Sally, who also retired in 2015, had racked up a combined 78 years of service at the highly respected local institution. (LFCLASC.)

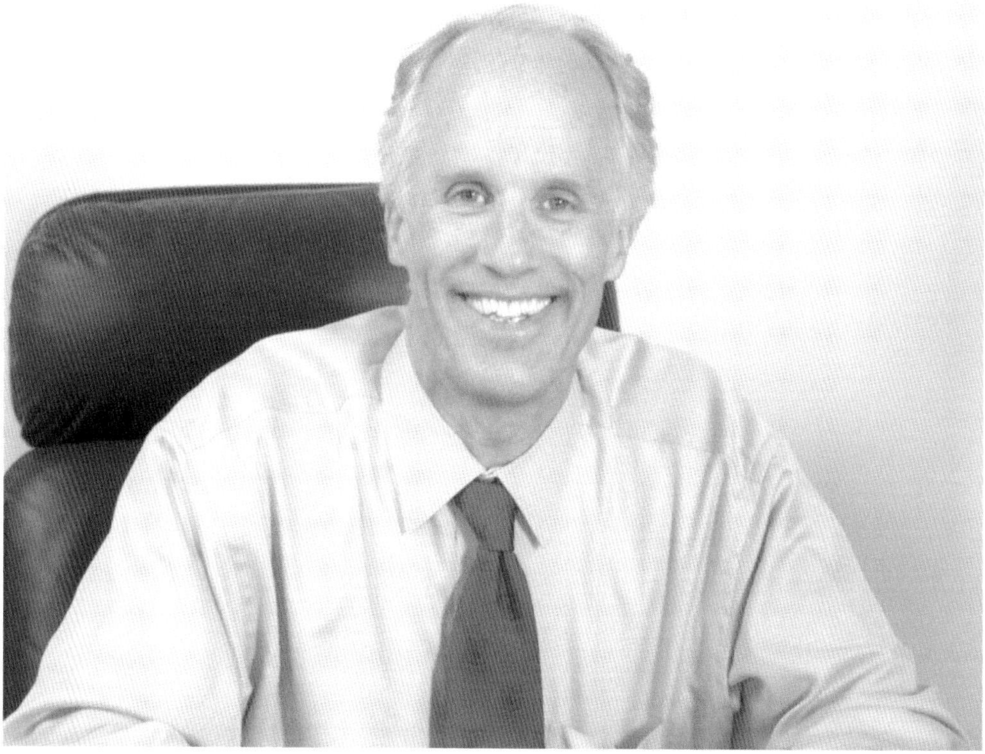

Stephen Schutt

Steve Schutt arrived on the Lake Forest College campus as its new president on July 1, 2001, less than three months before 9/11 and preceding two recessions. Nonetheless, he increased enrollment and has overseen significant new construction and renovation, including the following: Donnelley and Lee Library (2004); Mohr Student Center (2006); Sports Center expansion (2010); expansion of the Gus and Margie Hart Dining Hall, Stuart Commons (2011); and a replacement of Moore Hall (2012). (Lake Forest College.)

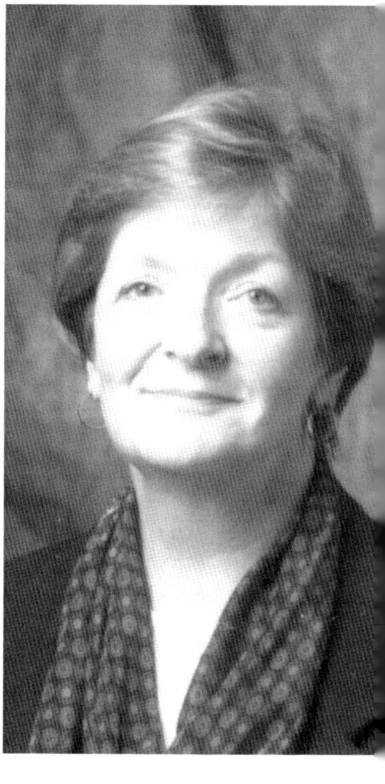

Leslie T. Chapman (c. 1946–2014)

Resident Leslie Chapman earned her bachelor of arts degree from Lake Forest College in 1979 and a master of business administration degree from Lake Forest Graduate School of Management in 1982. She served as vice president for business affairs and treasurer for the second half of her four-decade Lake Forest College career. She was for 12 years the treasurer of the Lake Forest–Lake Bluff Historical Society and had a lasting impact, preparing for the purchase of the organization's new home in 2015. (LFCLASC.)

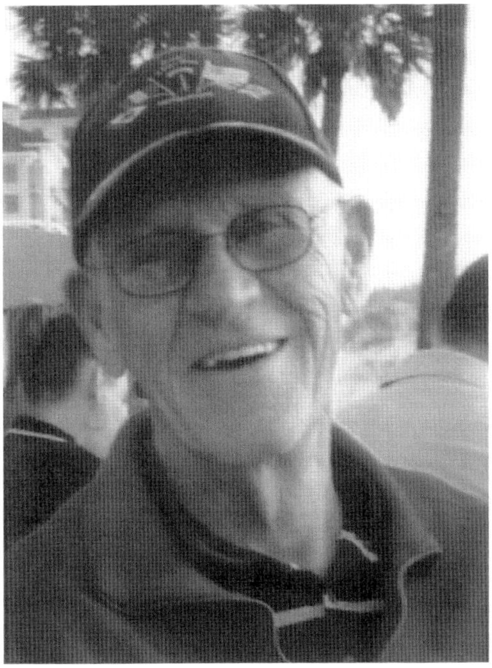

Maurice F. Dunne Jr.
"Business is always growing and you should be growing with it," declared "Moose" Dunne in a 2013 online interview with Maddie Coppa. Resident Maurice Dunne, who earned his master of business administration degree from the University of Michigan, served three decades as president of the Lake Forest Graduate School of Management. He directed the middle period of growth of the institution, now located on the west side. (LFCLASC.)

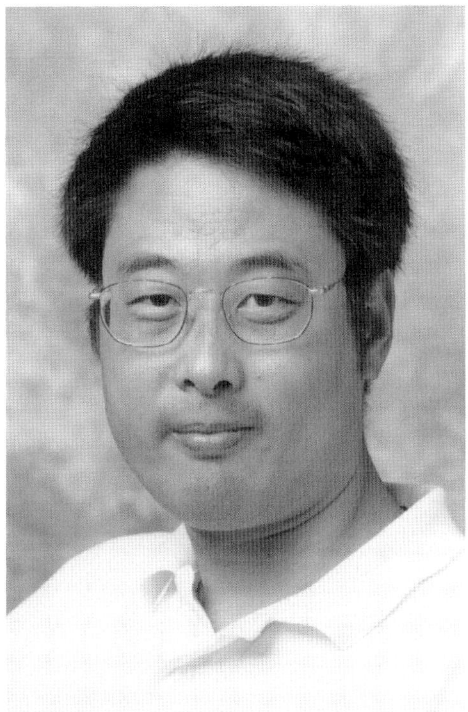

Shiwei Chen
Resident Shiwei Chen, professor of history and chair of the Asian Studies program at Lake Forest College, has recently researched the 1941 college commencement speaker, Dr. Hu Shih, who at the time was China's ambassador to the United States. Shih was an old friend of Lake Forest College's president, Rev. Dr. Herbert Moore, when both were at Cornell in the 1910s. Chen earned a bachelor of arts degree from Yunnan University, a master of arts degree at Peking University, and his doctorate of philosophy from Harvard. He also oversees the college's study programs in China. (Lake Forest College.)

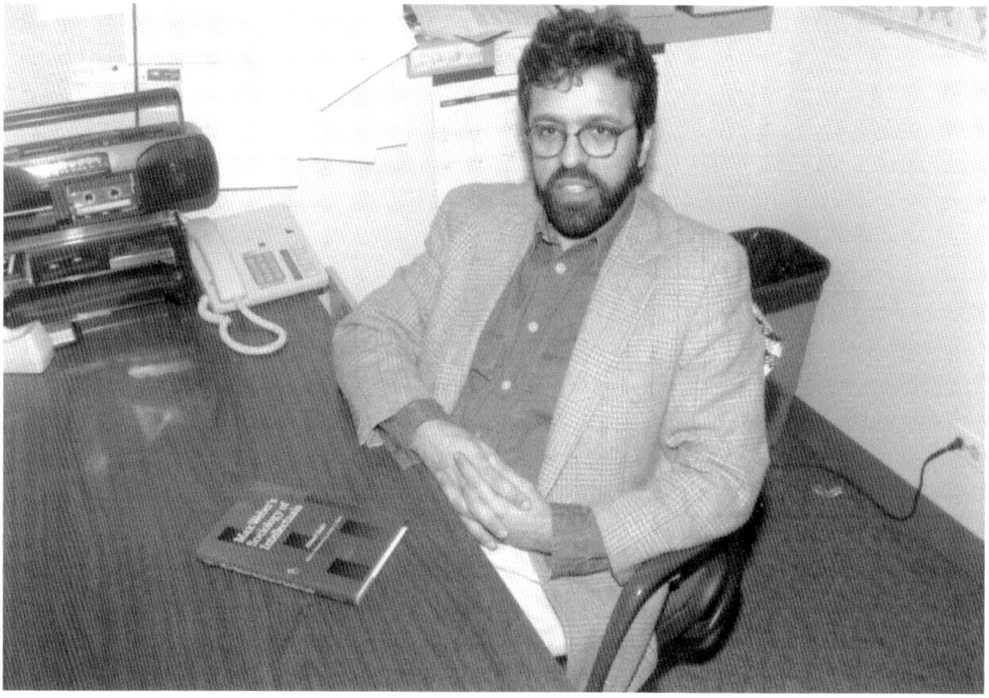

Ahmad Sadri
Iranian-born Ahmad Sadri is the Gorter Professor of Islamic World Studies and professor of sociology at Lake Forest College. He earned his doctor of philosophy degree from the New School in New York City. Sadri is noted for his 1993 book *Max Weber's Sociology of Intellectuals* and is the acclaimed translator of the Persian epic poem *Shahnameh* (2013). He is frequently heard discussing Iranian politics on WBEZ public radio's *Worldview.* (Lake Forest College.)

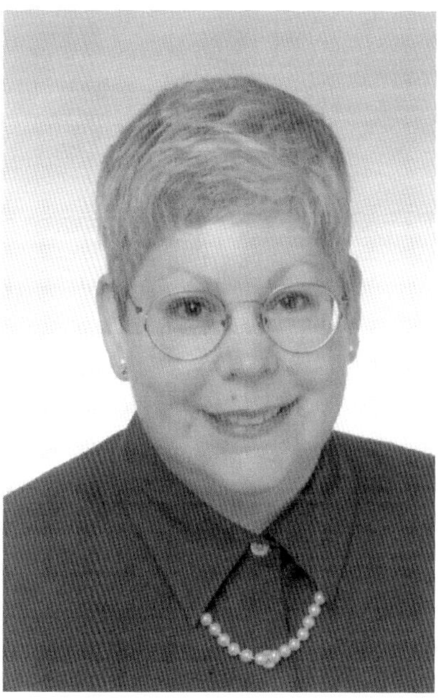

Kaye Grabbe
Grabbe, who earned her master of library and information science degree from Dominican University, has, since 1988, led the city-governed Lake Forest Library through growth and a major transition to the digital age. She has subtly expanded the landmark 1931 library building within its 1977 footprint and, with support of the Friends of Lake Forest Library, restored its dome, original windows, and roof while also conserving to high standards its remarkable museum-quality artworks. (Lake Forest Library.)

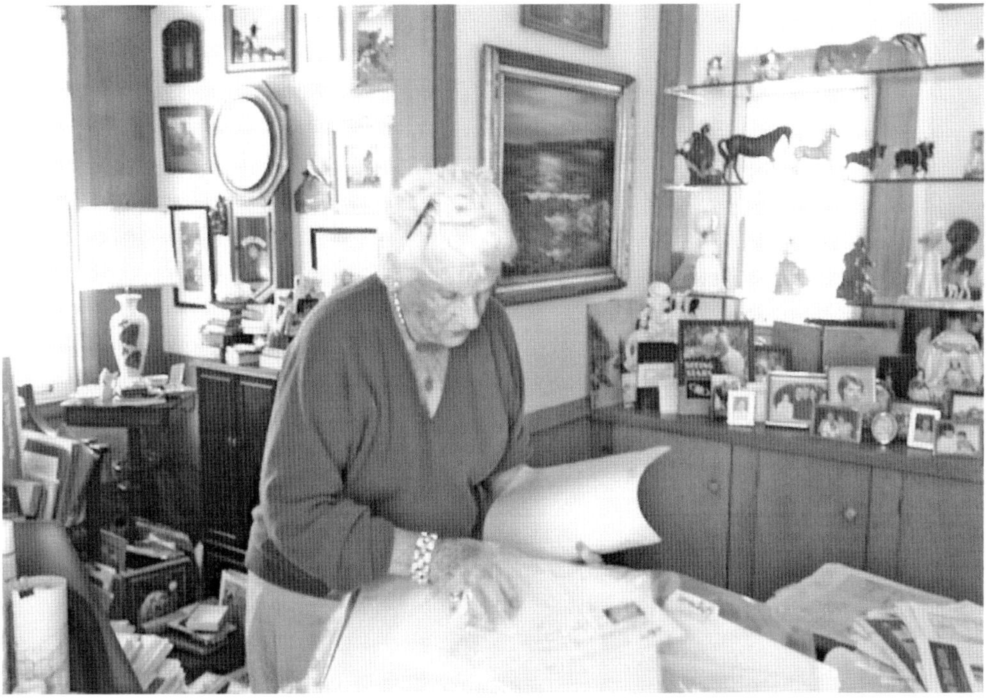

Shirley MacDonald Paddock

Shirley MacDonald Paddock has lived in Lake Forest all her life. Her childhood years were spent on the Howard Shaw–designed estate of Edward Larrabee Baker at 1110 North Sheridan Road. In 1949, her family moved to Mills Court. She graduated from Lake Forest High School, but in an era before accommodations for learning disabilities were introduced. Though bright, her apparent dyslexia kept her from further formal study. She next cleaned houses, nurturing her fascination with local history. In 1954, Shirley married Wisconsin native Harold L. Paddock, and they raised three children on Noble Avenue. Shirley and Harry were career District 67 nonteaching staff members, part of a rich local tradition of service in city operations.

Shirley Paddock's passions turned to history and genealogy, both of which called on her to overcome her reading challenges. Her sophistication in genealogy aided in the research for the Lake Forest College history, *30 Miles North*. Paddock traced her husband's family to its *Mayflower* roots and her own MacDonald family to its English and Scots origins through Canada. During this period, she spoke at Glastonbury Abbey in Glastonbury, Somerset, England, on English immigration to Lake County, Illinois.

In retirement, she has worked on several Arcadia books about Lake Forest. A more complete list of her publications can be found on Lake Forest College's library catalog website. She has contributed significant historical and visual material to Lake Forest College Library's Special Collections, as well as to the Lake Forest–Lake Bluff Historical Society. Shirley Paddock introduced historical study of the local support and westside pioneer farm communities, while also adding depth to what is known about the Chicago-based founders and the country club and estate group of the 1890s to the 1970s. In 2005, she identified a log home on Mills Court, masked under clapboard siding, and helped save it. The former Green Bay Road area pioneer residence was probably built in the 1830s by the Swanton family, who also probably occupied it. John Bryan soon moved the structure, had it analyzed, and then restored it at his Crab Tree Farm in Lake Bluff.

Paddock has served on the boards of Lake Forest–Lake Bluff Historical Society, Lake Forest Foundation for Historic Preservation, the History and Archives Committee of the First Presbyterian Church, and the Millburn Historical Society. Thanks to her remarkable efforts, the rich fabric of the exceptional history of Lake Forest has been preserved and generously shared. (SMP.)

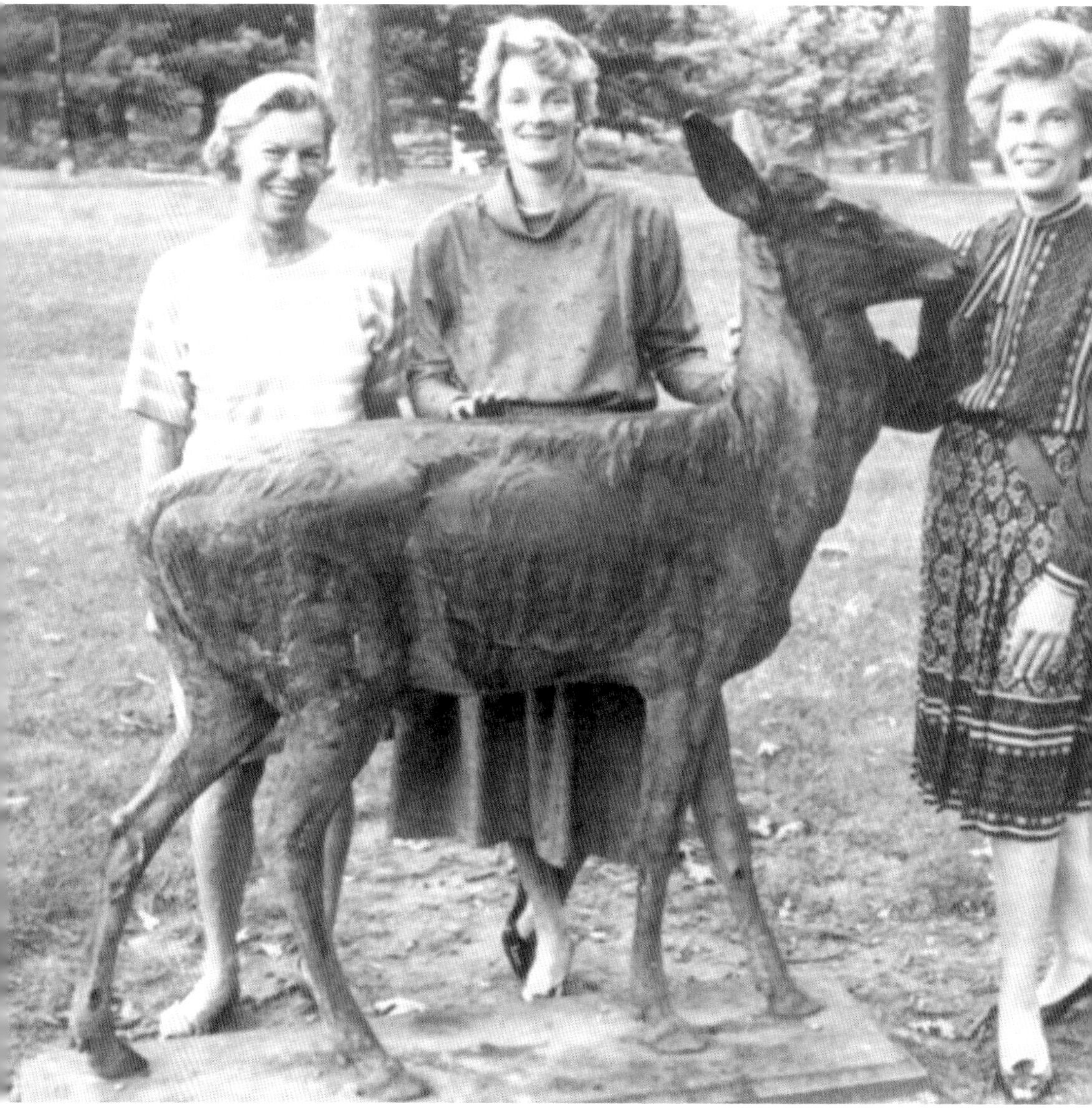

Lake Forest Garden Club Friends at Triangle Park

This 19th-century deer sculpture stands in Triangle Park, a small eastside heritage parcel that, since 1917, has been a Lake Forest Garden Club project. Shown here are club members Adair Foster (left, see page 72), Linda Armour (center), and Carol Swift (see page 47). (Lake Forest Garden Club Archives, LFCLASC.)

CHAPTER THREE

Architects, Preservationists, Gardeners, and Conservationists

After Chicago business leaders had made possible the move to Lake Forest and educators had taken up the duties of teaching and safeguarding the children and youth, veritable armies of specialists in architecture and landscape design were deployed to create site-specific, one-off buildings and grounds for the institutions and residences. Succeeding generations of these highly trained and experienced persons have stepped in to create what often are masterpieces in these design areas. In addition, especially in the last half-century, volunteer preservationists, gardeners, and conservationists have shared responsibility with the professionals to make Lake Forest a uniquely designed and protected community even while it expanded westward. Today, Lake Forest's historic visual character stands as a remarkably planned, custom-designed, and protected whole—without precedent in the midcontinental region.

Alas, the authors have located no photographs of important early Lake Forest designers. One was St. Louisian Almerin Hotchkiss, who laid out the mostly curvilinear east Lake Forest street plan in 1857. Frank Calvert had a local nursery and landscape design business by 1860. Asher W. Carter (1827–1916) designed the first hotel (1858) and the first academy (1859), but there are no known images of him. Similarly, Rufus Rose, who designed the 1870 D.J. Lake house at 644 East Deerpath Road, is known to the authors only by name.

So the illustrations here begin 30 years after Lake Forest's founding, with the designers of the 1887 Presbyterian church, Henry Ives Cobb and Charles S. Frost. Most local buildings and most garden and landscape acres in town are one-offs, unique designs for their sites. Gardens and landscapes roughly laid out by a professional designer were often shaped and tended by trained gardeners of the old Victorian style, such as Sylvester MacDonald (page 48), or by committed amateurs, often women who banded together in clubs for mutual support and education beginning by 1912, when the Lake Forest Garden Club was organized. The current number of local garden clubs has not been ascertained by the authors, but at one point in the 1990s, there were nine, as counted by the Lake Forest Library.

After these early days, and with the founding of Onwentsia in 1895, estates blossomed east and west, bringing in perhaps over 100 new Paris-trained and -influenced designers of homes, interiors, and gardens. Often, these individuals were based elsewhere, such as innovative decorator Elsie De Wolfe, from New York, and landscape architect Warren Manning, from the Boston area. But others did live locally or in the Chicago area. There were over 50 classically educated and trained architects who designed houses in Lake Forest from the 1890s to the 1940s. Some of these studied in Paris at the École des Beaux-Arts; others studied at US architecture schools that modeled their programs on the École's methods; and still others worked for architects who had trained in these programs. Many were products of multiple methods of gaining classical training. For example, Alfred H. Granger, after attending college at Kenyon, went to MIT, the first US architecture school structured like the École's program. Then, on the advice of Charles F. McKim, Granger attended the École in Paris, but, as Granger reported in his 1914 biography of McKim, he did not take the *diplome*, as McKim had advised him and others. In the early 1890s, Granger worked for Paris-trained W.L.B. Jenney, along with fellow MIT graduate Howard Shaw, who worked there with some interruptions from 1891 to 1894.

Also in that period and working in Jenney's office was James Gamble Rogers, who later married a daughter of the Albert Days family in town. Rogers designed Gorton School (now Gorton Community Center) and, in 1903, the Anderson Block, the brick Georgian three-story office building on the northwest corner of Deerpath Road and Western Avenue. The École-educated Rogers is better known for his Deering Library at Northwestern University and his similar collegiate Gothic work at Yale University.

Shaw's first—and, for a while, only—draftsman in 1897 was Robert Work, who attended the École-modeled program for architecture at the southside Armour Institute, now IIT. Work was a key Shaw staff member overseeing the construction of Market Square in 1916. By 1917, he had left that firm to be the licensed architect partner of David Adler, who did not receive a license to practice and sign plans until 1928. That year, Work went into partnership with Russell Walcott, whose brother Chester had studied at the École.

After World War I, two architects who designed locally were Stanley D. Anderson, grandson of town founder James Anderson, and third-generation Chicago-area resident Walter Frazier. They both studied at the École in Paris and came home to join Chicago firms—Anderson went to Shaw's, and Frazier went to Holabird & Roche. Anderson's practice, which developed by the mid-1920s, was classical throughout his career, while Frazier was influenced by the new trends 1920 in Paris in the Le Corbusier manner and the Art Deco/International style. Frazier and his partner Howard Raftery, based in Chicago and later west suburban Geneva, started out with classical projects. But, by 1930, they were embracing Art Deco and then, after World War II, Miesian International forms, as seen in the 1955 Waukegan Road Elliott Donnelley estate. By the 1960s, the firm was headed back toward the classical style, as postmodern style trends began to assert themselves, notably in the 1965 Edward B. Smith house, on the site of Byron L. Smith's 1895 Briar Hall. While designers of many houses in Lake Forest are still not identified, they all shared knowledge of and adhered to classic principles—harmony or suitability in their context, hierarchy of form for height and materials, clear circulation in the plan, and fine proportions. This was the prevailing local visual character by the early 1940s.

These same principles prevailed for landscape design, whether formal or naturalistic. Generally, though, these designers did not live locally: Jens Jensen was in Highland Park; Warren Manning, the Boston area; Rose Standish Nichols, Boston; Charles A. Pratt, New York; and Ralph R. Root was in Urbana in his Lake Forest period, and then in Chicago.

Modernism in architecture tended to favor self-referential style over compatibility, notable in I.W. Colburn's 1960s house on Lake Road at Spring Lane, facing Forest Park. But this embracing of modernism was a brief flirtation here.

By the 1960s and 1970s, new, related impulses energized the local scene: land conservation came with the founding of the Lake Forest Open Lands Association (LFOLA) in 1967; and historic preservation got a boost, especially with the founding of the Lake Forest Preservation Foundation (LFPF) in 1976. Both led to adjustments to local ordinances. The clustering of houses was now allowed for internal subdivision development planning. This facilitated the protection of large tracts of open space within underlying density requirements. For preservation of architecturally significant and historic structures and landscapes, ordinances were passed. In addition, limits were placed on the scale of houses on lots to preserve the open-space landscape. By 1998, the city had its own Historic Preservation Commission. Preservation became a specialty on staff, as forestry already was. A goal for preservationists has been to add to city-staff trained licensed experts in design—architectural and landscape.

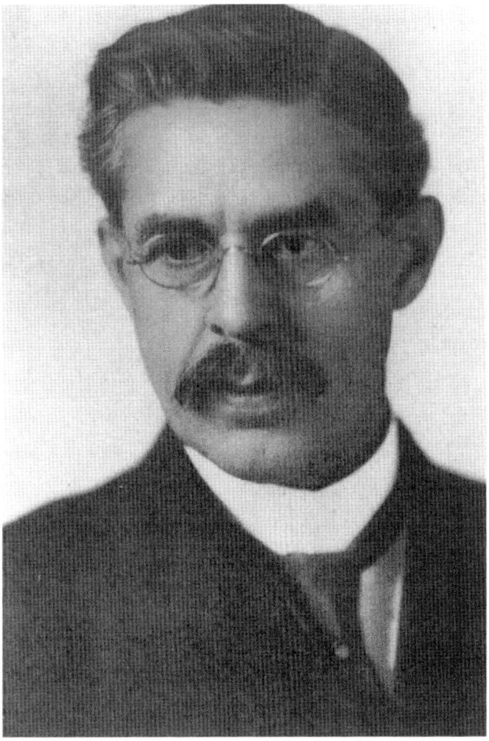

Charles Sumner Frost (1856–1931)
Noted architect Charles Frost was educated at MIT and lived in Lake Forest after 1898 at his home, Eastover. Some of his best-known work in Lake Forest was accomplished with his brother-in-law and partner, Alfred Granger. Among these works are the following: city hall (1899), the train station (1900), and Lake Forest College's Lois Hall (1899), Reid Hall (1900), and Lily Reid Holt Chapel (1900). The partners built stations for their father-in-law, Marvin Hughitt, builder of the C&NW Railway. (LFCLASC.)

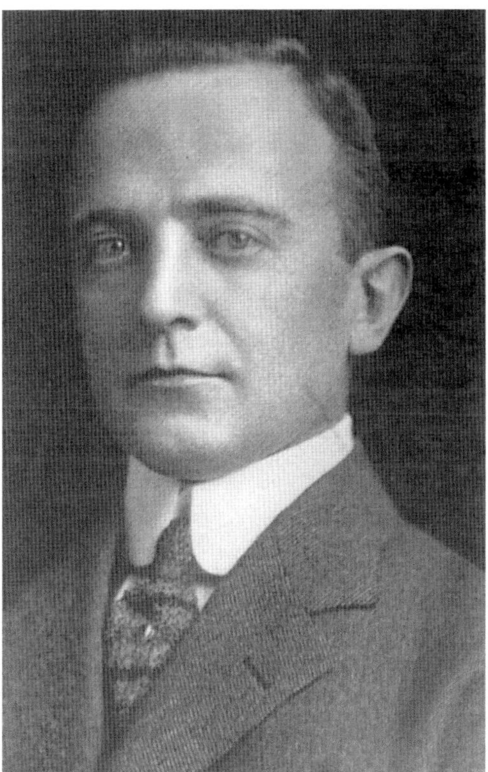

Alfred Hoyt Granger (1867–1939)
Ohio-born Granger earned a bachelor of arts degree at Kenyon College and attended graduate school at MIT. He came to Chicago with architect Charles Coolidge around 1891 to work on the Art Institute for the 1893 World's Fair. He also practiced in Cleveland (1893–1897) and in Philadelphia (c. 1910–1917), then again in Chicago and locally until his death. Granger chaired the 1922 Tribune Tower competition committee. As an author, he wrote, notably, *Charles Follen McKim* (1914) and *Chicago Welcomes You* (1933). (LFCLASC.)

Henry Ives Cobb (1859–1931)

Chicago-based architect Cobb practiced in Chicago from 1882 to about 1900. With Charles Frost as his partner (1882–1889), he designed the Presbyterian church (1887) and Ferry Hall's expansion (1888), as well as four houses near the church. His large, shingle-style home (1893), which he designed, stood on Green Bay Road. By 1895, it was the clubhouse for Onwentsia, serving as such until the late 1920s. Cobb's design for Ferry Hall led to his creating the plan for the University of Chicago from 1890 to 1900. (University of Chicago.)

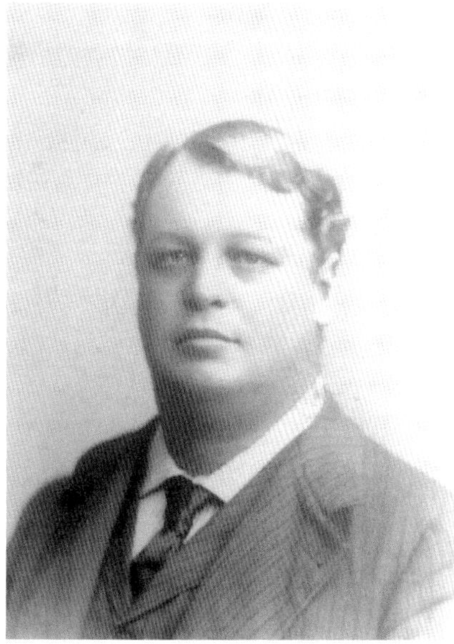

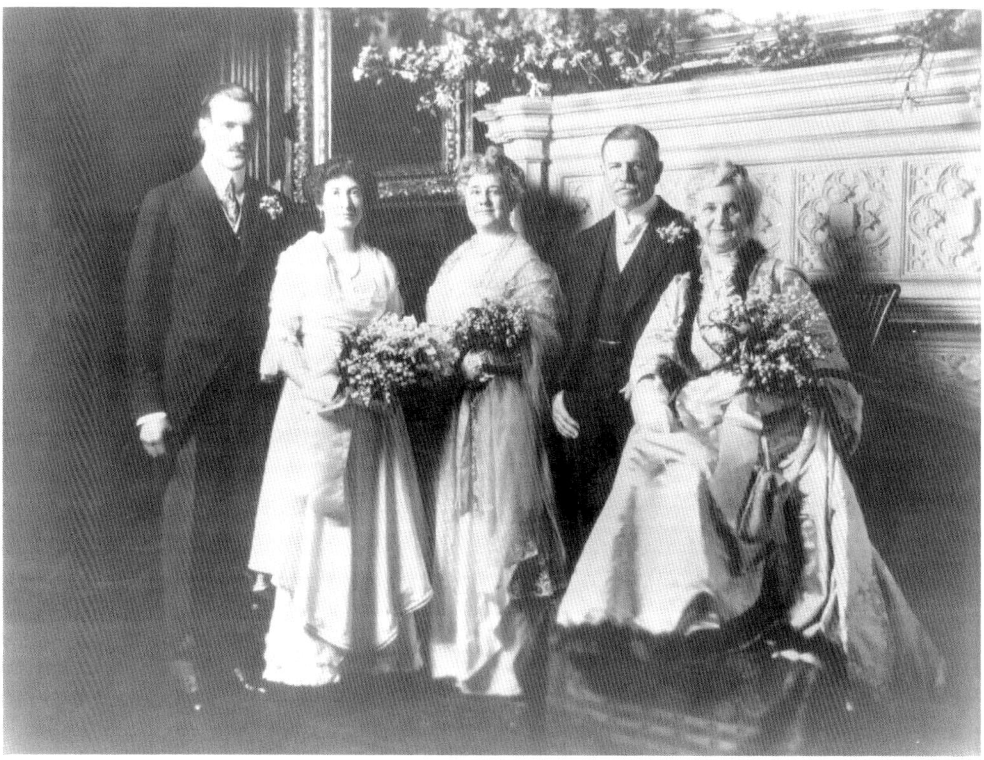

Harriet Hammond McCormick (1862–1921)

Harriet McCormick was a gardener, landscape reformer, and founder of the Lake Forest Garden Club in 1912 and the Garden Club of America (GCA) in 1913. Her Walden estate, begun in the 1890s, is illustrated with photographs in her book *Landscape Art: Past and Present* (1924). This 1915 photograph shows Harriet (center) with her son Cyrus III (far left) and his fiancée, Dorothy Linn, and Harriet's husband, Cyrus II, and her mother-in-law, Nettie Fowler McCormick (far right). (Wisconsin Historical Society.)

Howard Van Doren Shaw (1869–1926)

Second-generation Chicagoan Howard Van Doren Shaw earned a bachelor of arts degree from Yale in 1890 and completed MIT's architecture program in 1891. He was a 1926 AIA Gold Medalist. Shaw, who had his own practice by 1893, had begun his Lake Forest life and career by 1897, buying a Swanton family farm on Green Bay Road, north of Laurel Avenue, to develop two estate houses for clients (William Castleberry and Dr. Nathan S. Davis Jr.) and to create his own English Arts and Crafts summer place, Ragdale. A decade later, he developed a larger, related Swanton-Atteridge farm farther south, building six long, narrow estates with houses west of the road. The west-facing homes, with sunset views of the Skokie River, included the following: Brewster, brick, 1907; Clow, stucco, 1916; Donnelley, brick, 1911; Scott, stucco, 1910; Coonley, brick, 1911; and McBirney, stucco, 1909. East of Green Bay Road, he planned West Park, with its middle-class neighborhood.

By 1916, Shaw led in creating Market Square, an elemental English Arts and Crafts and classical complex that became, according to Richard Longstreth, a model for future shopping centers. The group of Chicago estate owners who were backers of the new City Beautiful downtown Lake Forest concept in mid-1912 bought up the stretch of Western Avenue west of the 1900 Frost and Granger English-style train station. A first plan was done by December 1912, apparently with associate David Adler's design input (the eagle on the fountain design was his emblem). But, with its shallow, longitudinal park, the complex would not generate the rent needed to pay a return on the Chicagoans' investments. Generally, the style reflected English town planning of the period (*LFEPC*). Finally, by 1915, a third plan by Shaw and his firm created a long park perpendicular to Western Avenue, increasing by 300 percent the Western Avenue front footage for prime rent. This changed both the character of the classic Palladian central building and also increased the height of the two towers, the north one restyled in a Wren manner. Most of the work was accomplished by the end of 1916.

The round relief medallion seen here is by Shaw's sculptor daughter Sylvia. This is a polymer recasting done by Paul Myers and given by him to Special Collections, Lake Forest College Library. (LFCLASC.)

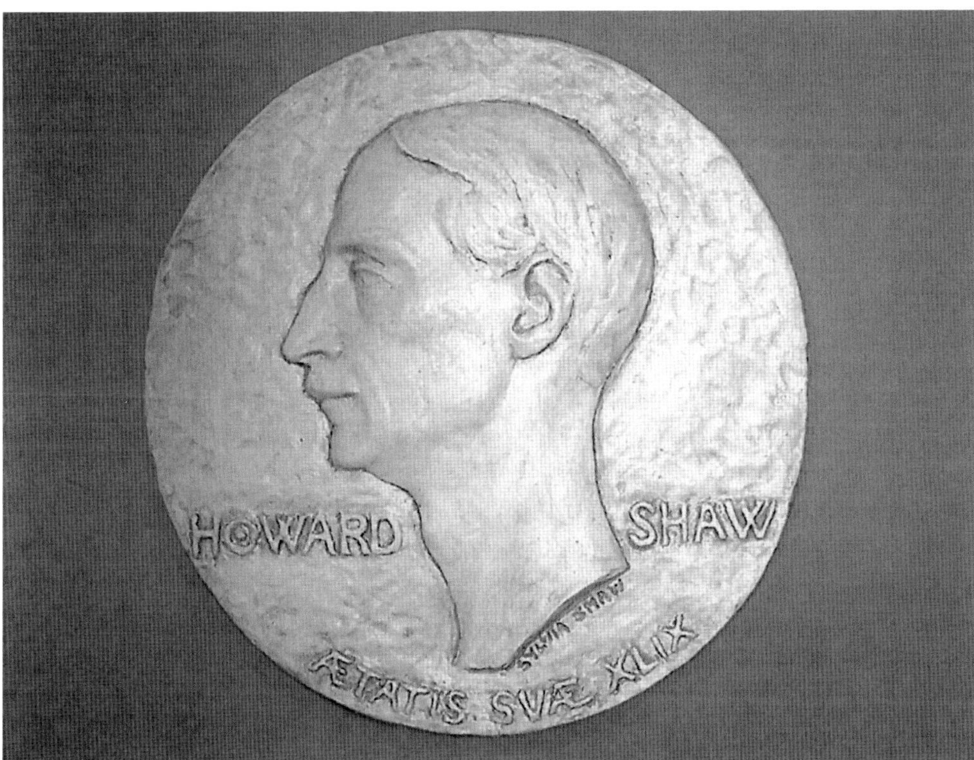

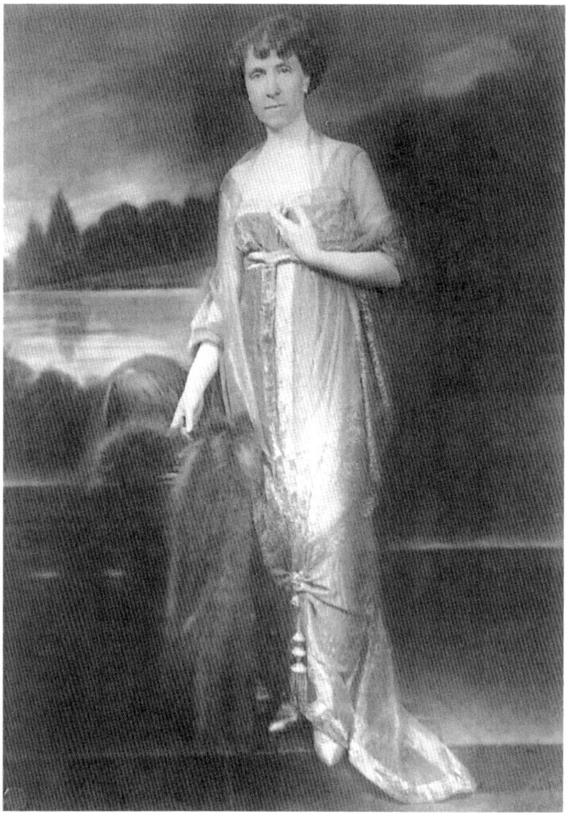

Edith Rockefeller McCormick (1872–1932)
The most stunning and well-remembered local estate—on both sides of the Atlantic—was that of Harold and Edith Rockefeller McCormick. The estate, Villa Turicum, comprised 200 acres on the south Lake Forest lakefront. Built from about 1908 to 1912, it was the vision of Edith, the daughter of wealthy John D. Rockefeller, with her New York architect Charles A. Platt. Later divorced, she was a grand dame in Chicago society for a generation. (Todd Protzman-Davis; LFCLASC.)

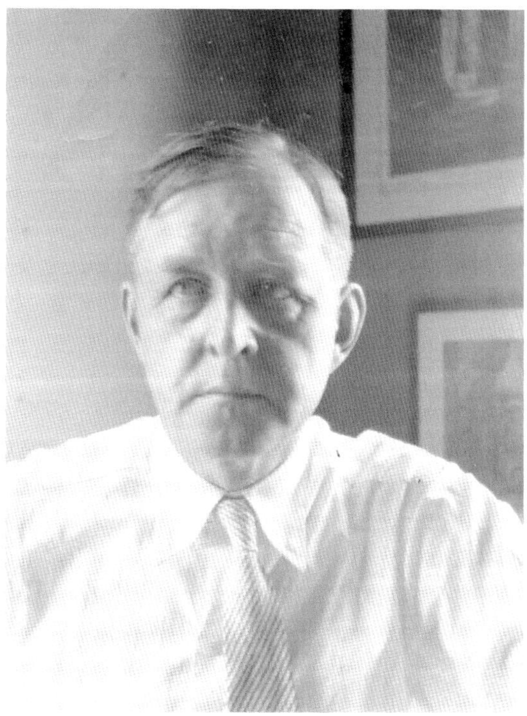

Edward H. Bennett (1874–1954)
English-born city planner Edward Bennett received his *diplome* from the École des Beaux-Arts in 1901. He arrived in Lake Forest in 1907 while working with coauthor Daniel Burnham on the 1909 *Plan of Chicago*. He later married and lived here permanently; his grandson E.H. Bennett III is still a resident. In the 1920s, he created the city zoning ordinance and introduced the Plan Commission, also laying out the Knollwood Club subdivision (*WLF*). (LFCLASC.)

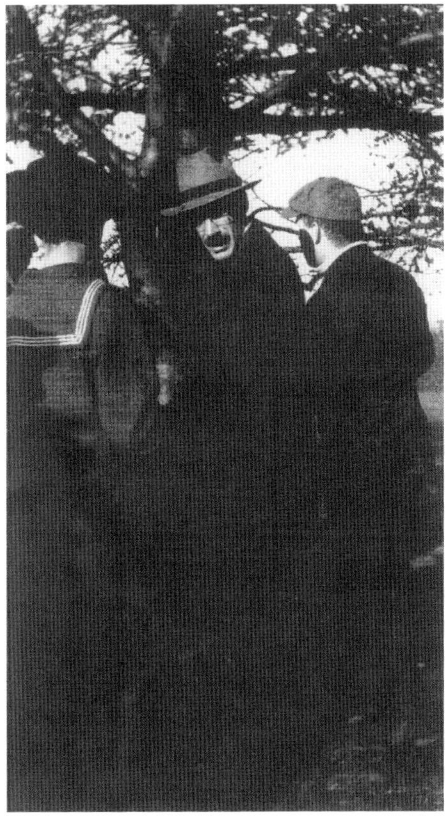

Ralph Rodney Root (1884–1964)
Root, center, educated at Cornell and the Harvard School of Design, taught landscape design at the University of Illinois from 1912 to 1918. He discovered and publicized Lake Forest's remarkable gardens, and he practiced here and in Wisconsin with a Chicago office as Root & Hollister. Promoting formal versus classic naturalistic design, he wrote *Design in Landscape Gardening* (1914), *Lake Forest* (1916), and an *Architectural Record* (January 1924) article on the local garden type. (LFCLASC.)

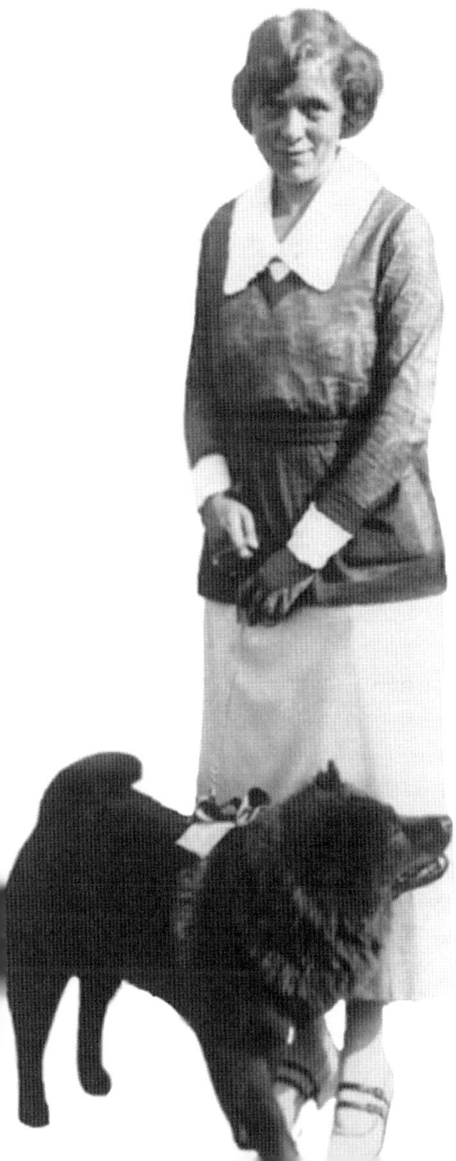

Jean Morton Cudahy (1883–1953)
Cudahy was president of the Morton Arboretum, following her father, Joy Morton, in 1934. She built the educational center there around 1940. Married to Joseph M. Cudahy, she was a director of Garden Club of America, New York, and a member of garden clubs here and in Palm Beach. She and her family had two David Adler houses in town: a 1914 home south of Deerpath Road, west of 41, and a 1930 house west of West Park. (Morton Arboretum.)

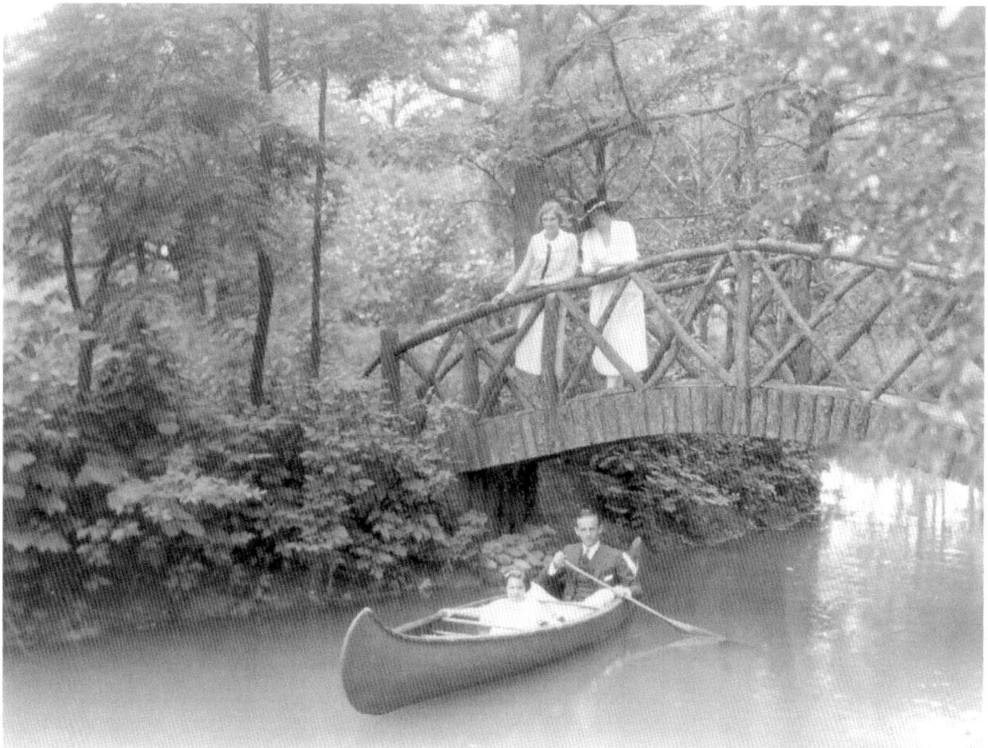

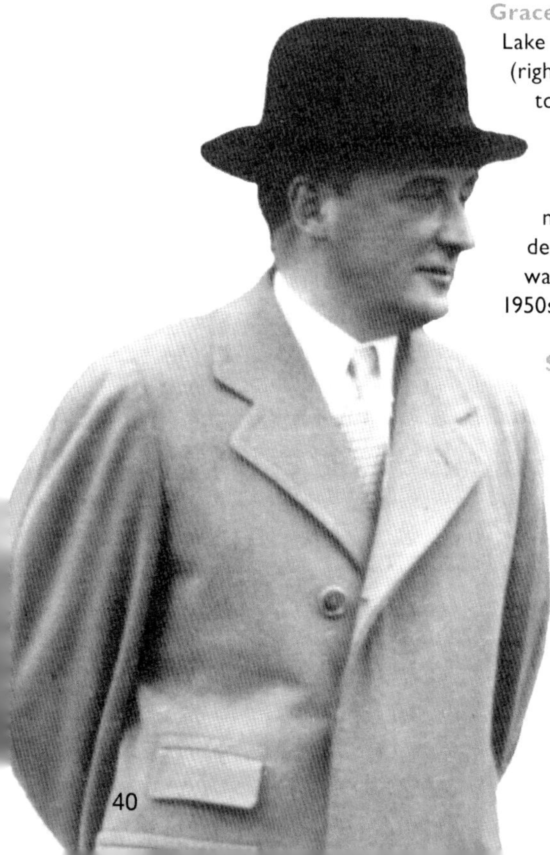

Grace Farwell Winston McGann (1868–1949)

Lake Forest Garden Club member and artist Grace McGann (right) stands on the rustic bridge over the pond connected to an island west of the second Fairlawn house, built in 1923. Her daughter-in-law Lucia Wood Winston stands next to her. Grace's son Farwell Winston and her granddaughter Ann are in the boat. Farwell served as mayor from 1925 to 1928. The pond and landscape were designed by F.L. Olmsted around 1868–1869. The water was drained when the estate was subdivided in the mid-1950s. (LF-LBHS.)

Stanley Davis Anderson (1896–1960)

Third-generation resident architect Anderson attended Lake Forest College, the University of Illinois, École des Beaux-Arts, and Penn State. He created English-style residences and notable commercial and public buildings from about 1920 to 1960. The latter included the Georgian-styled block of Deerpath Road west of Western Avenue (1925–1931), five Cotswold cottages (1926–1927) for Lake Forest College, and the Georgian Lake Forest High School (1935). He worked for Shaw until 1925, then at Anderson & Ticknor until 1941. After that, he practiced privately. (Paul Bergmann.)

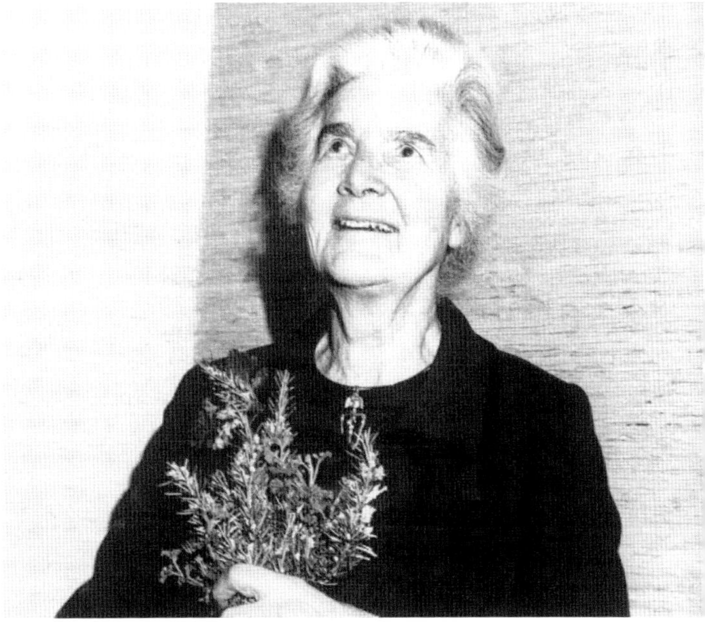

Edith Foster Farwell (1893–1977)
Farwell's Onwentsia Road herb gardens were nationally known in the middle of the 20th century, through books like her own *My Garden Gate Is on the Latch: The Story of My Garden*. Active in the Lake Forest Garden Club and serving as its wartime president, she also led 1930s and 1940s children's gardens and home-front Victory Gardens. President of the Chicago Horticultural Society Woman's Board (1957–1969), she won the society's Hutchinson Medal in 1951. (LFCLASC.)

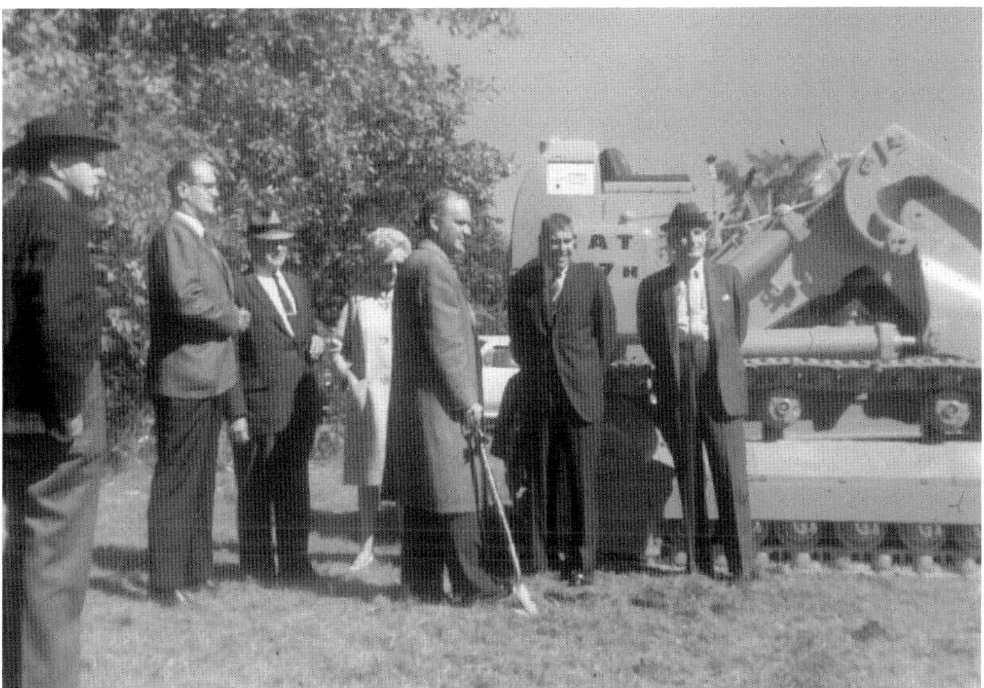

William Allan Pinkerton Pullman (1901–1988)
When resident and developer of hardy boxwood W.A.P. Pullman (shown center with shovel) died, he was hailed by Kenan Heise in the November 23 *Chicago Tribune* as the " 'father' of the Chicago Botanic Garden [CBG]." As president of the Chicago Horticultural Society (1959–1968), he convinced the Cook County Forest Preserves to acquire—and dedicate to the society—Skokie marshland at Glencoe for a botanic garden, founded in 1965. (Lenhardt Library of the Chicago Botanic Garden.)

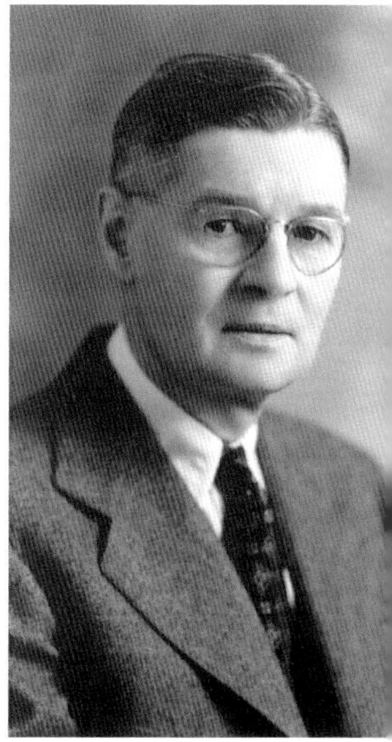

Otto George Schaffer (1886–1970)

Otto Schaffer, a 1914 graduate of the University of Illinois, taught landscape architecture at the University of Illinois at Urbana-Champaign from 1926 to 1954, ultimately chairing the department and becoming a fellow of the American Society of Landscape Architects (1943). His father was Gottlieb Schaffer, Clayton Mark's head gardener. Otto worked on designs for Triangle Park (1917) and West Park (1922). He attended Lake Forest College in 1910–1911. In 1964, he received an alumni award there. (Archives, University of Illinois.)

Irving W. Colburn (1924–1992)

Boston-born architect I.W. Colburn received his bachelor of arts degree from Yale in 1951. He is notable for his stunning New Formalist residences and institutional buildings designed while he was based in Chicago from the 1950s into the 1970s and later for preservation in suburban Boston. In 1958, he designed his AIA award–winning lakefront McLennan house, Lake Road. Other striking work included introducing, as planner, a new style at the University of Chicago. Jay Pridmore has published a 2015 study of Colburn and his work. (LFCLASC.)

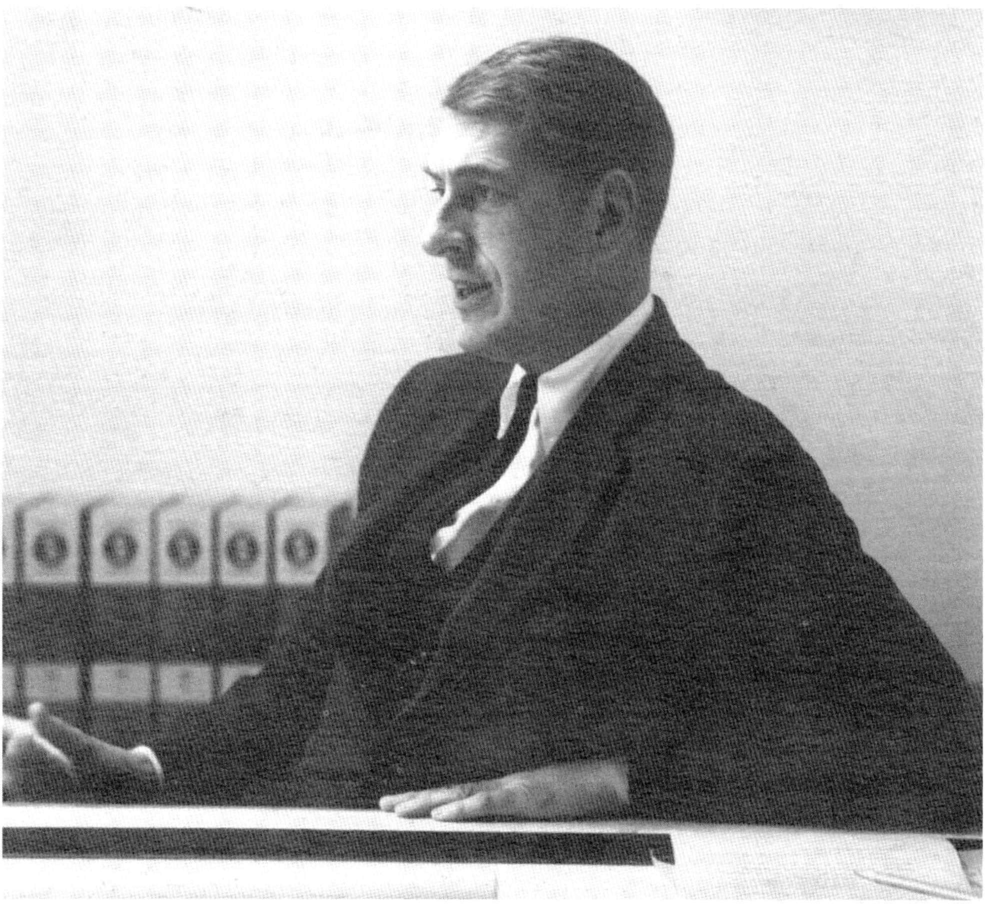

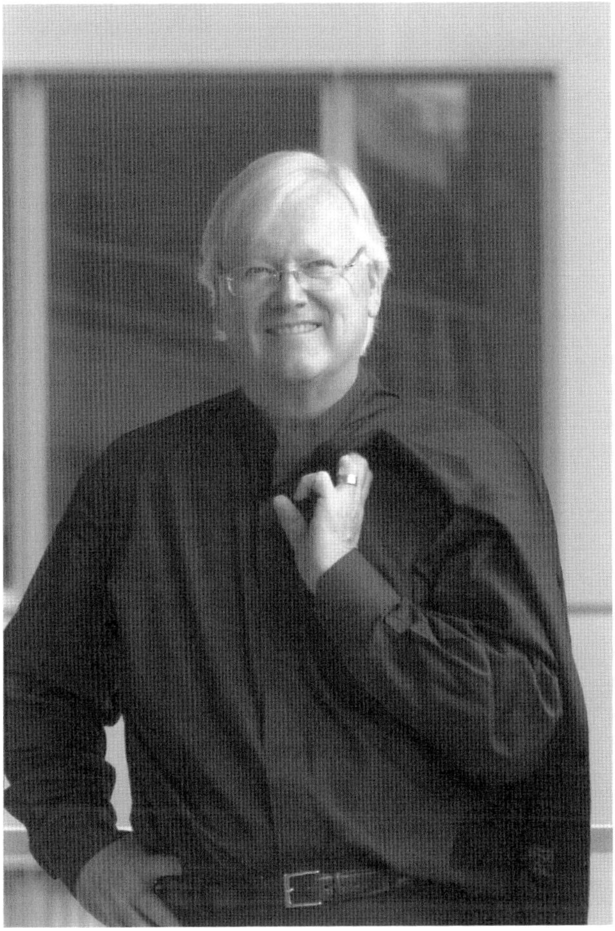

Adrian Smith
A top global architect based in Chicago and living in Lake Forest, Adrian Smith has preserved his 1920s Mount Vernon–like country house, set back on a broad lawn on North Waukegan Road's west side. The Smiths developed part of the former property, which was south and west of their home, in the Summerfield Drive neighborhood. He and his wife, Nancy, also acquired and restored Alfred E. Hamill's west-central Lake County countryside retreat, Elsewhere, designed in part by David Adler.

A 1969 graduate of the University of Illinois at Chicago's architecture program, Smith began working at Skidmore, Owings & Merrill in 1967, in the era when the firm designed Chicago's John Hancock Building (1969) and the Sears Tower (1974), the latter then the world's tallest building (1,451 feet). In 2015, the Lake Forest resident has under construction his design for the soon-to-be tallest building (3,300 feet) in Jedah, Saudi Arabia: the Kingdom Tower. His 2010 Burj Khalifa in Dubai is currently the tallest (2,722 feet). Smith's Chicago-based firm, the 2006-founded Adrian Smith + Gordon Gill, employs some 200 highly skilled staff members, bringing to Chicago the high-level intellectual work and jobs these megaprojects entail. His last tall Chicago project was the Trump Tower (1,389 feet) in 2009, not including its 2014 postconstruction signage.

In 2011, Smith was selected for the second Local Legend Award of the Lake Forest–Lake Bluff Historical Society. He is recognized as a Chicago business leader as well as a gifted, skilled, and persuasive designer, and his career recalls that of visionary Daniel Burnham. His great plans incorporate a kind of magic that has the power to stir clients' blood—from Chicago to the Middle East, from China to South Korea. (Adrian Smith.)

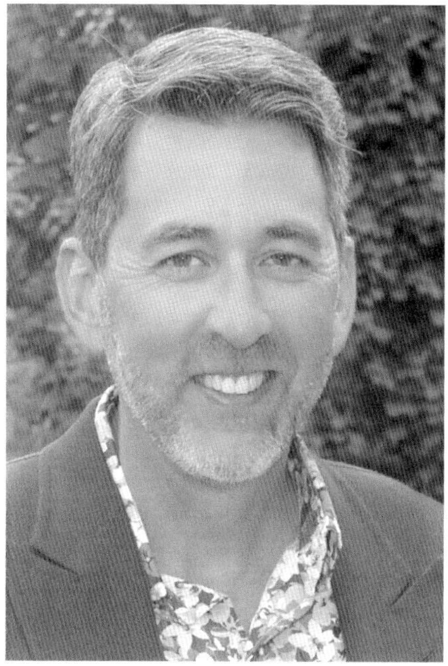

Craig Bergmann

A 1981 graduate of DePaul, Bergmann started his landscape design practice in 1982 and has since been applying his unique horticultural and design talent to North Shore gardens and beyond. He creates and restores gardens for great houses and small places. In 2011, with interior designer Paul Kluge, Bergmann purchased and has been restoring as studio and living space the Adler-designed residential group of structures at Elawa Farm. One of Bergmann's most notable garden restorations was that for the Ibero-Moorish garden of the House of the Four Winds (1909), originally designed by Howard Shaw and Boston's Rose Standish Nichols. The original arbor vitae were overgrown, allowing no light into the garden, and Bergmann substituted European hornbeam to make possible three growing seasons there. The pools and fountains were restored, too, by the Fernando firm around 2002.

Bergmann began gardening as a youngster, and this passion for plants developed into a uniquely effective eye for design in the first decade of his practice. By the mid-1990s, his evocative "Secret Garden" at the annual March Navy Pier Garden Show was a revelation that grew crowds of awed visitors. This showmanship as recently as the April 2015 Chicago Botanic Garden Antiques Show was outstanding and a draw for the event in its own right. He also ran the Onwentsia courtyard plant and garden ornament shop for the Lake Forest Garden Club's 2015 June House and Garden Walk.

Bergmann's consultations and horticultural and design projects have ranged from the garden restoration and early development at Camp Rosemary, by the early 1990s spreading over several acres, to the charming ravine-edge formal garden for an adaptively reused 1890 Lawrence Gustav Hellberg castle-like stable on a one-acre parcel. He also restored a small parterre by landscape architect Helen Brown Milman for the current owners of the 1930 Art Deco Milman house on Green Bay Road, designed by her architect husband, Ralph. In 2011, Bergmann led the restoration of Lake Forest College's 1909-completed Glen Rowan, the former Barnes estate of Howard Van Doren Shaw, contributing the design and committing to creating seasonal container gardens as donations as well. Other non-college funding came from the Lake Forest Garden Club with in-kind contributions from Stonework by Fernando, Lake Bluff—the firm that restored to the water features at the House of the Four Winds.

For three decades, Bergmann has contributed to garden restoration and development locally, a commitment only heightened by his purchasing the A. Watson Armour residential compound at Elawa Farm in this decade. This commitment to preservation and classic garden development over three generations has earned him truly legendary status here. (Craig Bergmann.)

Stephen Christy

Stephen Christy completed his graduate study as a landscape architect by writing on Midwestern native landscape proponent Jens Jensen. When Christy's mentor, Prof. William Tishler, put together a series of profiles of landscape architects for a pioneering 1989 National Trust for Historic Preservation book, *American Landscape Architecture: Designers and Places*, he charged Christy with writing one of the key articles—on regional master Jens Jensen, a resident of Highland Park and, after 1935, Ellison Bay, Wisconsin.

By then, Christy was the first executive director and first full-time employee for the 1967-founded Lake Forest Open Lands Association (LFOLA). Beginning in 1984, Christy was bringing to life Jensen's natural restoration ideals at Lake Forest in places like the Shaw Prairie, west of Green Bay Road. Indeed, in the early 1990s, Christy had his office in the basement at Howard Shaw's Ragdale, owned by the city and overlooking the prairie leading down to the Skokie River. Christy has worked with an inspired and tireless LFOLA board of directors to preserve hundreds of acres of land, particularly on the west side of Lake Forest and in Mettawa, and he has worked with the city to allow new forms of development that preserve open space. He has planned for trails and points of entry to Open Lands preserves and worked with a variety of mostly volunteers to carry out early spring prairie burns, to remove invasive species, and to build amenities, such as bridges.

Christy's private consulting and landscape practice has included the landscaping of the Lake Forest beach for the city, working with Lake Forest Garden Club, around 1988. Almost three decades later, this has evolved as a mature landscape of lawn, trees, and ravine edge with native plantings. It also has been the model for rehabilitation of the bluff-top portion of Forest Park, above the beach, including the recently restored bluff side's natural meadow planting.

Stephen Christy's adherence to Jensen's ecological and native design principles, and his assertive work to protect and appropriately design open space in Lake Forest, have contributed greatly to the 21st-century character of the city. With three decades of steady LFOLA and community commitment, the project comprises over 800 acres, with scores of trained staff and volunteers. Christy—and his vision of 30 years ago—ranks among the major molders of the townscape, as well as of the prevailing local land ethic. (Stephen Christy.)

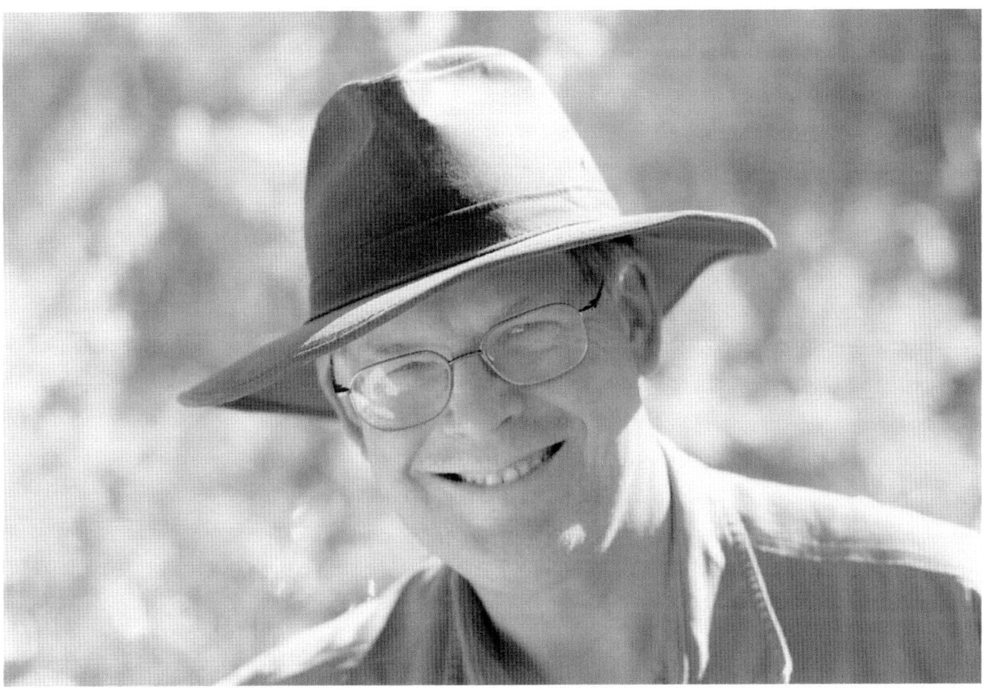

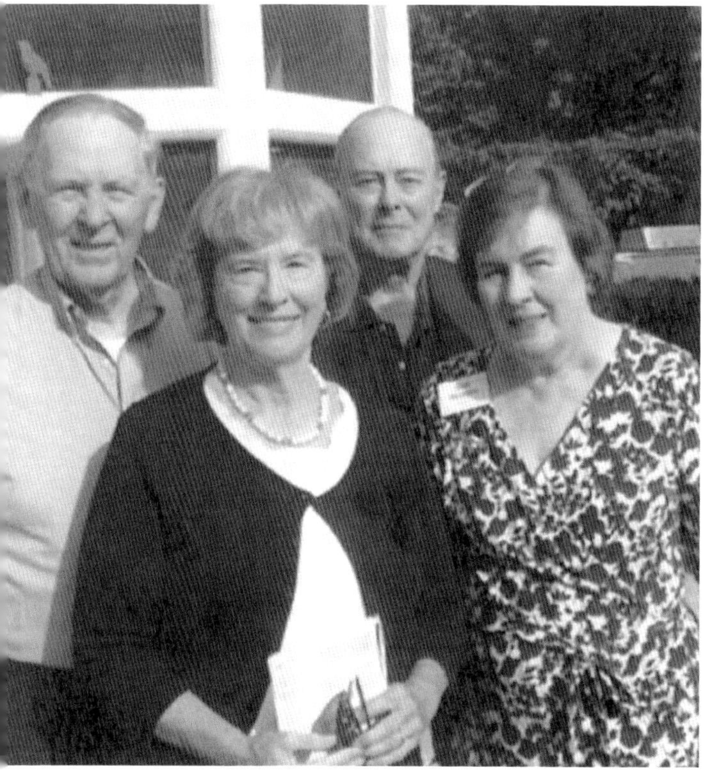

Gail Hodges

Former chair of the Lake Forest Building Review Board (1990–1993) and alderman (1993–1999), Gail Hodges is shown here, right, next to her husband, Jim, with Bob and Nancy Salzwedel at a preservation foundation event. She served as president of the Lake Forest Preservation Foundation from 2013 to 2015, reprising a role she had played in 1980–1982. While serving on the city council, she was engaged in the restoration of city hall and contributed to passage of the 1998 Historic Preservation Ordinance, which provided protections for historic districts, often estate areas. (Gail Hodges.)

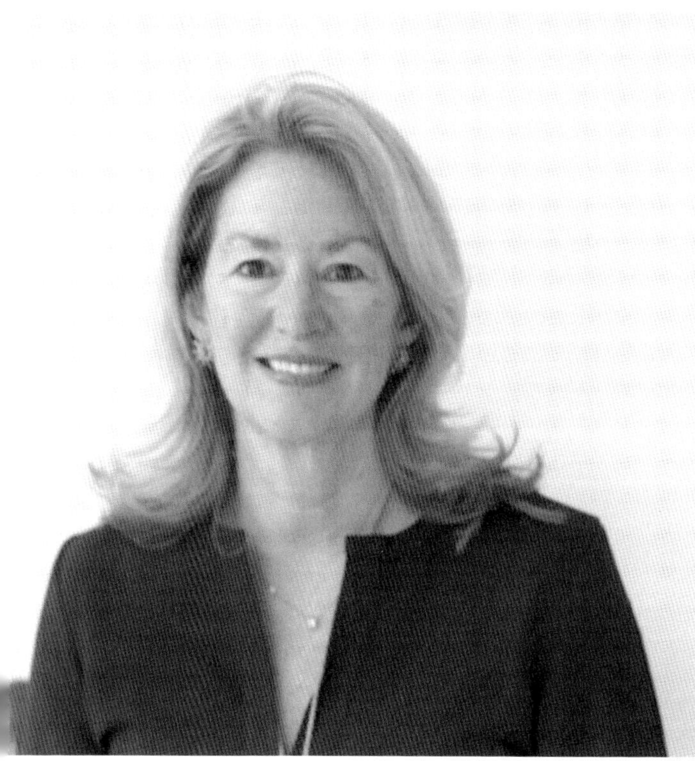

Marcy Kerr

Michigan native Marcy Kerr has been executive director of the Lake Forest Preservation Foundation (LFPF) since 2007, ramping up the organization's effectiveness. Long an active volunteer for the First Presbyterian Church, Infant Welfare, Lake Forest schools, and other groups, she has brought this experience to the foundation, along with her enthusiasm, warmth, organization, and tact. (LFPF.)

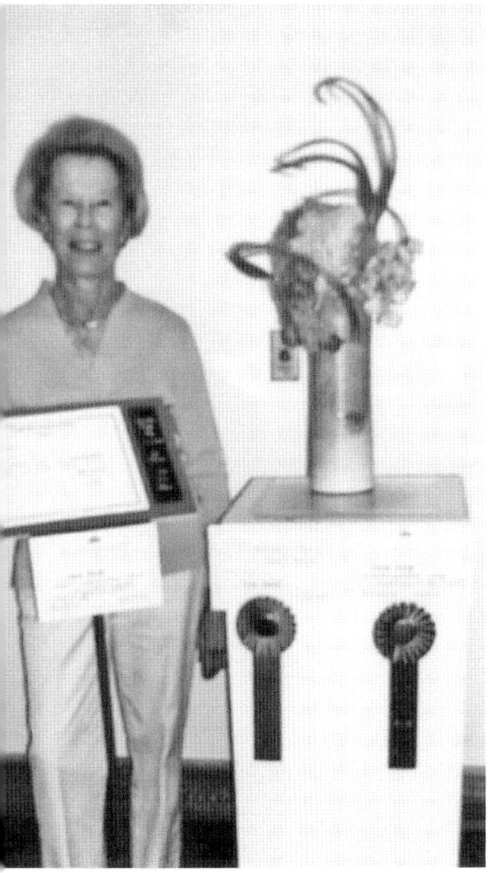

Carol Coffey Swift

Mrs. Edward Swift III is a world-renowned floral artist and winner of a medal for a huge arrangement at the Chelsea Flower Show, London, in 1992. The medal for flower arranging in the select Garden Club of America (GCA) is named for her. Swift has exhibited globally, and her work appears in major books. She has been a leading officer in the GCA and locally. (Art Miller.)

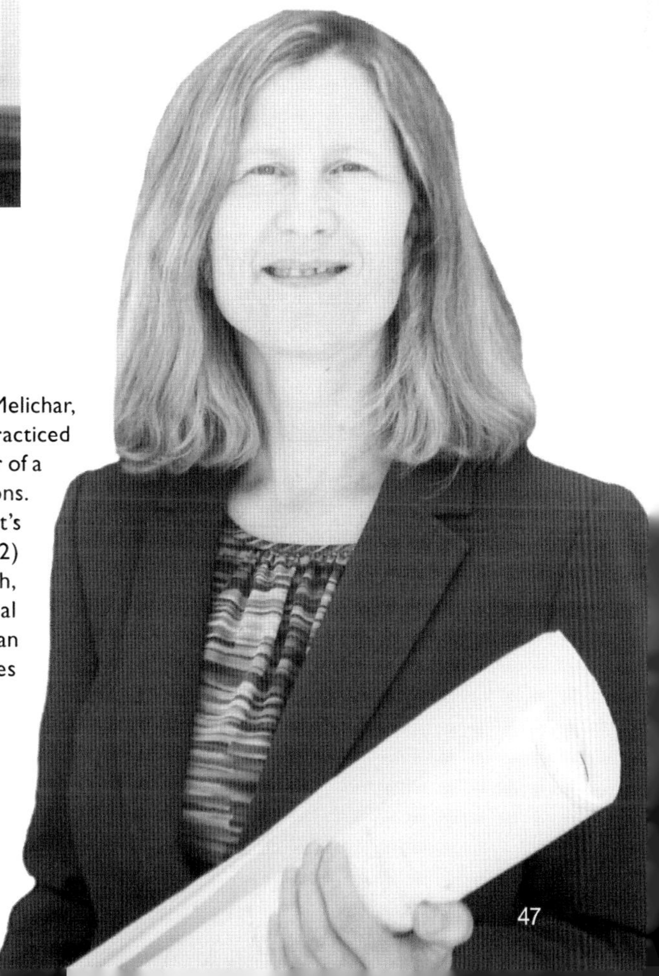

Diana Melichar

Architect and interior designer Diana Melichar, educated at Tulane and Columbia, has practiced architecture in Lake Forest for about a quarter of a century and has had many residential commissions. Notable projects include the Northern Trust's east side compatible addition (*DLF*, page 42) and her west Lake Forest Northern branch, both reflecting the Georgian stability of local banking. Her firm's westside train station is an anchor of that area, redeveloped two decades ago. (Melichar Architects.)

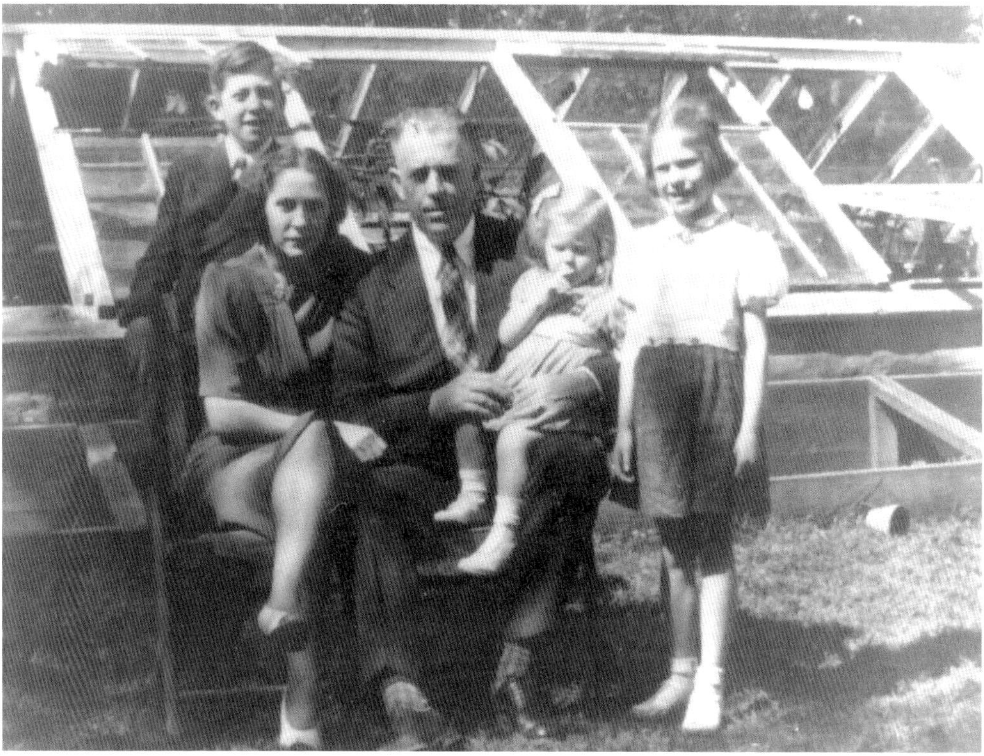

Sylvester MacDonald (1895–1981)

Ontario native and gardener Sylvester MacDonald came to Lake Forest in 1925, first serving as an under-gardener at Ragdale. By 1930, he worked at the E.L. Baker place (designed by Shaw in 1907) as gardener/driver, with his family living on the property. A North Shore Horticultural Society member, MacDonald won many awards. He is shown here at the Baker place's greenhouse with his family: from left to right, his son Kenneth, wife Avis, daughter Jeanette on his lap, and daughter Shirley. (SMP.)

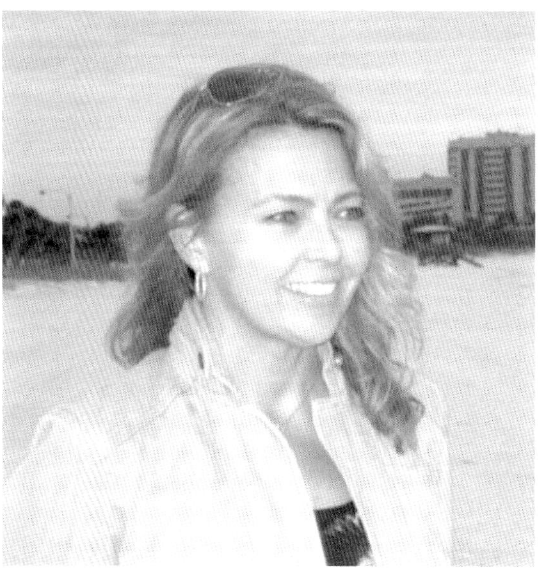

Sharon Harvey

With her husband, architect David Poulton, interior designer Sharon Harvey, a member of the American Society of Interior Designers, set up a design-build practice in the Poulton Group a quarter of a century ago, with offices in Market Square's iconic north tower. She received her bachelor of fine arts degree from the University of Colorado. Well-known local projects range from the stunning Italian villa for the Krebs family to the highly contextual country place at 240 North Ahwahnee Road, which looks like it was built a century ago. (Poulton Group.)

Marion Cartwright

Gardener, horticulturalist, native-plant expert, and organization volunteer Marion Cartwright (left) has been a leader in the restoration of native habitats and of gardens locally for Lake Forest Open Lands and Forest Park. She and DeeDee Borland revived the gardens at the city's Elawa Farm. Part of the large local Stuart clan noted for its civic dedication, she is descended from Dr. McClure, Presbyterian pastor from 1881 to 1905. Shown on the right is Ann Batenburg, who helped in the garden's first year. (Marion Cartwright.)

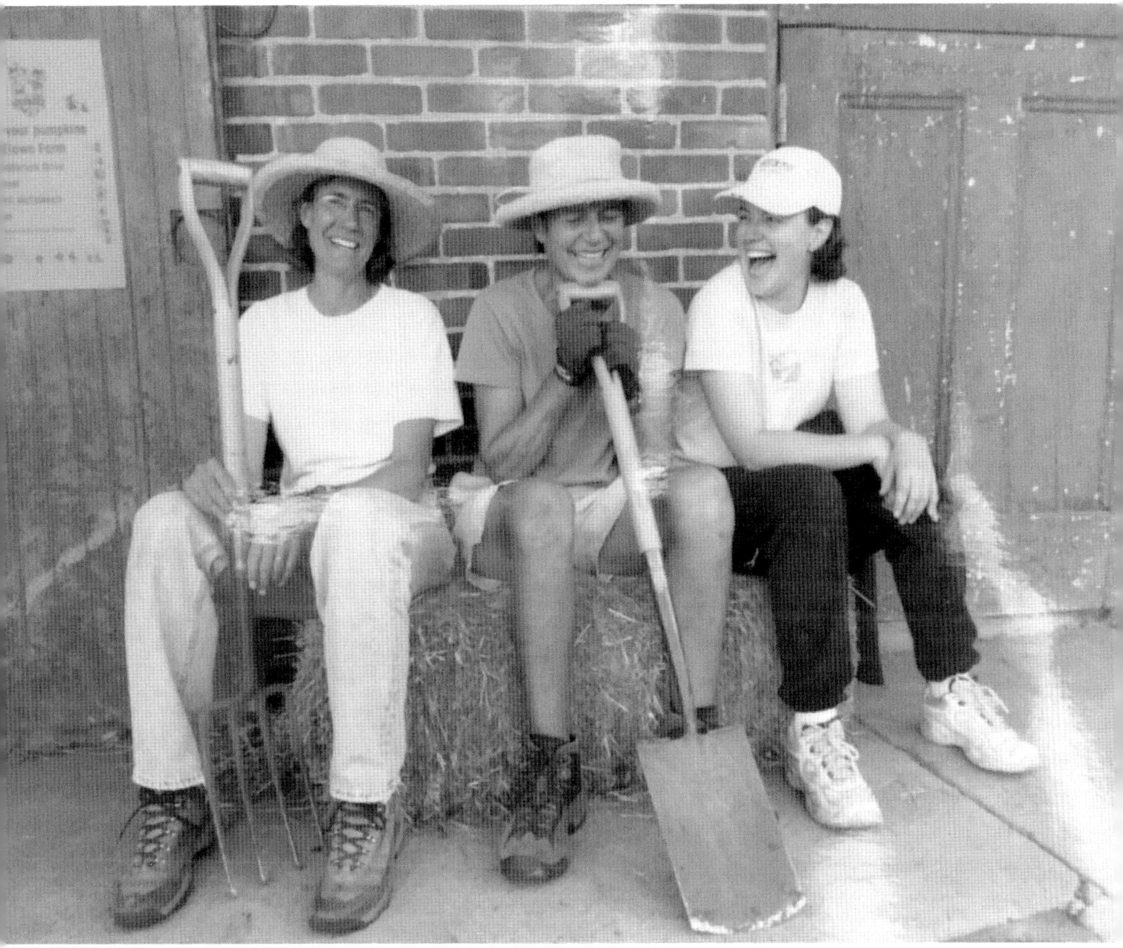

Dorothy J. Borland

DeeDee Borland (Master's School, Dobbs Ferry, New York; bachelor of arts, Univesity of Colorado; certificate, New York Botanical Garden) (center) loves to garden. She has lived much of her life in town, but while in New York for her husband's publishing business, she studied commercial horticulture. She and Marion Cartwright directed the garden at Elawa Farm, a model of modern organic gardening, from 2004 to 2012. She serves on the farm's foundation board and volunteers in the garden's flower beds almost daily in season.

Clyde Carr (1869–1923)

Carr attended Lake Forest Academy, Princeton, and Northwestern. He was president of Ryerson Steel beginning in 1911, and he perhaps contributed most to the Chicago area through his key role in the 1909 *Plan of Chicago*. He was on the general committee chaired by Lake Forest resident Charles D. Norton (*LFEPC*) in 1907–1908 and was chair of the crucial Committee On Boulevard to Connect the North and South Sides, connecting Michigan Avenue south of the river to the two-level bridge and the new Michigan Boulevard north of the river to Lake Shore Drive. Carr's father was of Virginia origins, and his mother had a Scottish lineage. A second-generation Chicagoan and a Lake Forest Academy alumnus, Carr had the social connections essential to convincing the elite, older residents of Pine Street (now Michigan Avenue) to make way for progress. He worked closely with Norton, who also perhaps brought him onto the Lake Forest College Board (1909–1913). He also served on the boards of the Orchestral Association and the Chicago Plan Commission.

Carr and his wife since 1894, Lillian, lived in Chicago at 1130 North Lake Shore Drive, Howard Shaw's innovative co-op apartment building at Elm Street, built in 1910. This was just three short blocks north of the upper terminus of Michigan Avenue, north of the Chicago River, that Carr had played a key role in creating. Indeed, through his work on the 1909 plan and with its follow-through plan commission, he contributed to the subsequent development of Streeterville and the Gold Coast. Michigan Avenue south of the river, along Grant Park, with Millennium Park and an expanded Art Institute, is one of the most vital streets in the nation.

In Lake Forest, Clyde Carr soon bought land at 55 North Mayflower Road, a block north of E.L. Ryerson's Havenwood, just being completed. After passing on a landscape plan by Jens Jensen, the Carrs chose a plan by Warren Manning, with its entry road farther south. Carr built his 1916 Wyldwood summer estate house, a French Provincial manor by New York architect Harrie T. Lindeberg, set in a nationally significant, naturalistic landscape. The Wyldwood house's entry features spectacular metalwork by New York craftsman Ira Bach. (LFCLASC.)

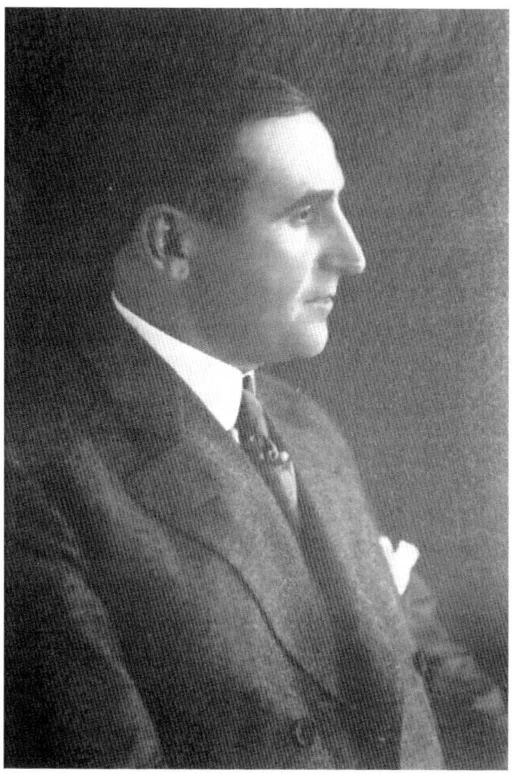

CHAPTER FOUR

Religious Leaders, Philanthropists, Organizational Leaders, and Volunteers

Religious leaders, along with the founding Chicago business leaders, their educators, and the designers of their buildings, were integral to launching Lake Forest. These selfless pioneers were the first in an evolving local group of other-focused reformers and givers. These include donors of money and goods, supporters of nonprofit organizations, and volunteers of all sorts who look beyond their self-interest to improve the lot of others. Lake Forest's DNA is Scots and mainline Protestant, originally Puritan-descendant strict observers. This meant quietly contemplative Sundays, no alcohol, modest dress, general self-control, and deep commitments to giving. Early on, this philosophy led to foreign-missions interest, especially by women, such as Sarah Rhea, her daughter Annie Rhea Wilson, and Mary Smith Farwell (*LFEPC*).

Sylvester Lind was a "first donor," or first pledger, though he never fulfilled his 1857 commitment to Lake Forest University. But, for the most part, pledges have been sound, and donations have often been breathtaking. Lake Forest Library (1931) was made possible by the daughters of John G. Shedd; the land for Northwestern Lake Forest Hospital was donated by the Dick family; and the early building for Lake Forest University was provided by the Durand and C.B. Farwell families. Between those two, their donations equaled two thirds of John D. Rockefeller's first $1-million gift for the University of Chicago. Sometimes, the most notable gifts are small donations, as evidenced by the many named benches at the beach or seats in the 2001 renovation of the high school auditorium. The big investors and donors over the last century have been the Onwentsia set. They have funded the West Park middle-class subdivision (1907) and Market Square; maintained the Alice Home Hospital in the 1920s; and funded the 1998–2000 Market Square landscape renovation and, lately, the rehabilitation of Forest Park. Small donations have been sought to broaden local shared commitment.

A major generator of funds for worthy causes during the last century has been benefit performances and parties. These events have supported settlement houses in Chicago in the 1910s and 1920s; hospitals in Lake Forest and Chicago; medical research; church benevolence giving (as with the annual April Presbyterian church auction dinner); and unique local campaigns, such as Bernie's Book Bank, a recently formed initiative to distribute new and gently used books to underprivileged grade-school students. Some of these events were great traditions of the pre-1970 era, such as the holiday debutant cotillion for Passavant Hospital in Chicago, drawing a large share of its debutants from Lake and Green Bay Roads in town. Annual galas for Lyric Opera, the Chicago Symphony, Ravinia Festival, Field Museum, Misericordia Home, and various hospitals and medical research institutions illuminate the regional social season and provide essential private funding in an era when public coffers are tapped out.

Before 1970, the *Chicago Tribune* and, more exclusively, the periodical *Town Topics* delighted in regaling their readers with these happenings. But that stopped, and, a generation later, local magazines, like John Conatser's *Forest & Bluff*, have picked up on the tradition and photographed and identified people at such benefit gatherings. The old guard may have avoided such public display, but, increasingly, scions of old families are appearing on the JWC Media pages. Thus goes the procession, to recall Henry Blake Fuller's 1895 novel about Chicago's evolving social scene, *With the Procession*.

The monetary gifts of many donors are equaled by the contributed time of selfless volunteers. The Lake Forest Open Lands Association maintains about 800 acres of restored natural landscape, managed mostly by volunteers guided by scores of useful, often very knowledgeable volunteers and a small cadre of staff. At Lake Forest College, one volunteer land steward, alumnus trustee Dennis Nyren, has donated countless hours, perhaps most visibly in the early 2000s, when he restored the long ravine edge between Washington and Sheridan Roads at Glen Rowan. This had been an overgrown and buckthorn-bound landscape until he returned it to life, with advice from landscape architect Cliff Miller, the equivalent of a six-figure donation to his alma mater.

So many people and institutions have expressed the fundamental instinct to give back and to help those in need, including the following: Boy Scouts and Girl Scouts; the American Legion, with its century-old Lake Forest Day project; the Friends of the Library; hospital volunteers; senior-center drivers; and those who work to help those less fortunate beyond the city limits, such as the Gorter and Hender families, who have pioneered recent sharing with North Chicago. There are as many ways to help as there are causes that cry out for support. Children of Lake Foresters have gone on to serve as missionaries in Persia (Annie Rhea Wilson) in the 19th century and to distribute aid in Kazakhstan and Myanmar (a son of Roger and Pauline Mohr) in the 21st century, and to run nonprofits in nearby towns with underserved groups—the recently deceased Garett Fitzgerald, son of former residents Kathleen and Thomas Fitzgerald, ran an Uptown Chicago community organization. Countless others give back on a part-time basis, bringing the local commitment to volunteerism to towns across the country.

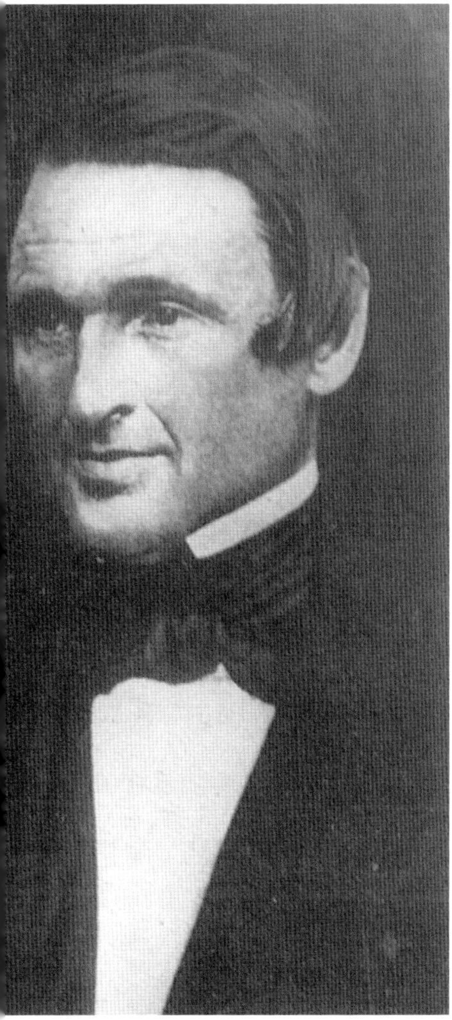

Robert W. Patterson (1814–1894)
Reverend Patterson and his Second Presbyterian Church were the founding spirits and sponsors of the town, organizing the Lake Forest Association in 1856. Patterson was the first president of Lake Forest College (1875–1878). When the Presbyterian church was built locally in 1887, the town's first stone building, it was constructed with limestone from Patterson's 1851 Chicago church building, which had burned down in the 1871 Great Fire. The patriarch spoke at the dedication. (LFCLASC.)

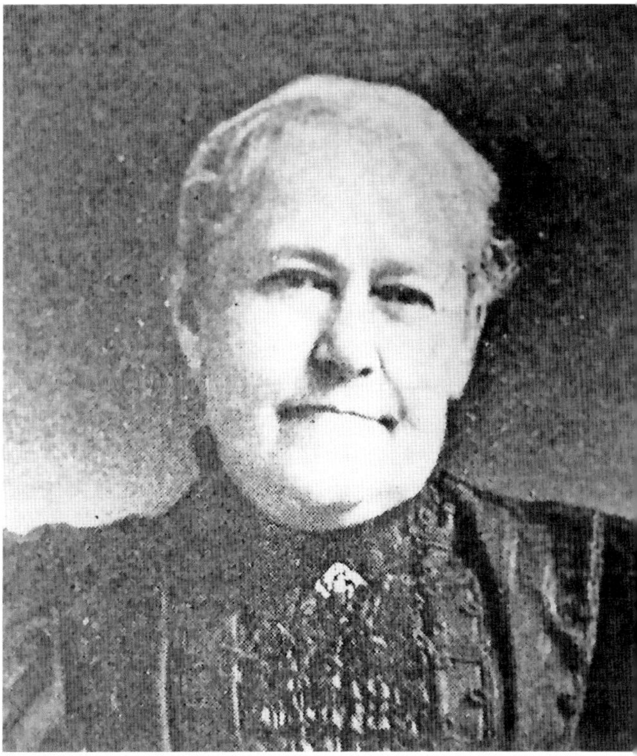

Sarah Jane Foster Rhea (1835–1918)
A former missionary in Persia, Sarah Jane Rhea, a widow with three children, settled in Lake Forest from 1873 to about 1900. She promoted support for Presbyterian foreign missions. Her home was a haven for workers visiting from Asia—a role passed on to Nettie McCormick. Rhea received many very large donations, and she founded the Presbyterian church's Steady Streams for children, to teach them philanthropy. (LFCLASC.)

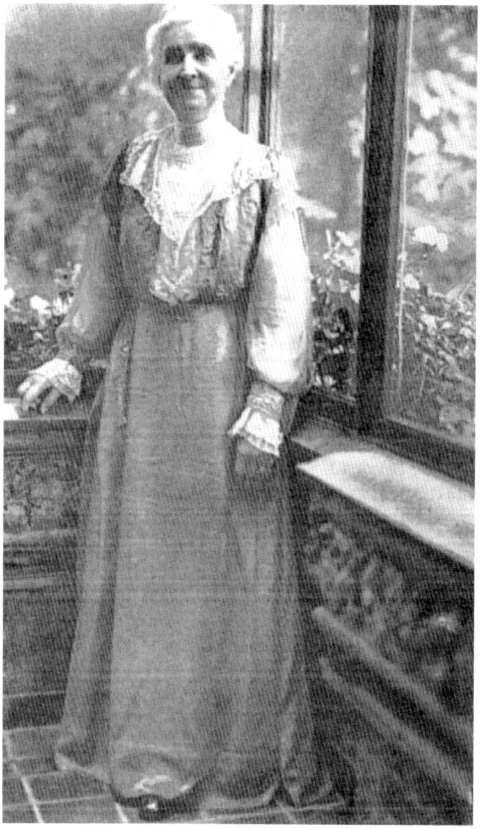

Nettie Fowler McCormick (1835–1923)
Outliving her husband, Chicago industrialist Cyrus McCormick I (1809–1884), by four decades, Nettie Fowler McCormick was the matriarch of a clan that developed summer places in town from about 1895 to 1916. Among these homes was her own, which she built with her daughter Anita Blaine. Nettie, a patron of Presbyterian foreign missions and education in China, entertained missionaries at her estate in summers. (LFCLASC.)

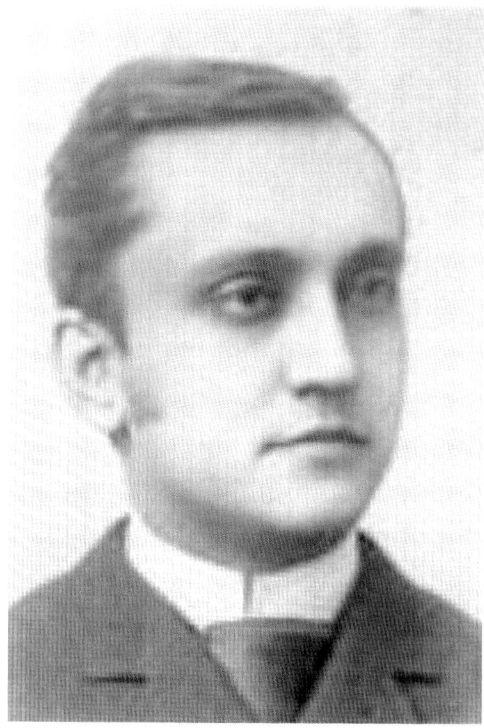

Nathan Smith Davis Jr., MD (1858–1920)
Dr. Davis was the son of the founder of modern medical education, whose medical school by the 1880s was under the umbrella of Northwestern University. Nathan Jr. became a faculty member in 1884, and he was appointed dean in 1901. In 1898, he acquired a Lake Forest Green Bay Road farm with Howard Shaw and another individual, with Shaw designing Davis's summer residence. A daughter married architect Henry Dangler, David Adler's first partner. (Find a Grave, Emma Duke.)

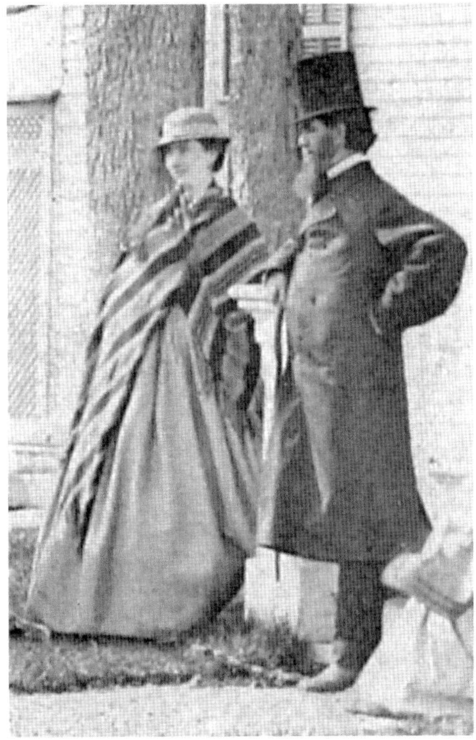

William Cowper Dickinson (1826–1899)
Rev. William Dickinson received his bachelor of arts degree from Amherst in 1848 and his bachelor of divinity degree from Andover. He was the first pastor of the Presbyterian church, initially in a temporary role (1859–62); he was later formally ordained there (1863–1868). Dickinson was the first college-level instructor for Lind University (1859–1863). His father, the Reverend Baxter Dickinson, and sisters ran the Dickinson Seminary, on College Road (1859–1867). At Amherst, he was in the circle of poet Emily Dickinson. He is shown here in 1866 with a sister, Martha. (LFCLASC.)

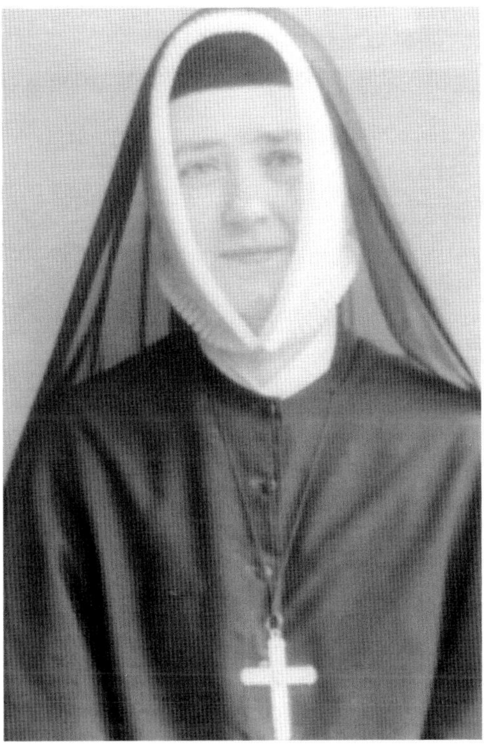

Margaret Burke, RSCJ (1903–1990)
Mother Margaret Burke was the second president of Barat College (1953–1975). By the early 1970s, she was wearing chic suits and dresses, symbolizing her ability to adapt to changes in the student body and the Catholic Church. John F. Kennedy's election as president in 1960 marked a sea change in access for Catholics, including into mainstream colleges, and Vatican II led to a decline in religious available for teaching. (Martha Curry, RSCJ.)

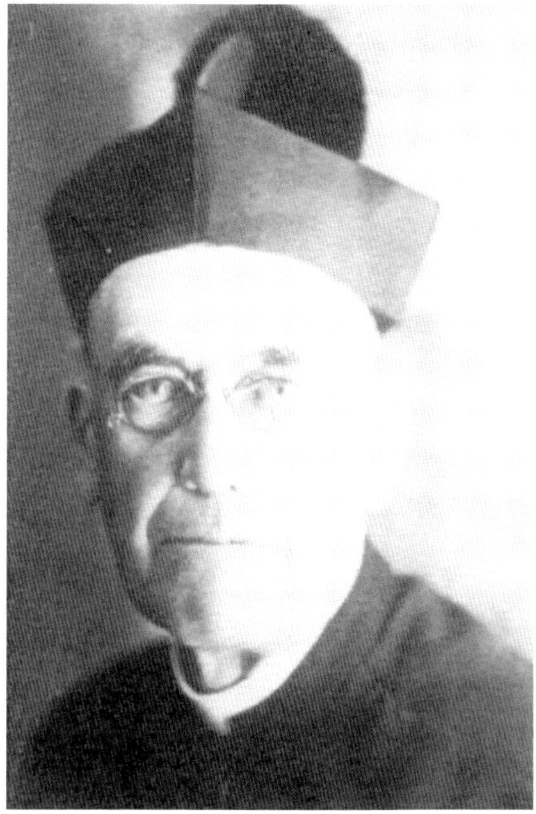

Francis J. Barry, DD (1867–1934)
Ireland-born Francis Barry attended St. Viator College in Bourbonnais, Illinois, and St. Mary's Theological School in Cincinnati and was ordained in 1894. He was pastor at St. Mary's in 1910, when the church was dedicated, and he oversaw St. Patrick's that year, when its fine old westside landmark church was built. According to local historian J.J. Halsey, in 1912, it was Father Barry's "great zeal and energy" that led to the "handsome" St. Mary's. (LFCLASC.)

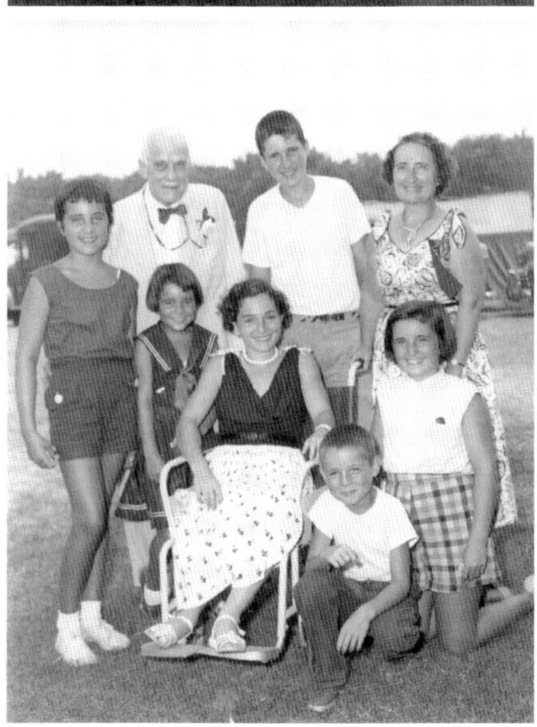

Theodore Proxmire, MD (1881–1959)
An early Lake Forest–based medical practitioner, Dr. Theodore Proxmire began his career in 1905, newly minted by a Chicago medical school. He lived on Deerpath Road, two doors from the Presbyterian church and half a block from the 1899 Alice Home Hospital (*LFEPC*, page 58). There, he delivered scores of babies, some of whom are seen here at a 1950s Lake Forest Day Reunion. His son William (1915–2005) became a noted Wisconsin US senator. (Louis E. Laflin Jr. Collection, LFCLASC.)

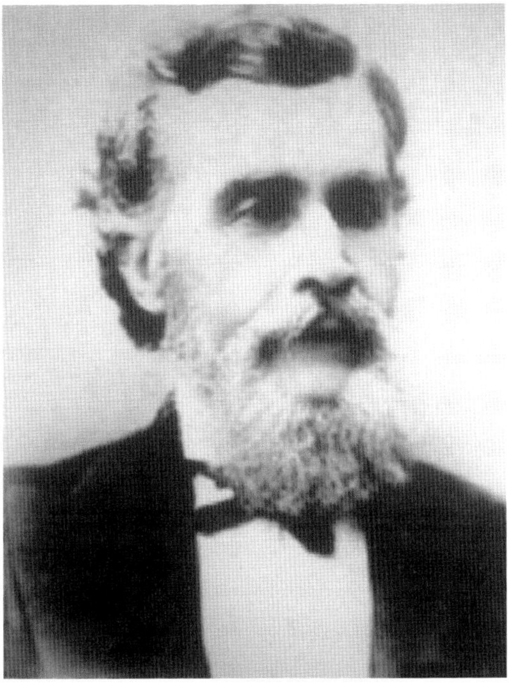

James Hughes Stokes (1815–1890)
Capt. James Stokes, an 1835 West Point graduate and official of the Illinois Central Railroad (1858–1861), was living in town, according to Edward Arpee's 1964 town history, when he volunteered for the Civil War. Stokes, after distinguished service, rose to the rank of brigadier general by 1865 and then entered the real estate field in New York. He is buried at Geneva, New York. (Find a Grave; John T. Griffith.)

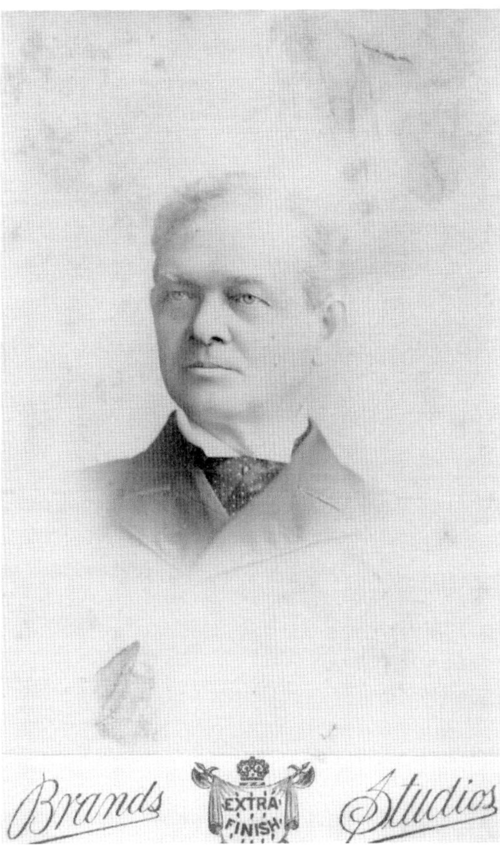

John Villiars Farwell (1825–1908)
John Farwell, who served as mayor from 1871 to 1872, cofounded with Dwight Moody the Chicago YMCA in the 1850s, funding the movement's first building. He left his successful business in the hands of his brother Charles in 1864 in order to support soldier medical relief. A few years later, Farwell went to England with Moody's evangelist crusade. In Lake Forest, J.V. Farwell was a member and leader of the Presbyterian church. (LFCLASC.)

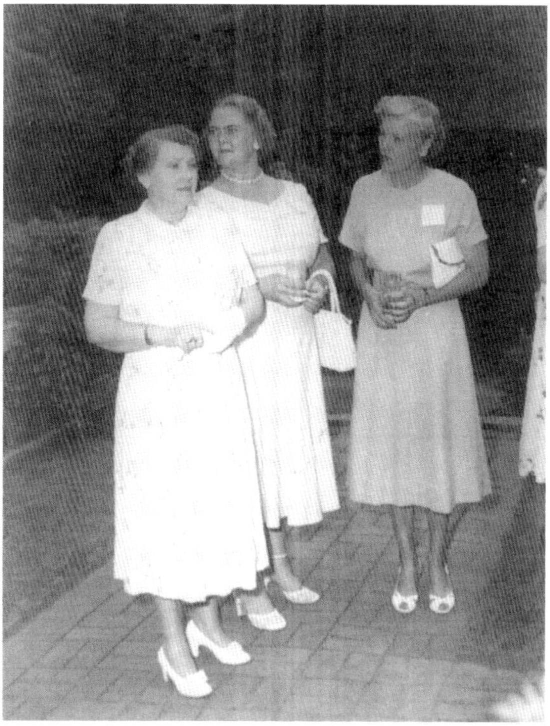

Clarice Walther Hamill (1884–1973)
Clarice Hamill is noted locally as a philanthropist for her 1955 donation to Lake Forest College of 6,500 uncommon volumes from the book collection of her husband, Alfred E. Hamill (*LFEPC*). She also was a gardener and the author of the personally hand-colored *Mexican Bouquet* (1946). She is shown here on the left with her daughter Clarice Barnes (center). (Louis E. Laflin Jr. Collection, LFCLASC.)

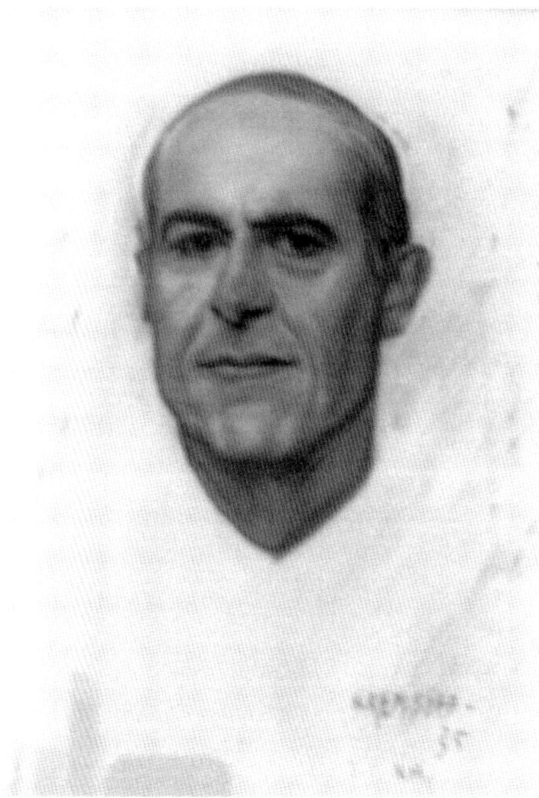

Alfred E. Hamill (1883–1953)
An investment banker, nationally known book collector, and philanthropist, second-generation resident Alfred Hamill presided over the construction and launch of the classic Lake Forest Library in 1931. A 1905 Yale graduate, he was a leader at the Art Institute and the Caxton Club and was also president of the Newberry Library. He wrote poetry, notably *This Last Devotion* (1941), under the pen name Hugh Western. See the article about him in *David Adler, Architect* (2002). (Lake Forest Library.)

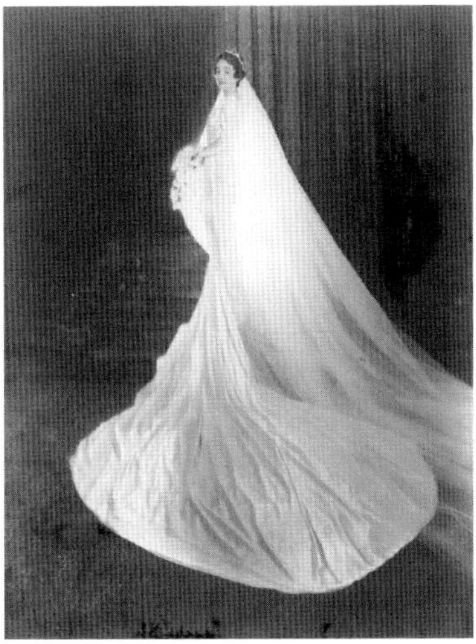

Jean Schweppe Armour (1914–1963)
As described by Rommy Lopat in her very informative article at Find a Grave, Jean Armour, the daughter of Charles and Laura Schweppe, was "the personification of glamour" as well as a donor and volunteer of note. She gave many Christian Dior and other couture dresses to the Chicago History Museum and volunteered for and was a member of the women's board of what now is Rush University Medical Center. (LF-LBHS.)

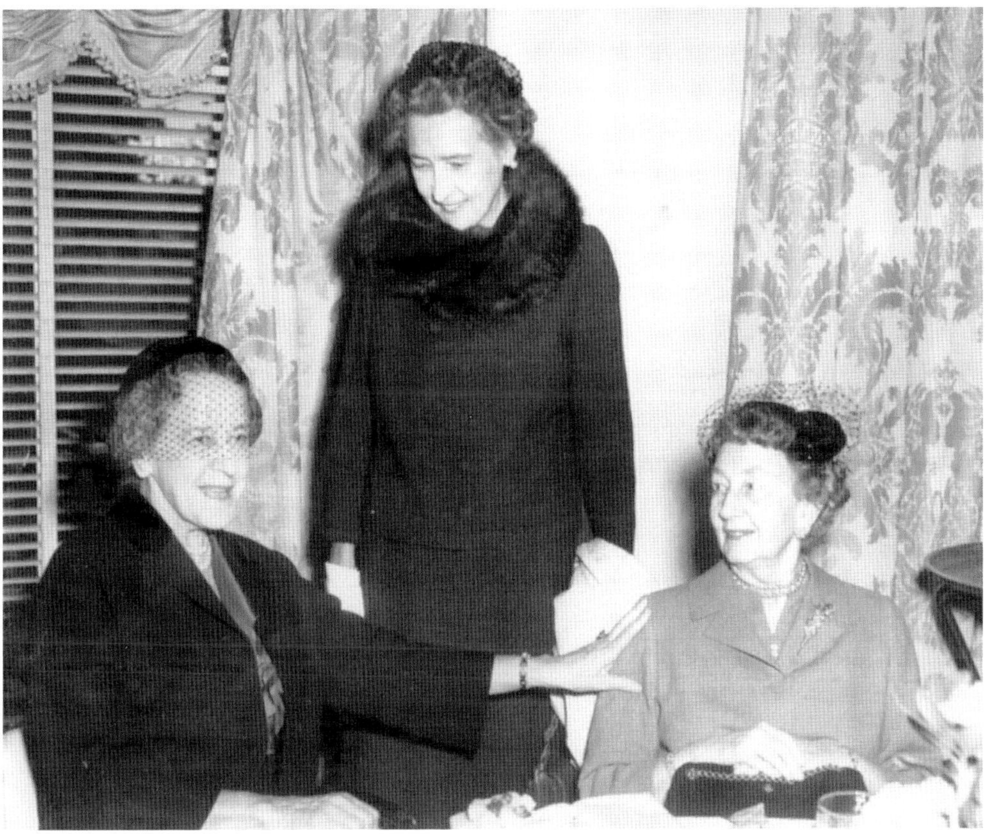

Helen Shedd Reed Keith (1884–1978)
Helen Reed, seated left, with her sister Laura Schweppe, standing, paid for the town's 1931 Lake Forest Library building on Deerpath Road, designed by Edwin Hill Clark, as a memorial to her late husband, Kersey Coates Reed, who had died early in 1929. Her 1932 home on Lake Road, designed by David Adler and standing opposite her 1927 redesigned garden, is among the most significant midcontinental classic residences. (DF.)

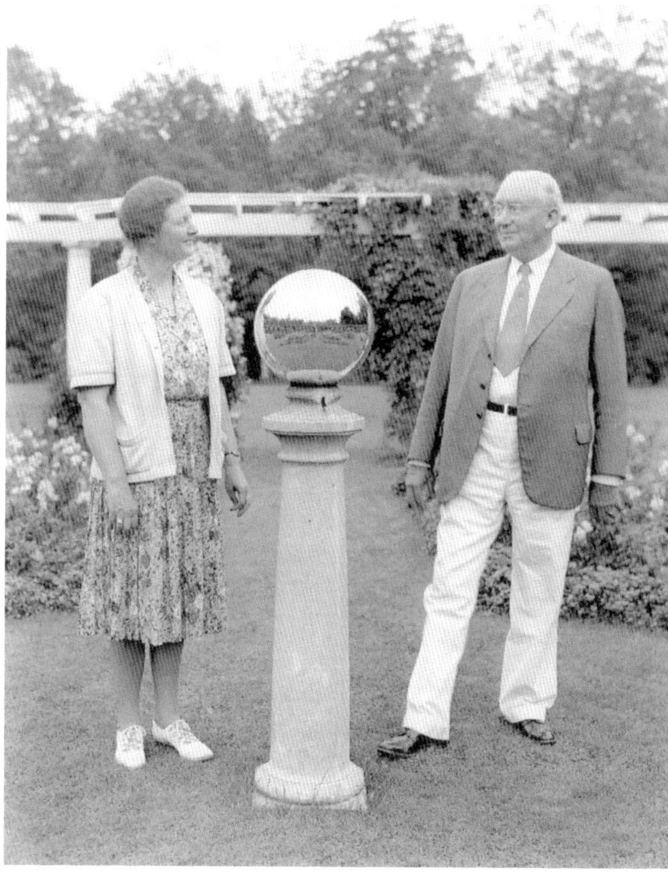

Clifford Webster Barnes (1864–1944) and Lilace Reid Barnes (1900–1989)
Lilace Reid Barnes was the daughter and only surviving child of Rev. Clifford W. Barnes and Alice Reid Barnes. Reverend Barnes was a notable Chicago reformer from the 1890s to the 1940s, and Lilace carried on her father's reform spirit and zeal. The father and daughter are shown here in the garden of their 1909 Shaw-designed house, Glen Rowan, on Sheridan Road. After Reverend Barnes's 1944 death, Lilace succeeded to his seat on the board of trustees of Lake Forest College, the first woman to serve on that body. The Yale-educated Barnes had succeeded his father-in-law, successful Chicago wholesale grocer Simon S. Reid (*LFEPC*), as head of the Reid family, which also included his spouse, Alice, and his sister-in-law, Grace Nash, in California.

As an associate of Hull House founder Jane Addams, Clifford Barnes fought for better living conditions for westside Chicago immigrants and for women's rights. When living at Hull House in the early 1890s, he rode on horseback down neighborhood alleys to inspect for trash buildup. He founded Chicago's Sunday Evening Club, which met at Orchestra Hall, for young people in 1908, and the Chicago Community Trust in 1915, for which he served as the first president.

Lilace Barnes, in turn, led the early-20th-century feminist and minority-rights campaigns of the YWCA—in Lake Forest and Chicago in the 1930s, throughout the United States in the 1940s, and internationally in the 1950s. In the 1960s, she was active in civil rights and crusaded for Chicago open housing. Around 1967, Lilace hosted a quiet meeting of Chicago real estate leaders and Dr. Martin Luther King Jr. at Glen Rowan. Lake Forest College student Bob Bullard tended bar for her on that auspicious occasion. It was held across the street from the college's Middle Campus. By 1968, she had transferred Glen Rowan to the institution and built a new Balfour Lanza–designed midcentury modern home in the ravine to the south. (LFCLASC.)

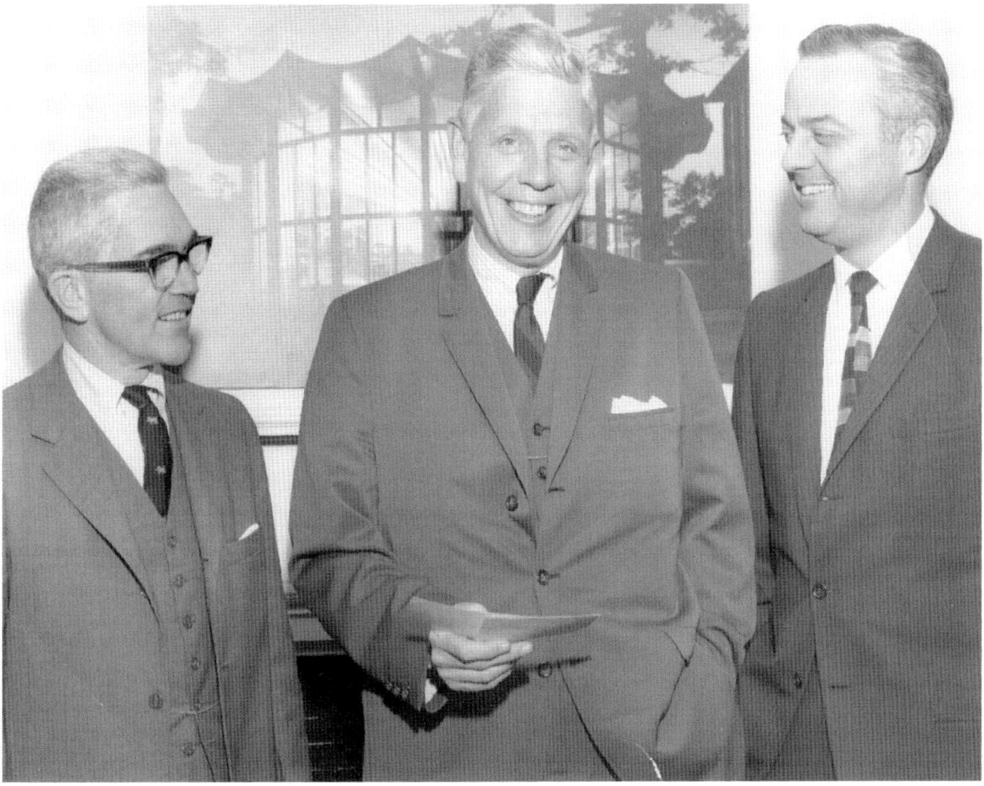

William Graham Cole (1917–2011)

Few educators from Lake Forest were of a higher public profile than religion scholar, author, speaker, and administrator William Graham Cole, center, shown here with business manager John Munshower, right. He was president of Lake Forest College (1960–1969) and the author of the 1959 hot read *Sex and Love in the Bible*. He presided over a baby-boom-era campus expansion but left financial challenges for his board of trustees and his able successor, Eugene Hotchkiss, who served from 1970 to 1993. (LFCLASC.)

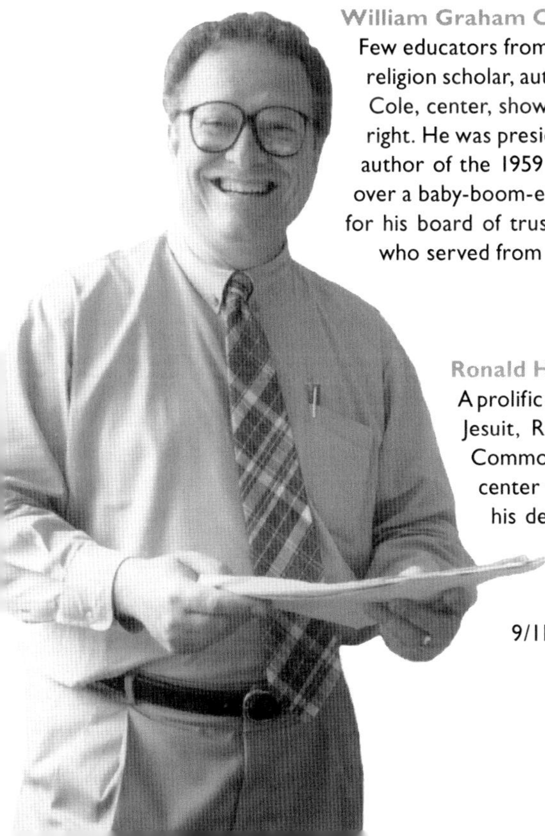

Ronald H. Miller (1938–2011)

A prolific author of books on religious subjects and a former Jesuit, Ron Miller in 1975 cofounded with Jim Kenney Common Ground, a North Shore–based interfaith center for inquiry, study, and dialogue. From 1974 until his death, he also was William A. Bross Professor of Religion at Lake Forest College. He died in New York, recently engaged in dialogue about the controversy of a planned mosque near the 9/11 Ground Zero site. (LFCLASC.)

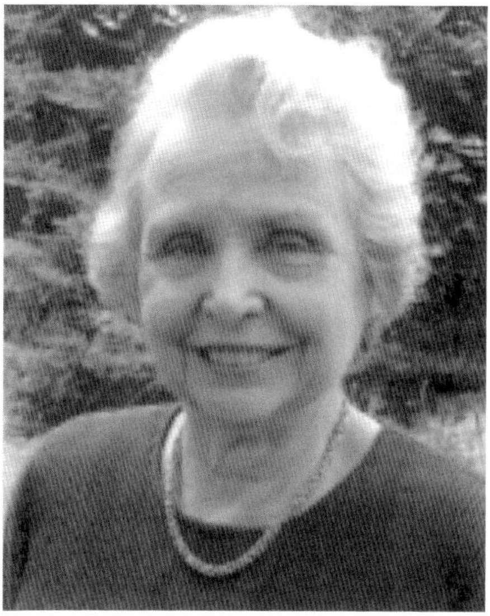

Marilyn Kearns Alaimo (1931–2014)

Marilyn Alaimo, a Lake Forest Cemetery Commission member and chair (1992–2000), received her bachelor of arts degree from the University of Illinois in 1953 and her master of business arts degree from Harvard. For 40 years, she was a volunteer and tour guide at the Chicago Botanic Garden (CBG) and, from 1987 to 1989, was president of the Garden Clubs of Illinois. She edited and coauthored *Stewards of the Land: A Survey of Landscape Architecture and Design in America* (1999). (Wenban Funeral Home.)

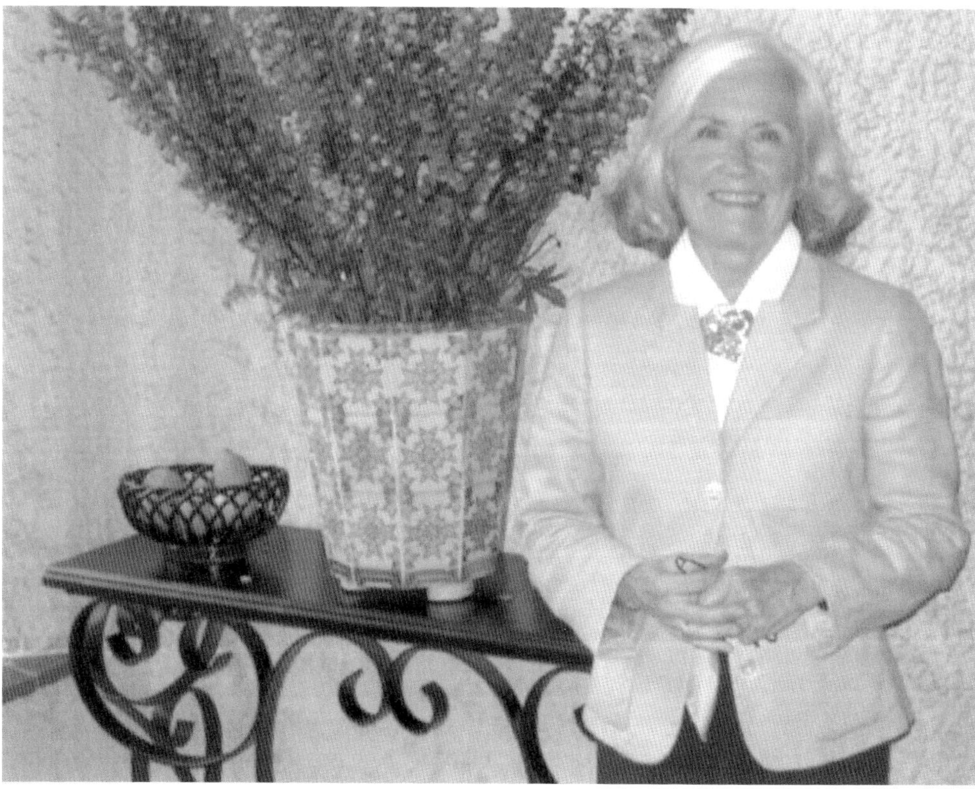

Carol Champ

Retired Army Corps of Engineers officer Carol Champ is a leading local volunteer. Her activities include the following: board member of the Preservation Foundation; a leader of the annual September Lake Forest Library book sale; and a connoisseur especially of Chicago and Lake Forest antiquarian books. She is a past president of the Friends of the Library. She and her husband, Alan, also serve actively with the American Legion's McKinlock Post in town. (*Daily North Shore.*)

Roger Mohr

Roger Mohr, who has lived in Lake Forest for over 40 years, has been a significant Lake Forester for three leadership aspects of his life: his career in Chicago advertising; his work with the Western Golf Association (golf sponsors of the BMW Championship event in 2015) and the Evans Scholar program; and his volunteer work with the City of Lake Forest, highlighted by his service as an alderman (2000–2006) and currently with the Lake Forest Preservation Foundation, chair of city relations.

Roger and his wife, Pauline Spicuzza Mohr, are from Milwaukee, and Roger apparently caddied, since he went on to be the first caddie scholarship program Evans Scholar to attend Marquette University, in that city, and graduate in 1953. Living on the grounds of the Knollwood Club for four decades reflects this lifelong golf interest. But Roger has given back, serving the game as chairman of the Western Golf Association (2011–2012), culminating his commitment to the organization. He served as vice chair (2008–2010) and as a trustee (2008–2015). He chaired the Evans Scholar Foundation (2010–2011), providing college scholarships for caddies, as well, raising funds to endow scholarships for more than 800 young men and women attending college every year.

After serving in the Army after college, Mohr entered the Arthur Meyerhoff advertising agency in 1956, and by 1965, he was president, a post he held for the next 15 years. The agency was acquired by BBDO Worldwide, and Mohr continued as president here, becoming BBDO Chicago chair in 1982. When Mohr retired in 1993, he was vice chairman of BBDO International.

Roger Mohr's city volunteer role overlapped with his Chicago business career, as he served on the Plan Commission from 1972 to 1975 and was chair in 1975—during completion of a major city comprehensive plan. From 1994 to 2000, he served in that capacity once more, and he chaired the Plan Commission again in 1999–2000. He then served on the city council as Third Ward alderman (2000–2006). He served on the Lake Forest Senior Resources Commission from 2000 to 2006 and was the chair from 2008 to 2010. He then served on the Lake Forest Senior Citizens Foundation (2011–2015). In 2014–2015, he served on the City's Larry Temple Award Committee, when the late Tim Christie received the award.

In this Western Golf Association photograph, Roger Mohr is shown in back on the left side. (Roger Mohr.)

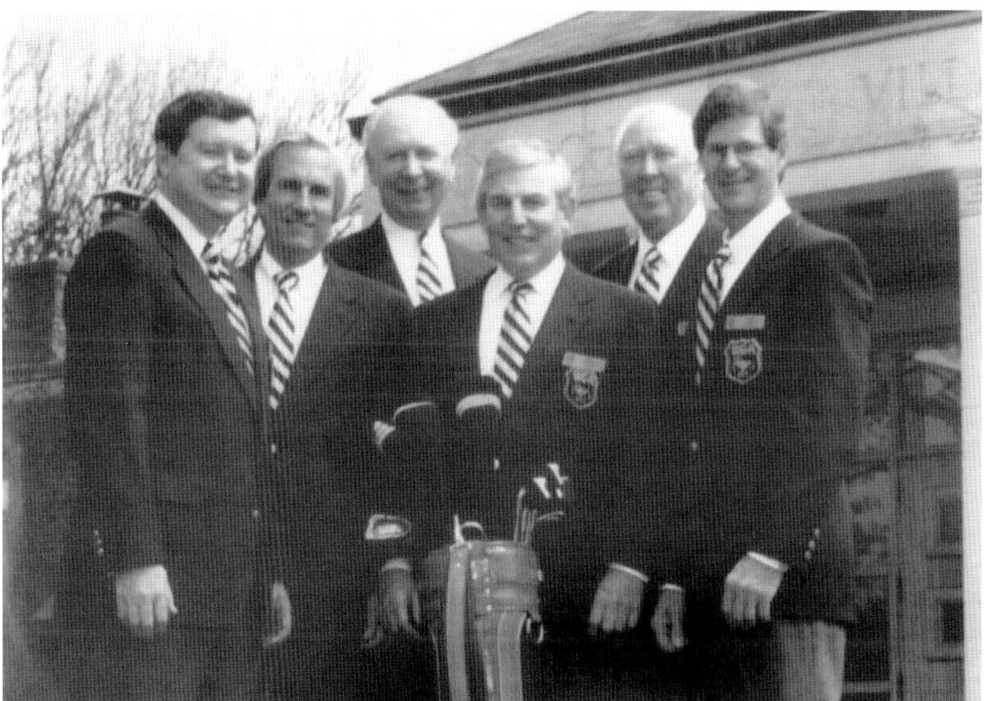

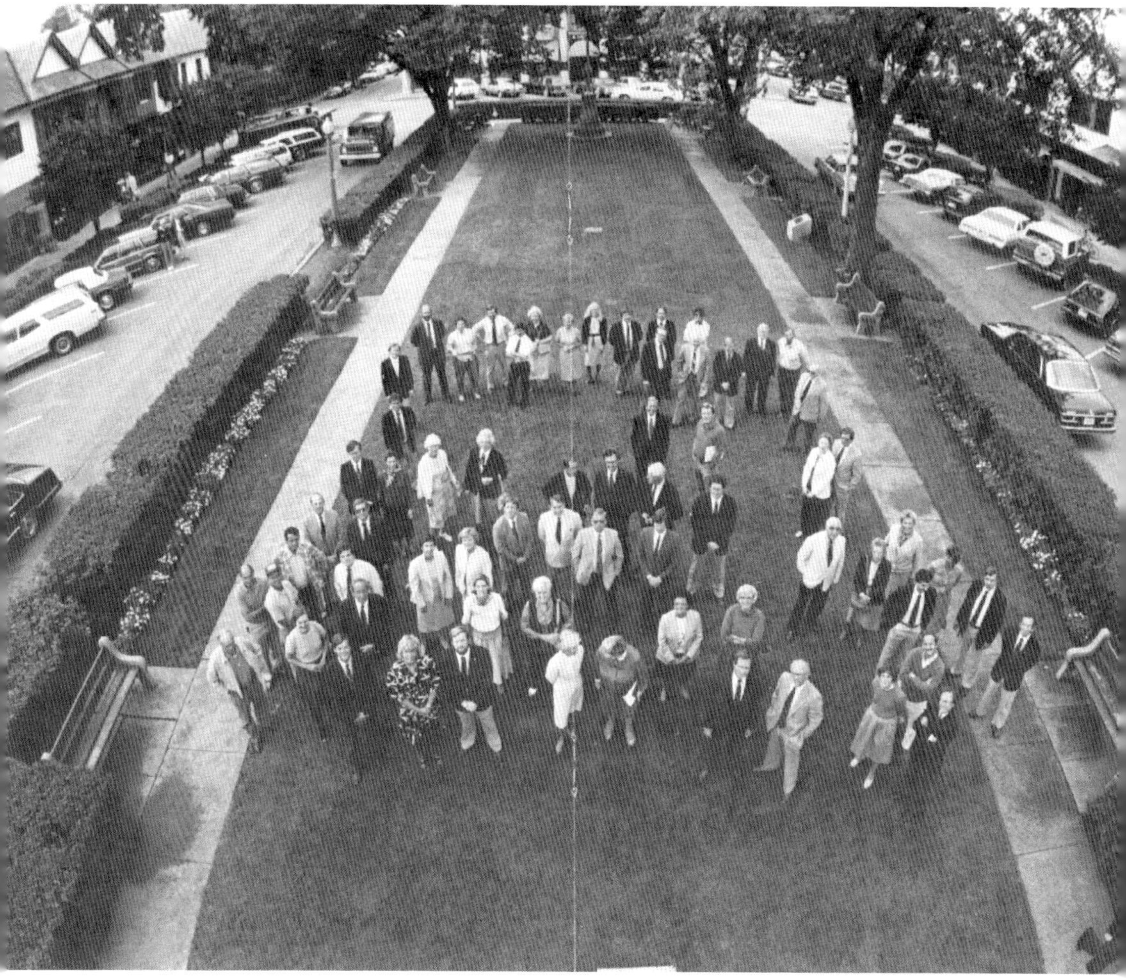

Local Leaders in Market Square

Gathered for this 1980s photograph for a city annual report are local business leaders, who signed their names at the photo shoot, here transcribed. Many of the names are accompanied by the person's business or profession. They are as follows: James Iacubino (Wenban's; *DLF*, page 40), Bob Pasquesi (Left Bank Restaurant), Paula Deruing, Floyd "Bud" Turner (Village Optical), Mary Lou and Chuck Helander (Helanders; *DLF*, pages 68 and 69), Ron Shlifka (Kiddles), Kathleen Van Ella (portrait agent), Gail Svendsen, Don Fiore (landscape, *WLF*), George Wiegold, Gordon Lackie (Griffith Grant & Lackie real estate), Maurice Dunne (Lake Forest Graduate School of Management), Jay Shlifka (Kiddles; *DLF*, page 71), Rick Price (insurance), Ellen Stirling (Lake Forest Shop), Joy Hodgen (Joytime preschool), Jim Randell, Bill Naslund, Bob O'Neill (attorney), Robert Bentley, Helen Foght, Paul Foght, Kathleen and Frank Swanton, Ann Fahey, Michael McClure, Carol Daniels, Sheldon Hill (architect), Donald Ruffolo (Don's Finest Foods), Dee Van Houtum, L. Robert Pasquesi (CPA), and Jim Marks. (City.)

CHAPTER FIVE

Local Business Leaders and Legends

Lake Forest's earliest industry was construction, with William Loughlin building the Lake Forest Academy frame building in 1858. The facility opened in January of the next year. Over the next century, many builders—in some cases, members of multigenerational firms—thrived here: Lind, Kelley, Griffis, Niemeyer, Avis, Kendler, Craig, LaDuke, (Randy) Holt, and Swanson, to name a few.

Soon, other businesses blossomed, serving the estate's builders: dry goods, building supplies and crafts, the depot and its freight warehouse, and more. Market Square was built in 1916 to compete for commuter dollars with Chicago stores like Marshall Fields; by 1931, Fields had its own branch store in the anchor building of the complex, remaining until 2006. Businesses evolved. For example, Helander's shifted from radio and early television sales to office supplies and then high-end stationery and printing. Big-box stores and malls offering discount prices killed off the east Lake Forest hardware stores—O'Neills' (*DLF*, pages 22 and 23) and Wells & Copithorne—by around 1990. Also falling victim were general merchandise stores, such as Garnetts and Hansens, and even the smaller chain store Woolworths. Grocery stores have evolved and changed. Don's Finest Foods, which developed out of the markets of Samuel Blackler and Janowitz's (*DLF*, pages 20 and 21), closed in 2008, replaced a few years later in its location by a Fresh Market, part of a chain.

During the heyday of the North Shore Line interurban railroad and before the prevalence of cars, neighborhood stores thrived, such as Maxie Cohn's at McKinley and Woodland Roads (*DLF*, page 85), perhaps three little ones in the Farwell's Crossing area, a Swedish store on Ryan Place (Johnsons'), and an African American establishment on Washington Road. After the eastside interurban line was closed in 1955 and cars became more widely available, these little stores disappeared.

Car dealerships are strangely absent, and gas stations are rare now in town. In the 1970s, there were a couple of gas stations with service bays on the corners of Bank Lane and Illinois Road. Both now are gone, though the Western Avenue BP and the Shell station at Deerpath Road and Oakwood Avenue remain, the latter only selling gas, with no service. Car maintenance in the 21st century is typically tied to the vehicle's dealership, and even those have left town for larger, less-expensive parcels of land. In the 1970s, James Swarthout had a Ford dealership at Western and Wisconsin Avenues, also the site of a former Knauz service station. Later, the site housed Lake Forest Sports Cars, and it is now a replacement office building housing the Bank of America. Wenban's, originally a livery stable, had a Buick dealership on the southeast corner of Deerpath Road and Oakwood Avenue, but by the 1980s, it had merged into the Knauz dealership at Western and Laurel Avenues. The Wenban site was developed as an office complex. Across Oakwood Avenue was McCallum Chevrolet (1950–1968). The Knauz

Chrysler, Buick, and European car dealership outgrew that far-from-the-center location by 1990 and moved to Lake Bluff, to a much larger building and a spacious tract of land at Routes 176 and 41. Today, Lake Forest has no car dealerships; four or five decades ago, there were four.

Service has always been the angle attracting customers to local businesses, rather than to shops in Chicago or, later, heavily commercial Vernon Hills. In the 1970s and 1980s, there was the remarkable, tiny, book-jammed Lake Forest Book Store, located south of Deerpath Road on Western Avenue. Its rent would have been miniscule compared to that of a car dealership. A harried parent in search of a birthday present could call the bookstore at 2:00 on a Saturday afternoon, requesting a book for a nine-year-old boy. The gift would be charged to the caller's account, wrapped, a card signed and addressed to the birthday boy, then picked up at the curb on the way to the party at 2:45. Similarly, the Toy Station was superb at selling assembled Radio Flyer wagons and other complicated, larger toys. Before abandoning the location in town, the owner, probably exhausted from the considerable demands of working in retail, opined that one could buy the same thing on the Internet for a third the price. It would not be assembled, though, and would arrive with perhaps unclear instructions. The Toy Station survived until recently in Libertyville, far from the time of Friday-afternoon visits by unaccompanied youngsters. In 2015, local kids can purchase frozen yogurt at the location, under Market Square's north tower.

A good example of competitive local service is Keith Einwiller's Wired, on Bank Lane. Einwiller competes with the big-box stores by offering service in the arcane arts of customized home-theater assembly and networking capability. The days of bringing a new television home and plugging it in are long gone for most nontechnical people. Similarly, caterers, including the formerly independent food store Don's, now the independent, chain-affiliated Sunset Foods, customize spreads for events small and large. Similar personalized services are provided by florists and floral designers, including the Looby family's Lake Forest Flowers (*DLF*, page 50), at Western Avenue and Illinois Road.

Restaurants and taverns have been perennial local businesses, with a good base of loyal diners. From the pre-1912 Matthews' restaurant and catering establishment west of the train station to today's Chief's, Francesca's, Lake Forest Wine & Cheese, Market House, Westwood Bistro, and the Grille on Laurel (*DLF*, page 88), there have been many good establishments since the liberalizing of liquor licenses in the 1970s. The Market House's predecessor, the Southgate Restaurant, ably run by Larry Ross, was a beneficiary of that action and also of the Market Square second-floor conversion, around 1984, from apartments to offices. In the 1970s and 1980s, the Gallery and Gordon's were made feasible by being allowed to sell alcoholic beverages.

The taverns serving beer and wine had appeared with the end of Prohibition in 1933. The Lantern is the main reminder of that midcentury era, when there were others, like McCormick's, on Deerpath Road and Bank Lane. Today, it is Dimitrio's second-generation jewelry store. Serving breakfast and lunch—but no alcohol—is Egg Harbor, the popular regional chain in an old A&P location south of Illinois Road. And anticipated anxiously is the return of the Deer Path Inn (*DLF*, page 15) in 2016, likely an effort to mount a fine-dining place to fill the gap left by the decline after the 2008 financial panic and the demise earlier in 2015 of Lovell's on the west side (*WLF*, page 109).

In all, the business climate east—and west, at Settlers' Square (*WLF*)—remains vibrant, with the support of the chamber of commerce, shared with Lake Bluff and led effectively by Joanna Rolek. As long as prosperity and resources exist, there will be customers with more cash than time or specialized knowledge.

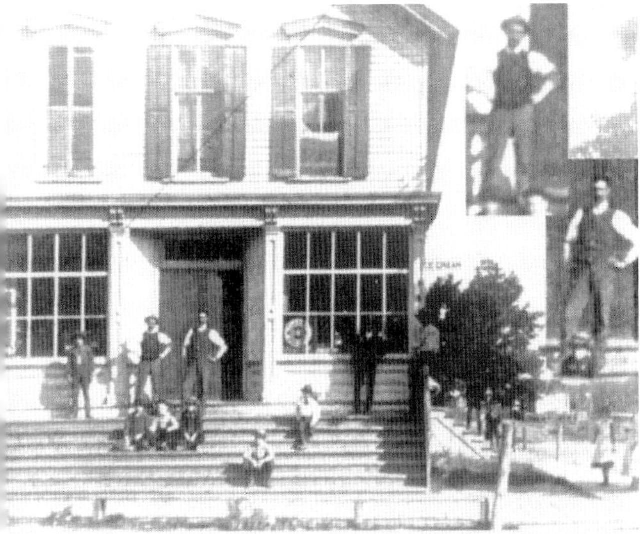

James Anderson (1831–1919)

Aberdeenshire native Anderson is shown on the left, standing in the doorway and in the insets. He began working for Sylvester Lind in a general store, ultimately taking it over. He moved the enterprise to the west side of the tracks, on Western Avenue, onto land he had received in trade for early work grading the campus and roads. He and a son-in-law imported the first Angus cattle into the United States in 1878. James Jr. (1869–1938) founded a surveying company, which continues in the 21st century. (David Mattoon and LFCLASC.)

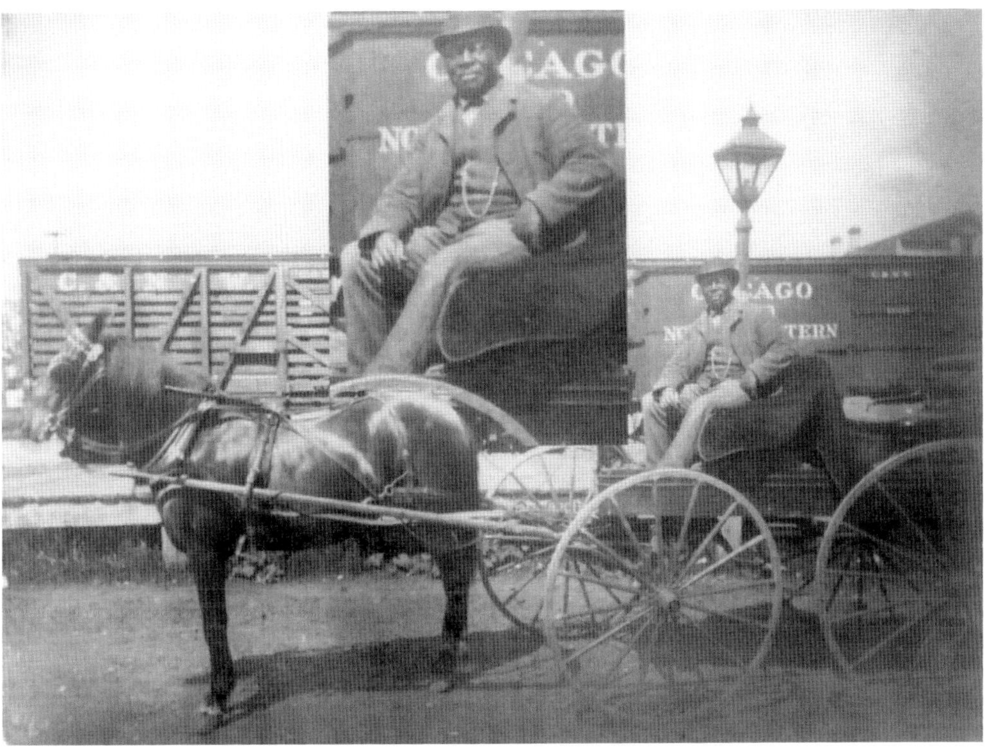

Samuel Dent (1835–1890)

Former slave and Union soldier Samuel Dent (*LFEPC*, page 32) was a local livery driver from 1872 until his death. He is an example of late-19th-century African American entrepreneurs who, with friendly support, built businesses rivaling their Irish and native-born competitors before disappearing in the first half of the 20th century. Dent was much loved and fondly remembered, and his memorial at Lake Forest Cemetery was donated by the community. Dent was interviewed for the *LFU Stentor* in 1890. (David Mattoon and LFCLASC.)

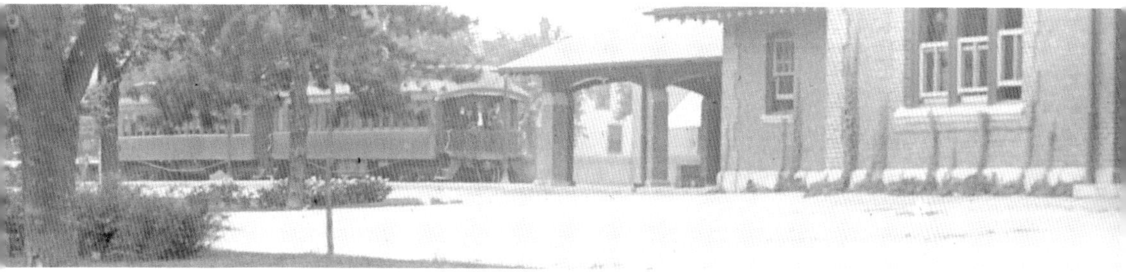

William A. Morgan

Morgan, shown with youngsters, was ticket agent at Lake Forest's east depots and the train station for 40 years, from the 1860s until his retirement in 1908. According to railroad historian David Mattoon, the commodious, upscale 1900 station (*LFEPC*, page 98), built to accommodate Onwentsia crowds, was the fourth. The previous station replaced the second structure, built in 1860 (*LFEPC*, page 26). Morgan was a pioneer member (no. 295) of the International Association of Ticket Agents, founded

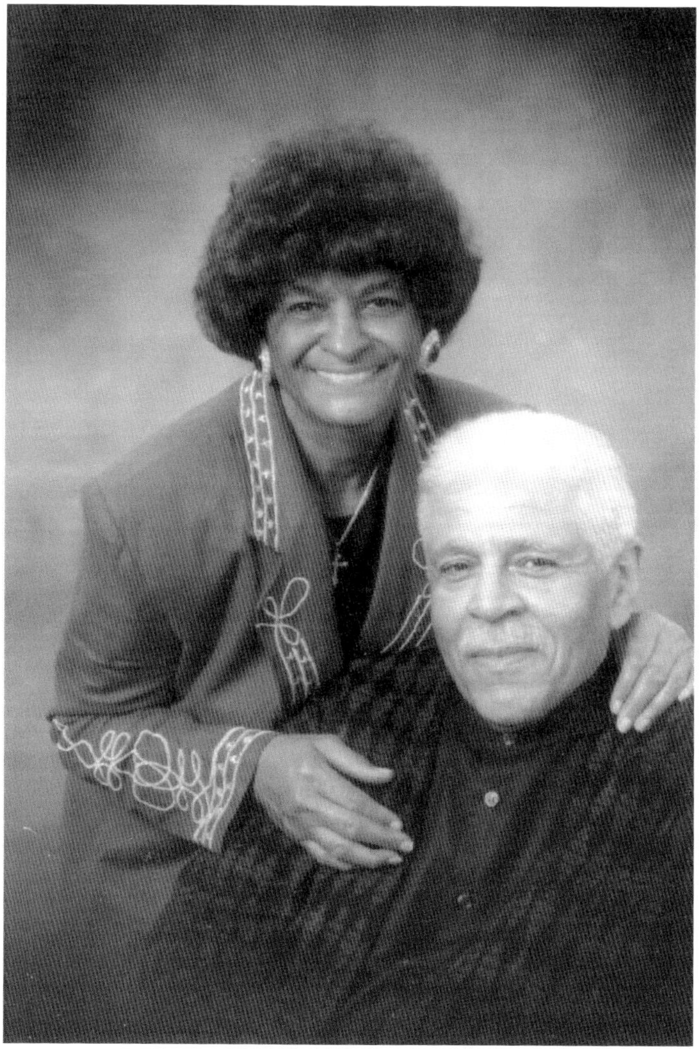

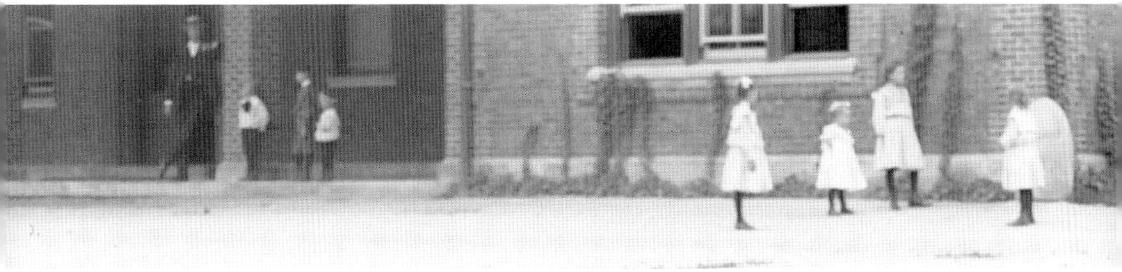

around 1888. These multitasking managers were central town figures, dealing with passengers, freight, and telegraph messages in the era before automobiles became standard and roads were improved. A respected local citizen, Morgan served two terms as city marshal on two different local party slates; everyone trusted him. Morgan is shown here at left in a detail from two station views by photographer William Henry Jackson taken after 1900. (David Mattoon and Library of Congress.)

James Casselberry (1927–2013) (OPPOSITE PAGE)
Casselberry and his wife, Mary, bridged two eras of racial diversity in town, between the historic African American service community dating to the 1850s and persisting into the 1950s and the college-based, more transient group of African American students in the city, especially since the early 1960s.

James Casselberry was born in Lake Forest in 1927 to Arthur E. (1896–1974) and Texanna Green Casselberry (1900–1984). His parents grew up on neighboring farms in Wedowee, in east-central, rural Alabama. Arthur's brother William and Texanna's sister Viola also married, and both couples migrated to Lake Forest, living first in the historic Washington and Illinois Roads African American community. The two Casselberry families soon moved north to the Spruce Avenue neighborhood. James attended Gorton School and graduated from Lake Forest High School in 1945. He studied two years at Howard University and then returned to Lake Forest, taking classes at Roosevelt and working. In 1950, he enlisted for two years in the Army, reaching the rank of sergeant.

Once back, in 1952, James met Frances "Mary" Williams, a Northwestern student, and they married that summer. They settled in Brockton, Massachusetts, where his father's development and construction firm built and sold properties. They moved back to Lake Forest with two daughters in 1959; James Jr. was born soon after. After a period working with Metropolitan Life, Jim joined his uncle William's waste-disposal, sewer, and septic business in the mid-1960s. In 1974, he bought the sewer and septic parts of the business, operating it as James Casselberry & Son until his retirement in 2006. The family built a house in the 1960s on the corner of Spruce Avenue and Sheridan Road, at 460 East Spruce Avenue—the first home on Sheridan Road for an African American family as the 1950s Jim Crowe rules subsided, though the address still read Spruce Avenue. Jim recalled that the Deerpath Theater was segregated until 1957, with African Americans sitting in the balcony. The loosening of class distinctions may have contributed to his return to Lake Forest. Jim was also active in Scouting, the American Legion, and the Presbyterian church, though, earlier, he had belonged to the First Baptist Church on Oakwood Avenue (*LFEPC*).

By the 1970s, Mary Casselberry worked at Lake Forest Hospital, and the family, one of the few left of this historic group, was welcoming into their home African American students of Lake Forest College. They were unofficial mentors, confidants, and friends to young people, typically urban, who found themselves in an alien suburban environment. These close ties were maintained. (James Iacubino.)

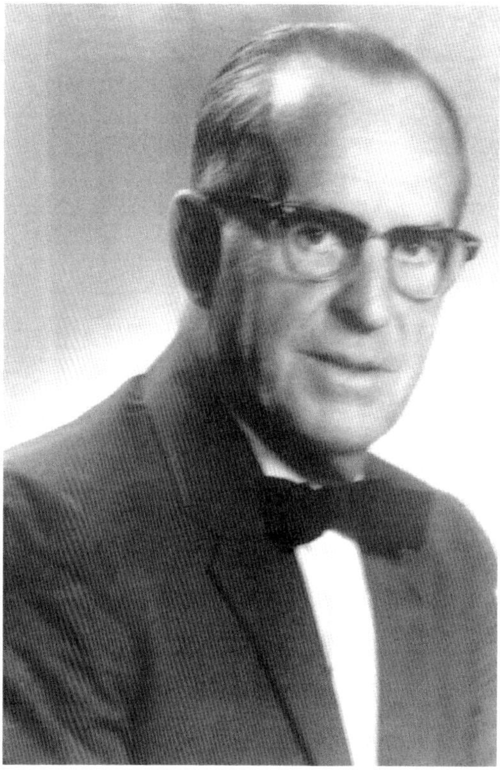

Melville C. Lackie (1900–1977)
Canadian-born Melville Lackie arrived in the 1920s, a nephew of local developer and real estate wizard John Griffith (*LFEPC*, page 87; *LFD*, page 31; *DLF*, pages 42–44), and married Katherine Lindenmeyer. The firm's president at midcentury, he continued real estate brokerage for many major Chicago business figures and for development of local subdivisions. Retiring in 1971, he was succeeded by his son Gordon, followed in turn by Gordon's son Scott early in this century. (Scott Lackie.)

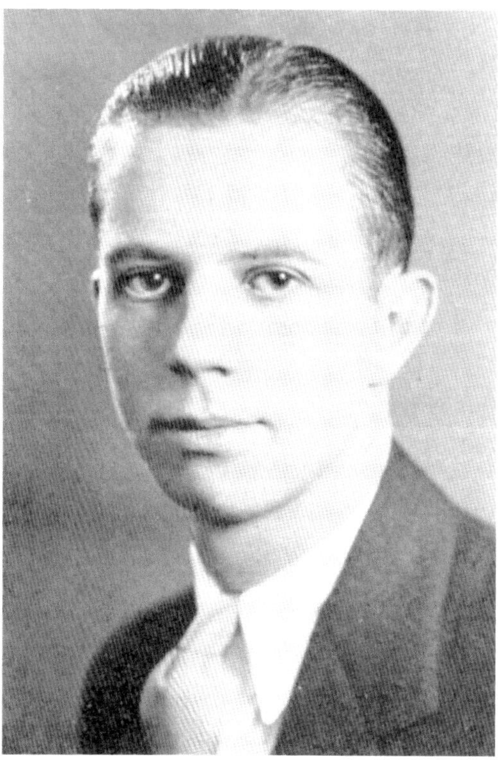

Barry Fitzgerald (c. 1911–2004)
Fitzgerald, a 1933 graduate of Lake Forest College, was assessor of Shields Township from 1962 to 1980. He came from a pioneer family in town. His cigar store in Market Square was open from 1924 to 1958. His grandfather, an Irish immigrant and Civil War veteran, owned the "Shoe Shop" on McKinley Road, opposite the train station. The store appears on the first published town map (1861, *LFEPC*, page 25). (LFCLASC.)

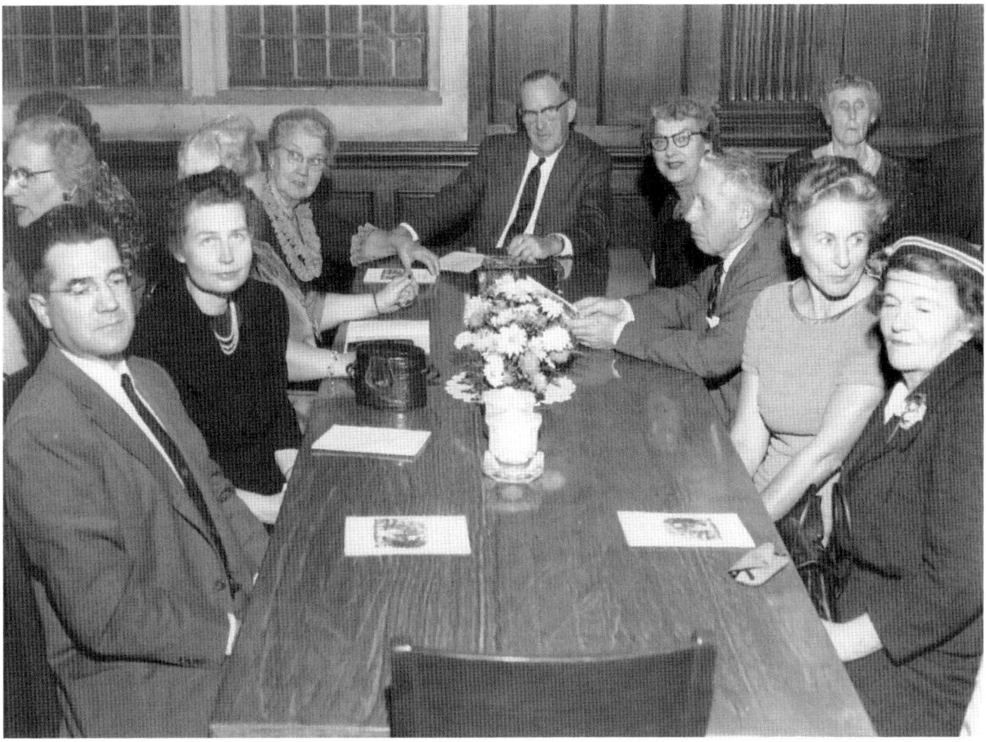

George G. Robertson (1899–1981)

George Robertson, shown seated at the table, third from the right, at the 1959 Presbyterian church centennial dinner, was employed as a hardware-store clerk when he joined the local Masonic lodge. He is best known for founding, in 1922, Robertson's men's clothing store, responsible for "the Lake Forest look," according to Shirley Paddock. By the 1950s, he had retired; E.W. Robertson was the manager, and Ted Washburn (Hempstead Washburn Jr.) was proprietor. (Louis E. Laflin Jr. Collection, LFCLASC.)

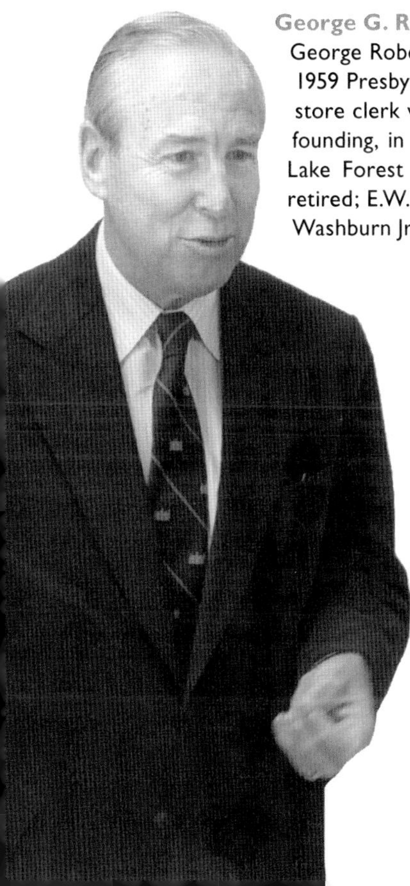

James A. Lovell

Capt. James Lovell completed his fourth mission as spacecraft commander of *Apollo 13* (April 11–17, 1970) and became the first man to journey twice to the moon. Before the Skylab program, Lovell held the record for the most hours logged in space. He retired in 1973, ran US Cellular, and, with his son, owned Lovell's (*WLF*, page 109), a westside fine-dining restaurant. (Lake Forest College.)

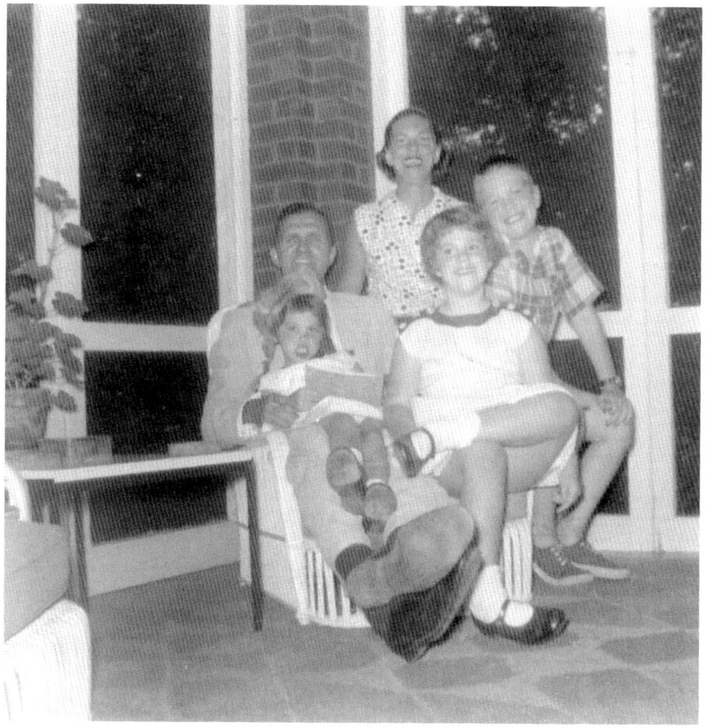

Adair Orr Foster (c. 1919–2002) and Ellen Stirling

Ellen Stirling is planning ahead seven years to the centennial of her third-generation designer women's clothing boutique, the Lake Forest Shop (*DLF*, pages 62 and 63), as reported in the *Lake Forester* of January 20, 2015. Her grandmother, Margaret Baxter Foster, founded the Market Square store in 1922 (the same year as Robertson's), and her parents, Volney and Adair Foster, ran it. They worked there before Ellen took over the business in 1986. Ellen serves as a director of the Lake Forest Bank.

Just as the area had one-off, uniquely designed houses and landscapes, North Shore women sought perfectly fitted, highly fashionable, and often name-couturier apparel. These gowns have been worn by North Shore women for benefit balls in the city and at clubs. In 1922, women's clothing was undergoing radical change—women had been granted the right to vote the year before. Thus, older patrons sought modern but less-daring clothing, while younger women were eager to explore new options—shorter skirt lengths, looser fits, and new hats for the new, bobbed hairstyles. Many also sought Paris gowns at the famous couturiers—earlier, Worth, and soon, the innovative Chanel. The Lake Forest Shop offered an alternative to the Rue St. Honore quarter, and it has served well local style and cachet.

As architectural and interior styles have alternated between modern and traditional approaches, these trends can also be found in dresses, slacks, tops, and wraps. The Lake Forest Shop has been a leader in these changes; designer Bill Blass declared Lake Forest women among the best-dressed in the country, and he credits Ellen Stirling for this local edge. Anyone who has seen Stirling arrive in a room understands intuitively what he meant.

The Fosters and Stirlings have lived on and near Green Bay Road, at first in the 1903 Arthur Heun–designed Herman Gade house on a wooded hill south of Two Gables, the Laurance Armour place. In the 1980s, Adair and Volney Foster built a new home on the west side of Green Bay Road and north of Onwentsia on Pembroke Lane and the golf course. The Stirlings live in the historic John Andrews King house, a bit farther south on Green Bay Road and across from the club. The photograph shows, clockwise from upper left, Volney Foster, Adair Orr Foster (Mrs. Volney), David Foster, Sally Foster (Carson), and Ellen Foster (Stirling) (*DLF*, page 62) on the porch of 335 Green Bay Road in 1955. (LF-LBHS and Ellen Stirling.)

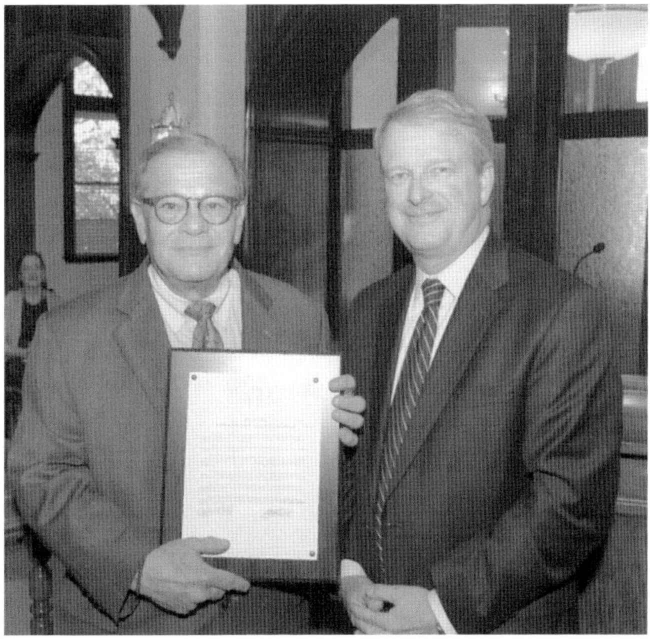

James Iacubino
Recently retired, James Iacubino (*LFEPC*, page 88), shown at left with Mayor Don Schoenfeider, worked for Wenban Funeral Home (*DLF*, page 40) after 1970. He purchased the business in 1976. Over the years, he has given educational sessions to physicians and others to assist grieving families. He helped as many as four generations in some families get through difficult times. James and his family—his wife, Dorothy, children Anthony, Anne, and stepdaughter Gosia, and grandchildren—live locally. (City.)

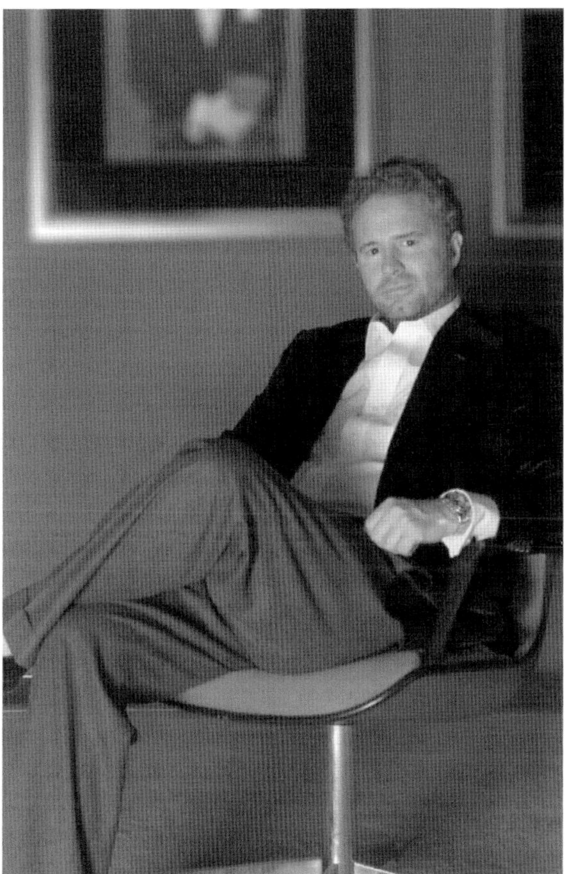

John W. Conatser
John Conatser, chief executive officer and founder of JWC Media, launched *Forest & Bluff* in 2001 with one idea in mind: "load its pages with the people of Lake Forest and Lake Bluff living their very best lives." The carefully designed, intriguing pages and hyperlocal feel of *Forest & Bluff* gave birth to other successful JWC Media publications, such as *Sheridan Road*, the *North Shore Weekend* newspaper, and the website *Daily North Shore*. (JWC Media.)

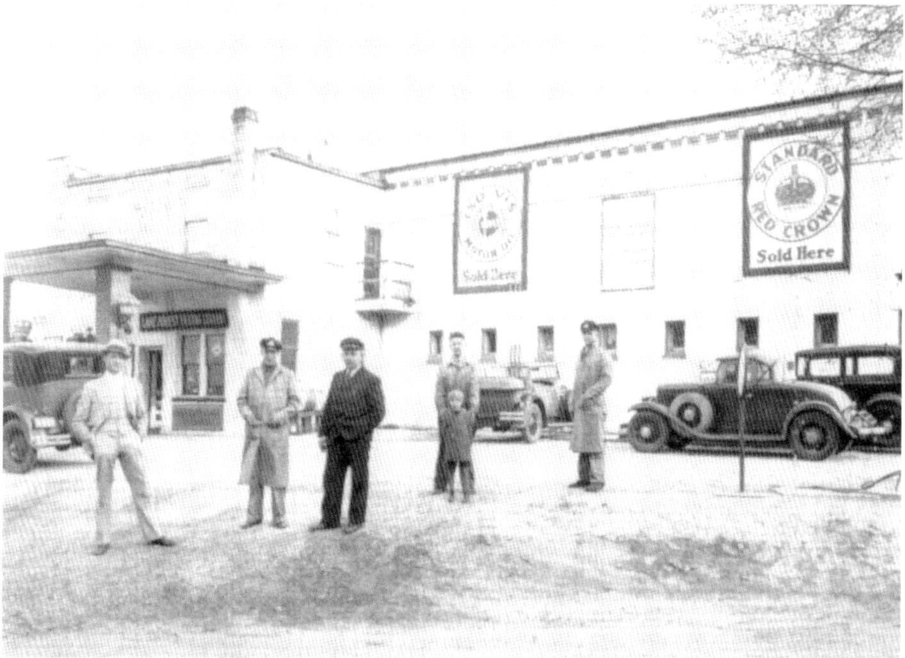

Karl Knauz (c. 1904–1972)

A small-business saga spanning three generations, Knauz Motors has been a Lake Forest concern for over a half-century, from 1935 until the late 1980s. In 1923, tool-and-die maker Karl Knauz, 19, left depressed postwar Germany for the United States, to Kenosha. At church, he met Emmy Becker, a cook in Lake Forest for the Thomas Dennehy family on Woodland Road. Karl and Emmy were married in 1927. For health reasons, Karl left factory work and became a butler and driver for Emmy's employers; they soon were working for Chicago mayor Carter Harrison Jr.

Karl Knauz took a key step in 1930, taking over a failed garage at today's Westwood Bistro and opening a car-repair shop and filling station. Shown here is the first location of Karl Knauz's garage (1930–1934), on the southwest corner of Western Avenue and Woodland Road. The site is identifiable to locals by the still-present steep entry driveway. Knauz and his team posed for this photograph. They are, from left to right, Knauz, Ed Wolf, Herb Peters, Siegfried Becker, and Bob Becker, Knauz's future right-hand man. Siegfried and Bob were siblings of Emmy Becker Knauz.

By 1935, Knauz partnered with Wallace Boutin to start a business on Western Avenue, just north of Westminster Avenue, in a new gas station and garage on what is now Swarthout property. Knauz's German-trained machinist skills were prized in the next decade, as people kept their cars longer, while Boutin ran the gasoline service. They also acquired a Chrysler dealership, small at the outset, which the firm held into the early 21st century. They bought land for expansion at Western and Laurel Avenues in 1941 and, in 1946, moved there.

By about 1950, the partners split, and Wally Boutin took the western portion of the land for a new dry-cleaning establishment, using petroleum-based chemicals he was already knowledgeable about. For the next half-century, he and, later, his son Jerry, operated this business. The site was eventually sold for a condominium complex. Karl Knauz retained the garage and car dealership and brought his son Bill into the business after the young man's service in the Korean War and some time in the European racing world.

By the end of the 1950s, Bill was able to introduce European cars on the North Shore, aided by the use of modern advertising. It was Karl Knauz, though, who secured the crucial North Shore Mercedes dealership through his Chicago Germania Club connections. He expanded and renovated the facilities for this new line (*DLF*, page 88). (Bill Knauz.)

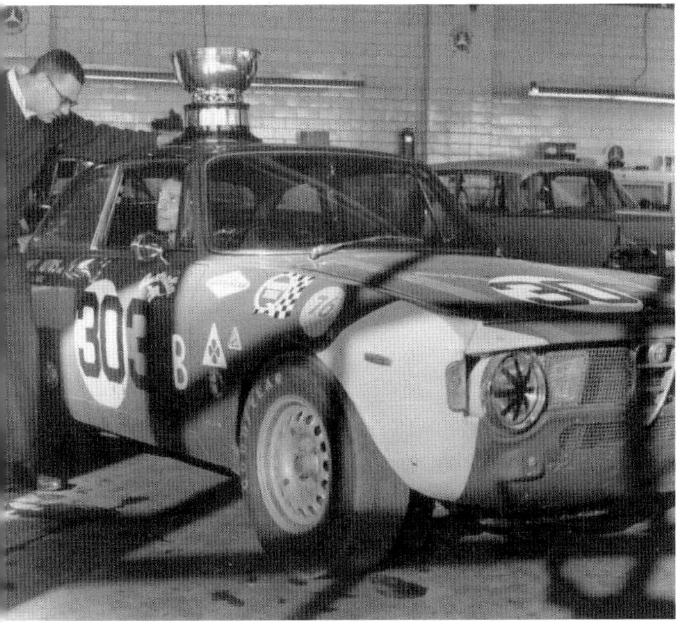

Heinrich Wilhelm Knauz

Second-generation resident Bill Knauz (left), a car and racing enthusiast, speaks with mechanic Horst Kwech, seated in a 1965 Alfa Romeo GTA. With this car, Bill won for the Knauz business the Sports Car Club of America President's Cup in 1966. The trophy can be seen on the car's roof. By the late 1980s, the company needed much more space as the economy improved, and Bill bought a factory on 29 acres at Routes 41 and 176 in Lake Bluff. (Bill Knauz.)

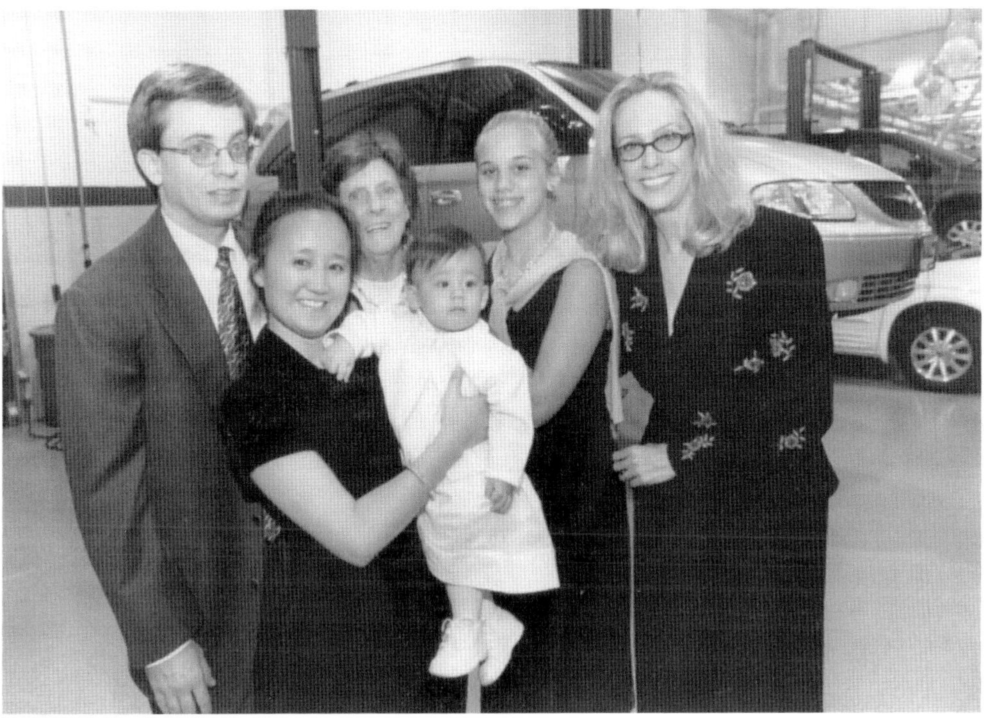

Kim Knauz Madden

Bill's daughter Kim, after working in the firm, retired when her husband, William Madden, joined Bill and soon thereafter took over operations. Shown here in 2001 are Bill's wife and Kim's mother, Ingebourg Knauz, (third from left) and Kim Madden (far right). Also shown are Bill and Inge's grandchildren Katie Madden (second from right) and David Knauz (far left), with David's wife, Kitty, holding their daughter Julia. David is the son of the late Karl Knauz II. (Bill Knauz.)

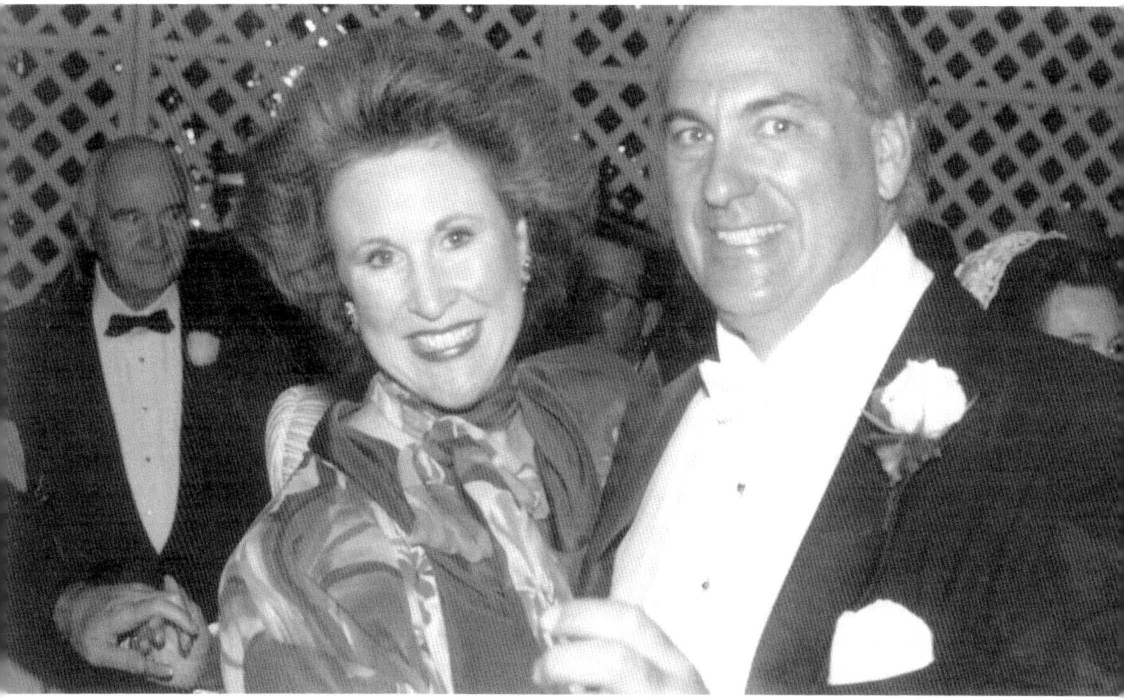

Bruce Southworth (c. 1941–2012) and Mary Southworth

For over three decades, Samlesbury Hall, owned by Mary Southworth, has facilitated preservation of the essence of Lake Forest through its English antiques and interior design. Samlesbury Hall, Ltd., is one of the Midwest's largest direct importers of 18th- and 19th-century English antiques. This Lake Forest heritage business specializes in beautiful gifts and holiday place settings. Mary Southworth's late husband, Bruce, was the master of ceremonies at his company, Southworth Productions, providing spectacular special occasions and celebrations for his clients of many years. An avid collector, Bruce is well-remembered for his love of dancing Christmas toys.

The Southworths contributed significantly to the preservation and stewardship of Lake Forest's architectural heritage through the restoration of The Evergreens, their landmark brick home dating from 1858. It was built for a founding father of Lake Forest, Dr. Charles Quinlan, on an estate once much larger. This first local estate residence was rescued by the Southworths in the 1970s, restored, and is preserved as an iconic mansion just east of Lake Forest Library. (Mary Southworth.)

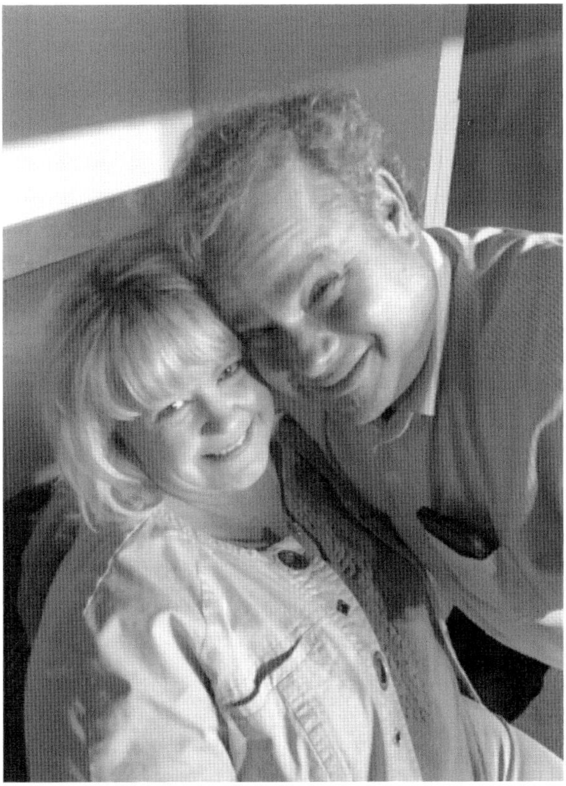

Steve Vignocchi

Vignocchi attended Lake Forest High School and graduated from Lake Forest College in 1993. He grew up a resident, always walking with crutches. While at the college, he worked in the archives, and he returned to work there on a project basis from 2008 to 2010. Reliable and determinedly independent, he finally—with reluctance—accepted a disabled parking placard. After working in archives at Baxter, in 2015, he took a new pharmaceuticals post, moving with his wife Nancy to Kentucky. (Steve Vignocchi.)

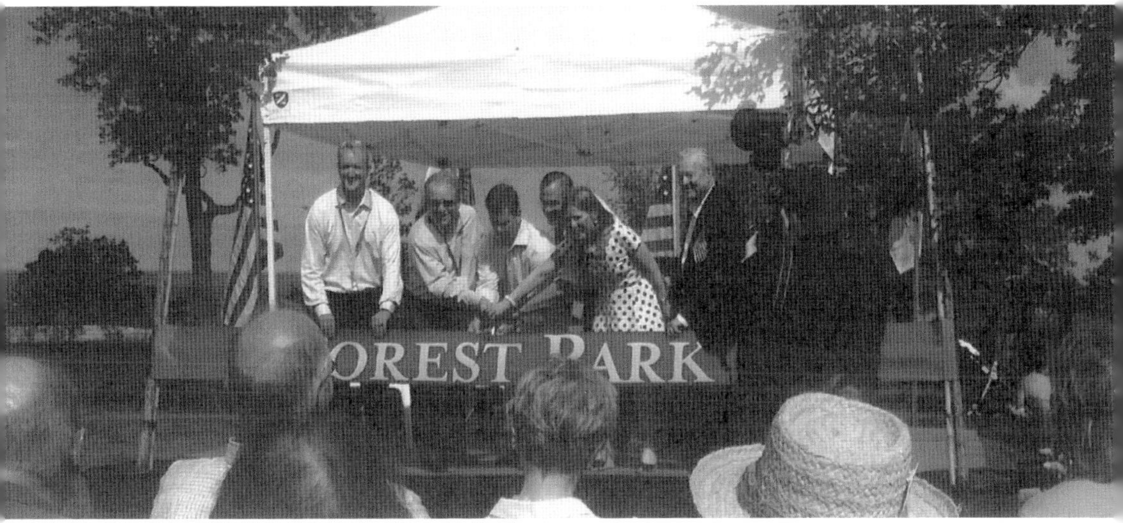

Susan Wright

In 2015, Wright joined Lake Forest Bank as a senior vice president, with a portfolio including community relations, business development, and relationship management. She is shown here representing the bank, a major sponsor, at the June 14, 2015, ribbon-cutting for the rehabilitated Forest Park with Brian McCaskey (far left) representing another major sponsor, the Chicago Bears. Also in attendance are Mayor Don Schoenheider, Congressman Bob Dold, project president Ralph Gesualdo, and event emcee Bill Kurtis (far right). (Arthur Miller.)

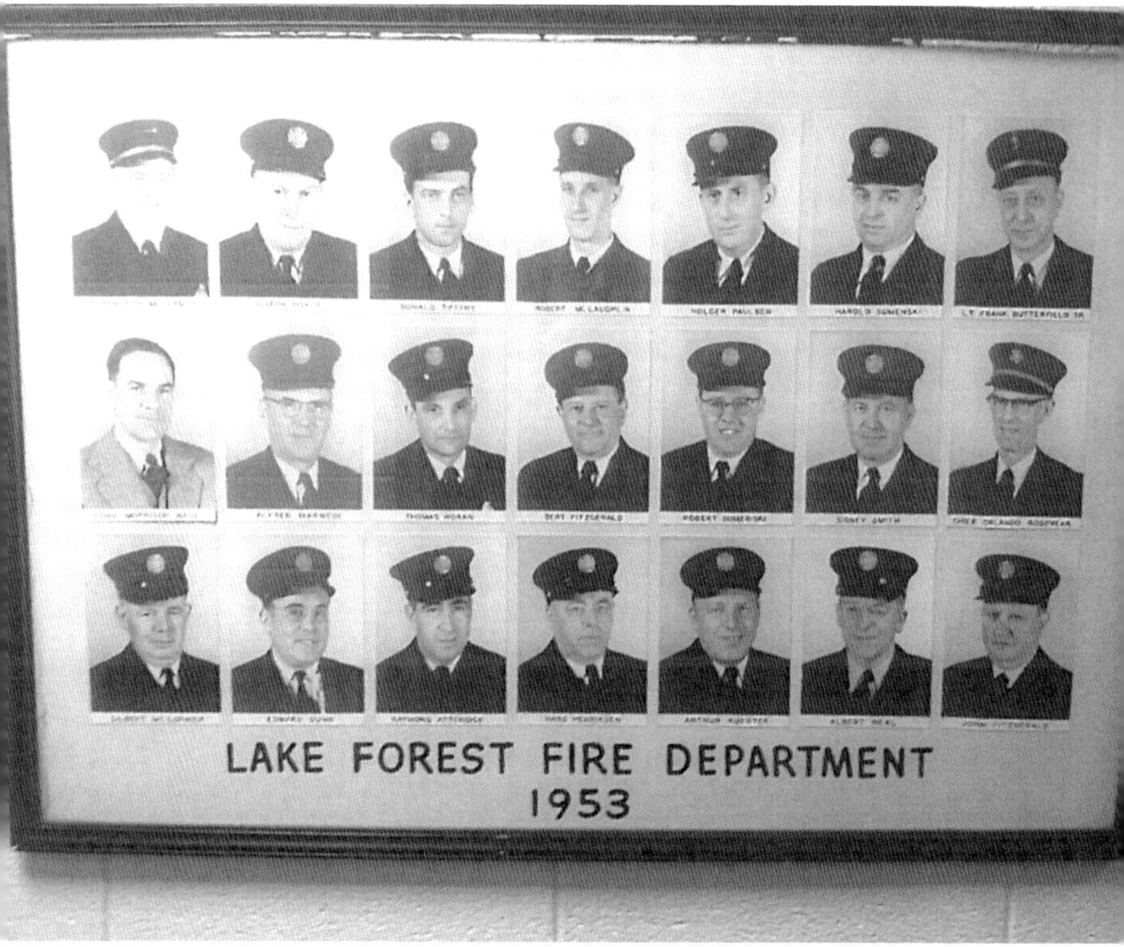

Firemen, 1953

Public service following World War II is exemplified in this 1953 fire department staff composite photograph, which hangs in the Public Safety Building. Shown are, from left to right, the following: (top row) Lt. Kenneth McCormick, Joseph Doyle, Donald Tiffany (see page 88), Robert McLaughlin, Holger Paulsen, Harold Sumenski, and Lt. Frank Butterfield Sr.; (middle row) Commissioner Morrison Waud, Alfred Marwede (see page 87), Thomas Moran, Bert Fitzgerald, Robert Sumerski, Sidney Smith, and Chief Orlando Rosevear; (bottom row) Gilbert McCormick, Edward Dunn, Raymond Atteridge, Hans Henriksen, Arthur Kuester, Albert Neal, and John Fitzgerald. For a photograph of the fire department staff in 1915, see *DLF*, page 17. (Arthur Miller and Lake Forest Fire Department.)

CHAPTER SIX

Government, Political, and Public-Service Leaders

Generally, Lake Forest has had a low-profile national political history, even though it was born out of the national conflict over slavery in the 1850s. Antislavery Republican Presbyterians sought a haven for Puritan descendants and Scots away from the freer lifestyle of the city to avoid pressuring political allies, the Germans, over Sunday and alcohol issues.

While relatively few local residents have held national and state public office in proportion to the town's historic economic clout, some have exerted indirect political power to promote their interests—financial, social, and altruistic. At least one son of a local family has gone to the US Senate, William Proxmire (D-WI), son of Dr. Theodore Proxmire. Most notable, though, is US senator Charles B. Farwell (R-IL), who served in Washington both in the House—intermittently between 1870 and the mid-1880s—and in the Senate from 1887 to 1891. He had an impact on national and Chicago affairs for two decades. Farwell had been Chicago's first political boss, as Cook County clerk. In addition, two generations of Republican-backing Stuarts served as US ambassadors: R. Douglas Stuart to Canada under President Eisenhower and his son Robert D. Stuart to Norway under President Reagan. The younger Stuart, who died in 2014, had also led the anti-interventionist America First in 1940–1941.

At the state and local levels, though, many have served as volunteers or nearly so: Corrine Wood (lieutenant governor); Susan Garrett (state representative and senator); Mary Beatty (Lake County board member); and Mike Rummel (mayor). Several members of the larger Farwell clan served as Lake Forest mayor, and Sylvester Lind was mayor four times. Even the township has been served by many, going back to William Atteridge in the 19th century and, in the mid-20th century, Barry Fitzgerald. Indeed, Illinois is notable for having the most units of government, over 6,900; Texas is next, with 5,100 such freestanding operations. This results from separate fire, sanitation, township, transportation, and arcane taxing bodies, sometimes overlapping and each with its own board of trustees. A notable, crucial example is Metra, the Chicago metropolitan area's multicounty commuter rail authority. Rail expert Norman Carlson serves on Metra's board, representing Lake County. For three decades, James Swarthout served on the 1914-founded North Shore Water Reclamation (formerly Sanitary) District Board of Trustees. He was succeeded by his son Thomas in 2012. Thomas is a former Lake Forest alderman.

Relatively few national candidates have drifted through Lake Forest at election time, it being a relatively "safe" Republican constituency, except to fundraise, as did Mitt Romney in 2012. A candidate for president from here was Adlai Stevenson, as a Democrat no less, in 1952 and 1956. He had rented in town seasonally before building his estate in Mettawa in the 1930s. Encouraged by progressive friends locally, he successfully ran for governor in 1948. A standout backer was Jane Warner Dick, who wrote about the 1952 campaign in her *Whistle-Stopping with Adlai* (1952). She later joined him in his 1961–1965 mission to the UN and also wrote a memoir, *Volunteers and the Making of Presidents* (1980).

Not to be overlooked are the many local volunteers—aldermen and members of the many boards and commissions. All are supported by dedicated staff, working within a nonpolitical city manager form of government.

While there were party-contested town elections in the early days, by 1935, the Lake Forest Caucus was organized to recommend candidates for the city council, mayor, and for the school boards—Lake Forest District 67 and Lake Forest High School District 115, which also serves Lake Bluff and Knollwood. Early on, the caucus was not open, at least to one left-wing, non-taxpaying faculty member living on campus in the early 1940s who reported his inability to attend. But in recent decades, certainly, the caucus process has been open, and its main work is recruiting capable local people to appear on slates for office at elections and to serve on boards and commissions. Each ward elects its own committee on candidates and welcomes new and long-term residents' participation in the myriad appointed bodies that advise the city council on matters relating to finances, development, and general governance.

An example of cross-department involvement was fire commissioner Morrison Waud (1910–2007), a grandson-in-law of Byron L. Smith, who served as mayor in the late 1950s. Most mayors, in fact, have wended their way up through the voluntary boards and commissions, often bringing useful organizational skills from their careers. Waud, who graduated from Princeton in 1932 and from Northwestern Law School in 1935, was managing partner for nine years of the elite Gardner, Carton & Douglas law firm. He retired in 1975, enjoying a further three decades with his wife of 72 years, Anne Byron Smith, who died 11 weeks before him in 2007. His son Cornelius B. Waud was also mayor, from 1996 to 1999.

City staff and volunteers at all levels—again, often multigenerational, like Alfred Marwede and his son Alfred Edward Marwede—were committed to the fire department from its origins. Fred Jackson, the retired longtime head of the recreation department, is a third-generation Lake Forest resident. His grandfather was an English gardener on Cyrus McCormick's Walden estate a century ago. Fred continues to live a block from the house on Illinois Road, near the former North Shore Line Calverts and Farwell Crossing stops, which McCormick built for the Frederic Jackson family in 1918 so his children could commute to high school in Highland Park. This community stability in city staff and volunteers has contributed to its sound, overall frugal governance.

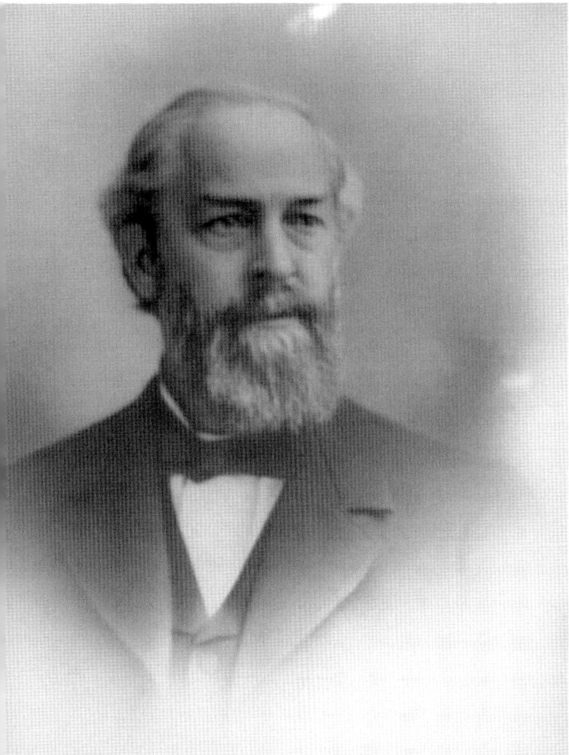

David J. Lake
Born in Mount Morris, New York, David Lake was mayor (1866–1867), trustee of the Lake Forest Association (1856–1862), and ruling elder of the Presbyterian church. He was a director and cashier of Manufacturer's National Bank, Chicago. Living at 644 East Deerpath Road, by 1867, he was the only Lake Forest Association trustee to live here. A son copublished issues of the first printed local newspaper, the *Gem* (1867). (City.)

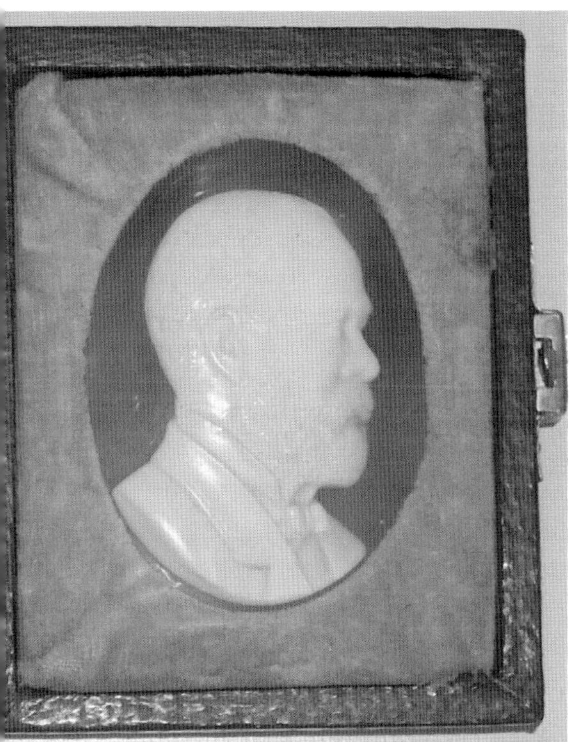

Charles B. Farwell (1823–1903)
Republican Farwell, Chicago's first political boss as county clerk (1853–1861), served in Congress (1871–1877 and 1881–1883), as well as in the US Senate (1887–1891), long enough to manage the floor fight to bring to Chicago the 1893 World's Columbian Exposition. He played a crucial, little-known role in the election of Pres. Rutherford B. Hayes and supported high tariffs to build up US and Chicago manufacturing. (Lucia Winston Heyworth Collection, LFCLASC.)

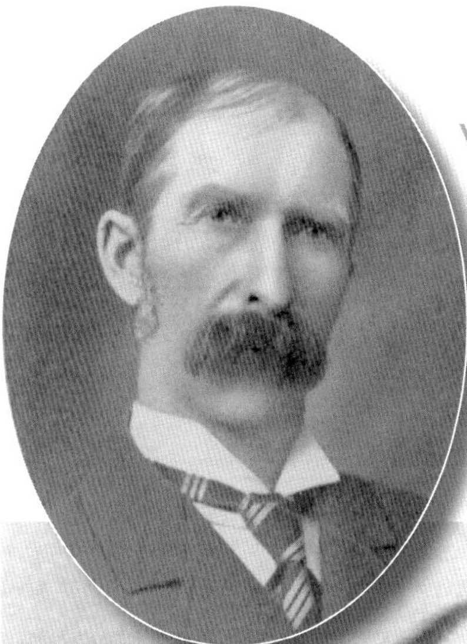

William Atteridge (1843–1910)

Green Bay Road farmer William Atteridge served in most elected offices of Shields Township from the 1860s to the 1890s, and he was supervisor for most of the decade between 1872 and 1882. He had been in the first class of Lake Forest Academy (1858–1859). Son of pioneer Thomas Atteridge and grandson of patriarch James Cole, both Protestants from Cork, Ireland, he farmed mostly west of Green Bay Road. (LFCLASC.)

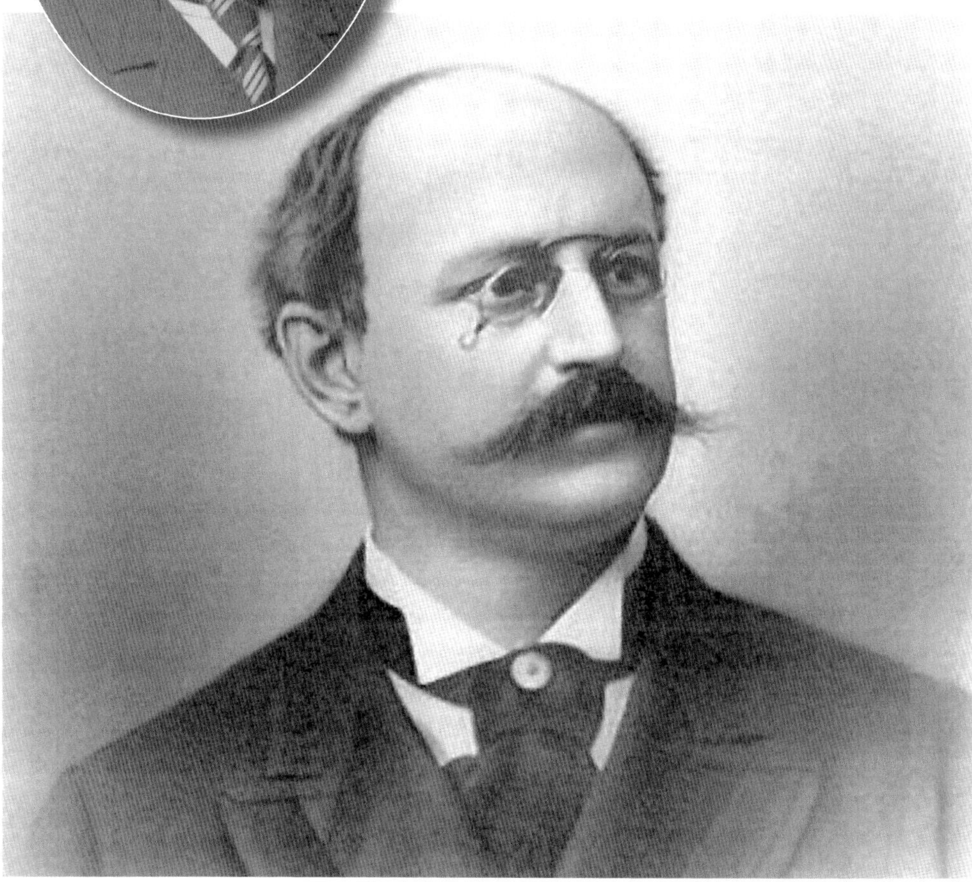

Walter Cranston Larned (1850–1914)

Larned earned his bachelor of arts degree from Harvard in 1871 and his bachelor of laws degree from Columbia in 1874. He served as mayor from 1889 to 1891. Born in Chicago, Larned married Emma Scribner, daughter of the New York publisher and granddaughter of rail baron John Insley Blair. Larned practiced law in Chicago and was an art critic and author of novels and *Churches and Castles of France* (1895). In 1887, he formed the Lake Forest Art Institute, for which the H.C. Durand Art Institute was built in 1892. (City.)

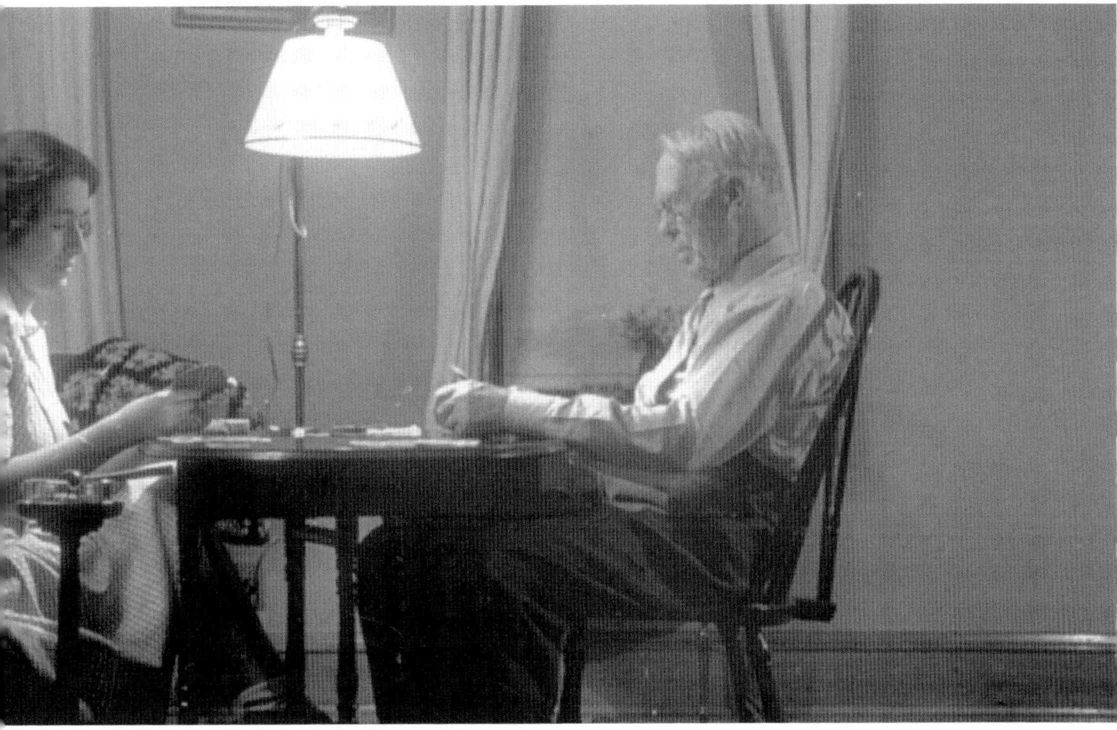

James Ferguson Blaikie King (1858–1943)
James King was Shields Township justice of the peace from 1893 to 1903. As John Halsey described it in his 1912 history, "Mr. King was a most painstaking and industrious magistrate and soon familiarized himself with the law for primary jurisdictions, thus giving his court a public respect so often not secured because not deserved by rural magistrates." He was Shields Township supervisor after 1911 and had been a member of the first fire brigade in the late 19th century.

But his main claim as a legendary local revolves around his role as city clerk (1894–1932). In that post, he oversaw the transition from the small, college-centered town of the 1850s–1890s to the future city stretching west to today's tollway. He issued the first printed version of city ordinances in the 1890s. In 1899, the city government was consolidated into city hall, with the library and fire department included. Soon, auxiliary space was developed for city departments nearby on Forest Avenue. He facilitated developing Market Square in 1916, coordinating for city infrastructure. In the 1920s, he worked with resident and planner Edward H. Bennett's Chicago firm to implement zoning, confining commercial development east of Green Bay Road and ending such development on Western Avenue at the Farwell's Crossing North Shore Line stop (Ryan Place). He and Bennett also created the Plan Commission in the 1920s, with Bennett the first chair. In 1925, the city also annexed southeast to Everett, controlling development farther west than any other North Shore suburb. This 1920s expansion, along with the zoning and Plan Commission of that decade, set the template for future city development.

James King provided municipal governmental stability, probably linked to Scots frugality and restraint. He worked with 13 mayors through the period of estate growth after the founding of Onwentsia in 1895 and until two years before federal income tax rates increased, ending that era of expansion.

James King first visited Lake Forest at age 20 in 1878. Like 19-year-old Alexander Kelley from Old Deer, Aberdeenshire, King arrived with the first Anderson-Findlay shipment of Aberdeenshire Angus cattle. And, like the future contractor Kelley, after a rough trip in 1882, King settled in Lake Forest. He, his wife, Ellen, and, eventually, their family of eight lived near other Scots on Oakwood Avenue, Scott Street, and, ultimately, at 857 Summit Avenue. He is shown here with his daughter-in-law Virginia King. (DF.)

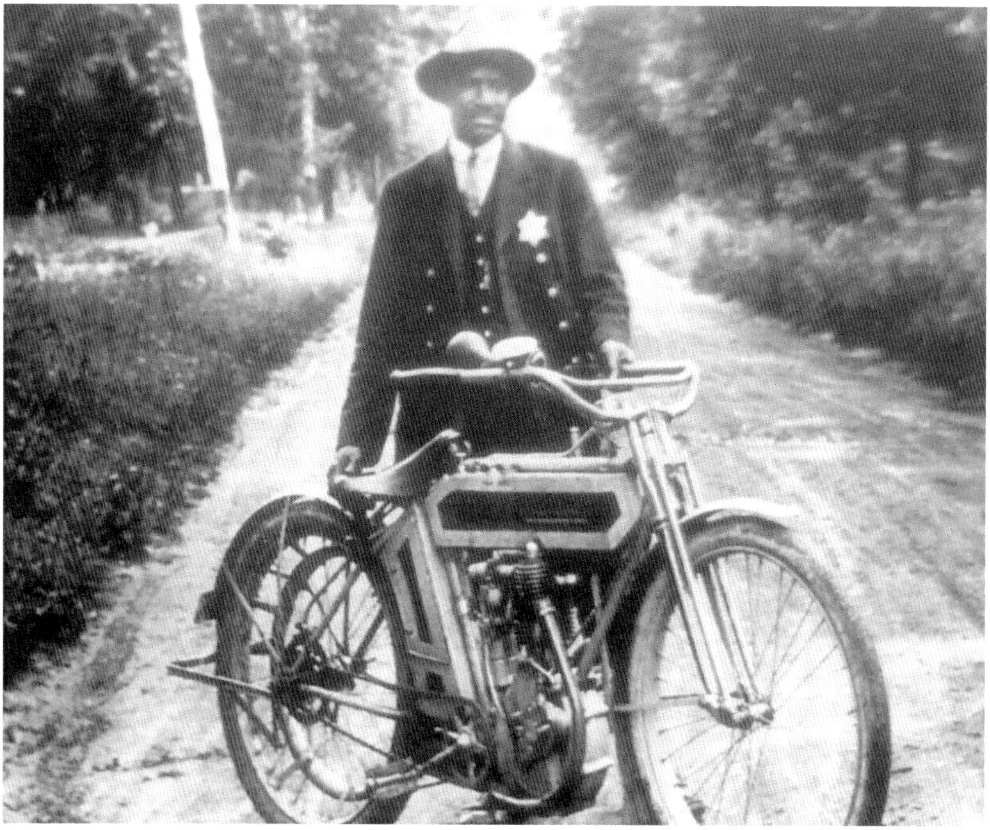

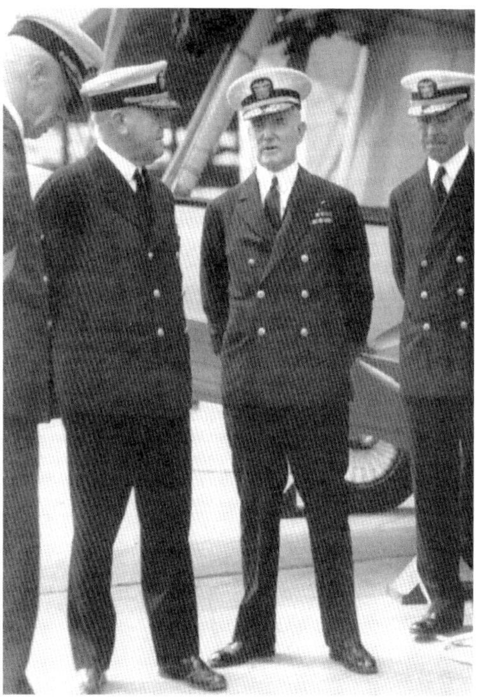

Walker Sales (1865–1919)

Lake Forest's second night-shift police officer, serving from about 1900 to 1920, was Walker Sales (*LFEPC*). By 1900, there were two, and perhaps three, African American neighborhoods, and Officer Sales's motorcycle would have allowed him to make rounds in each. Originally from Kentucky, Sales had been coachman for I.P. Rumsey in 1900, living with his family on that former Quinlan estate. (City.)

William Adger Moffett Jr. (1869–1933)

Rear Admiral Moffett, second from right, commanded the Great Lakes Naval Training Station from 1914 to 1918, the period of its rapid growth and development. With Dewey's fleet in Manila in 1898, before coming to the North Shore, Moffett also was decorated for his bold entry into a Mexican harbor around 1914. He lived in Lake Forest, and Edward Arpee wrote his biography, *From Frigates to Flat-Tops* (1953). (Arlington Cemetery.)

Neil N. Campbell (1890–1956)

When the City of Lake Forest adopted the council-manager form of government in 1939, Neil Campbell was the first city manager. Campbell was born in Paisley, Ontario. A 1910 engineering graduate of the University of Illinois, he soon was city engineer, working with city clerk James King. By 1921, Campbell also had a private surveying practice. In 1943, he and his staff redrafted the original 1857 plan of the town, preserving and perhaps recreating information lost on the original; they also used city and county versions of an 1895 redrafting.

Neil Campbell, whose city career began later in the estate era than did James King's, faced a different mix of challenges. By the late 1930s, high income taxes had stopped new growth of estates, and after World War II, high inflation and rising school taxes for baby-boom children led to the accelerated subdivision of estate properties. And this resulted in more new children arriving in the schools. Resources were scarce to address basic needs, much less the beautification ideals of leading citizens. Scots-derived thrift, as with James King, would have helped Campbell get through a very tough era for a community with wealthy tastes and expectations.

Neil Campbell lived at 215 North Washington Circle with his wife, Helen Fieldon Campbell, and there raised his family of three daughters, one of whom, Vivian, married 1939 Lake Forest College graduate Chester Petersen. The young couple continued to live at the homestead until 1978 (*LFD*, cover, page 2, and page 60). Vivian was secretary to the Presbyterian church's pastor, Oliver Brackett, in the 1930s. By the 1950s, she ran a baby-boom-era maternity shop in Market Square.

Here, Neil Campbell poses with his family around 1950. Shown are, from left to right, Campbell, Roger Petersen (son of Vivian C. Petersen), James Pollack (son of Dorothy C. Pollack), Chris Proctor (daughter of Jean C. Proctor), Helen Fieldon Campbell (with Scott Proctor), and Charles Pollack. (Roger Petersen.)

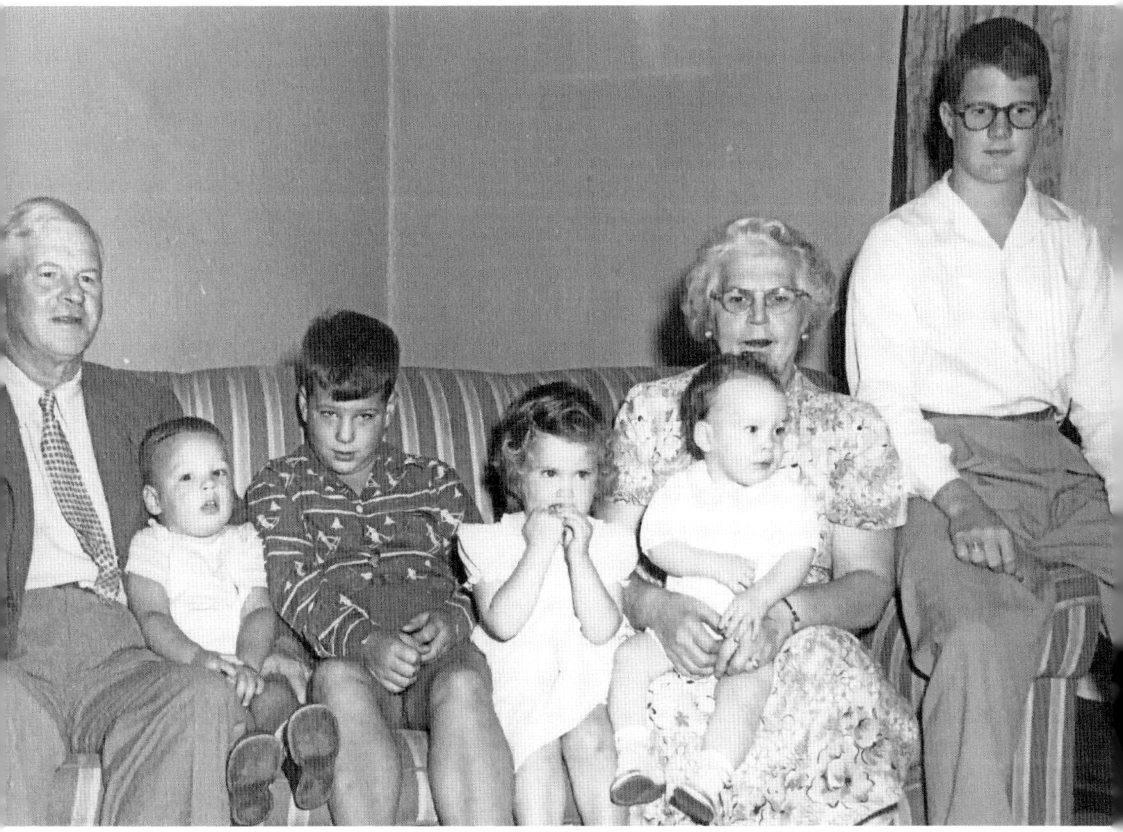

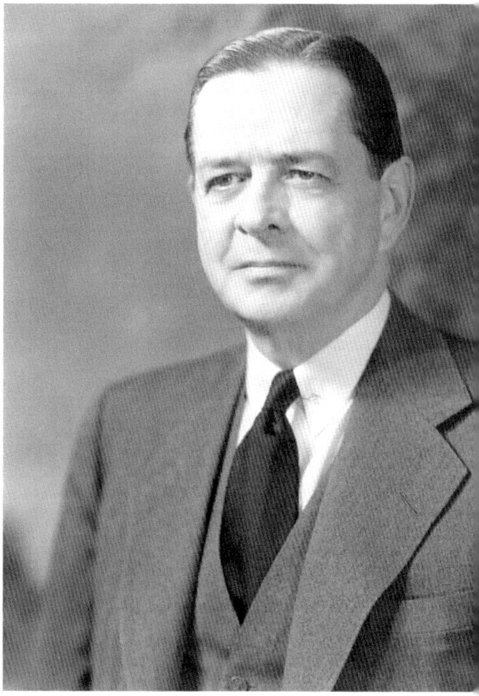

James H. Douglas Jr. (1899–1988)

Like the local Stuarts, resident James Douglas was descended from founders of Quaker Oats. A 1924 graduate of Harvard Law School, he had a distinguished record of national service: assistant secretary of the treasury in the Hoover and Franklin Roosevelt administrations (1932–1933) and, in the Eisenhower years, secretary of the Air Force and deputy secretary of defense (1953–1960). A Chicago attorney with Gardner, Carton & Douglas, he married twice, first to Grace McGann Douglas. (LFCLASC.)

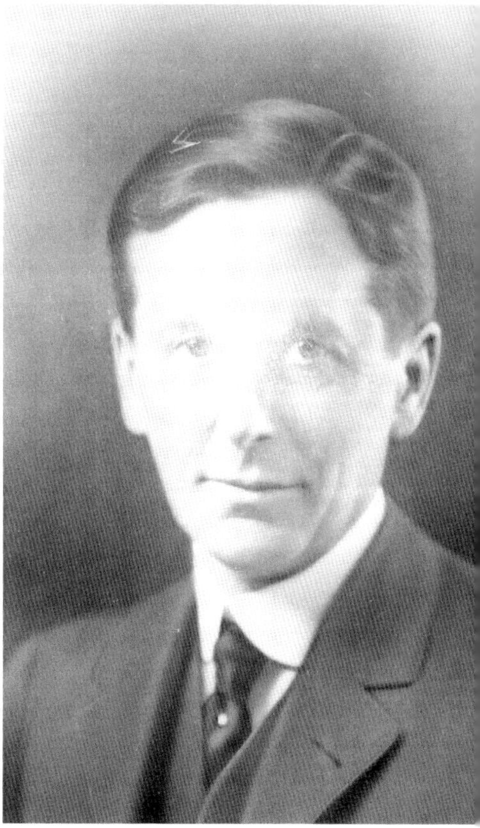

John Taylor Pirie Sr. (1871–1940)

Pirie, son of Scotland-born department store founder John Thomas Pirie (1827–1913) and Sarah Carson Pirie, served as mayor from 1911 to 1914. Rommy Lopat's Find a Grave article, drawing on the 1926 edition of *Who's Who in Chicago*, provides clarity about three generations of department store men named John T. Pirie: John Thomas; John Taylor Sr.; and his son John Taylor Pirie Jr. (1903–1980), the second husband of Ginevra King. (City.)

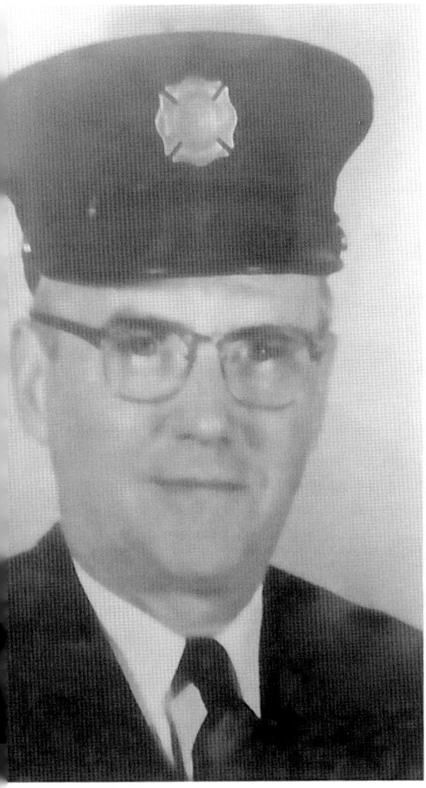

Alfred Edward Marwede (1902–1970)

Alfred Marwede was a second-generation volunteer fireman. His father, Alfred Marwede (1870–1928), helped found the first fire brigade and was chauffeur to J.V. Farwell (*LFEPC*, page 81). The younger Marwede was in the heating-oil business, and his son Alfred William "Bill" Marwede (1930–2014) was the owner of the Marwede's Dry Cleaning establishment in town. (Arthur Miller and Lake Forest Fire Department.)

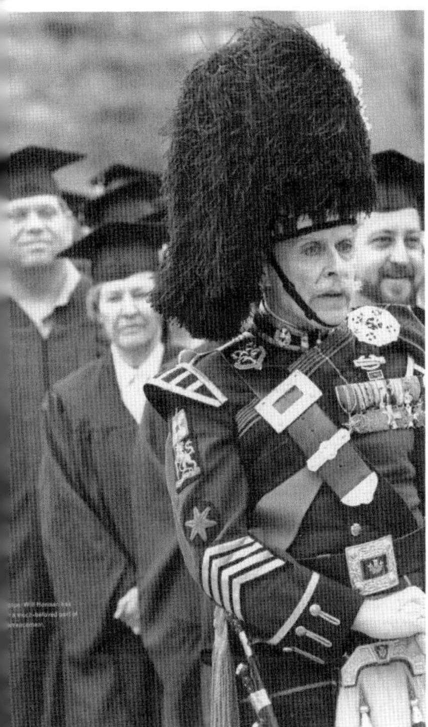

Virginia Feister Frederick (1917–2010)

Ginnie Frederick earned a bachelor's degree from the University of Iowa in 1938 and a master of liberal studies degree from Lake Forest College in 1999, the latter institution also granting her an honorary doctorate in 1999. She is seen here at center in 1999. Frederick was the first woman elected to the city council (1974–1979), and she then served in the Illinois General Assembly until 1994. She made custom women's dresses from 1947 to 1979 and was active in the League of Women Voters. Her 2001 autobiography, *Moving On—My Life Through the Twentieth Century and Today*, began as her master's thesis. (LFCLASC.)

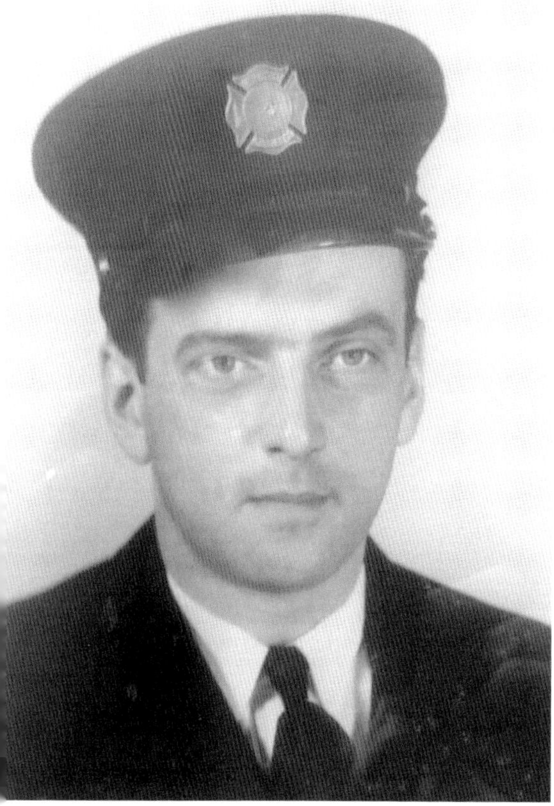

Donald Tiffany (1898–1984)

Don Tiffany was a local fireman, as seen here in the early 1950s, and a police officer and captain before retiring and operating the legendary Lantern Tavern and Restaurant on Western Avenue. A favorite spot of college students, alumni, and locals, it thrives still north of Westminster Avenue. He was succeeded in the business by his son Don Jr. (1942–2007). (Arthur Miller and Lake Forest Fire Department.)

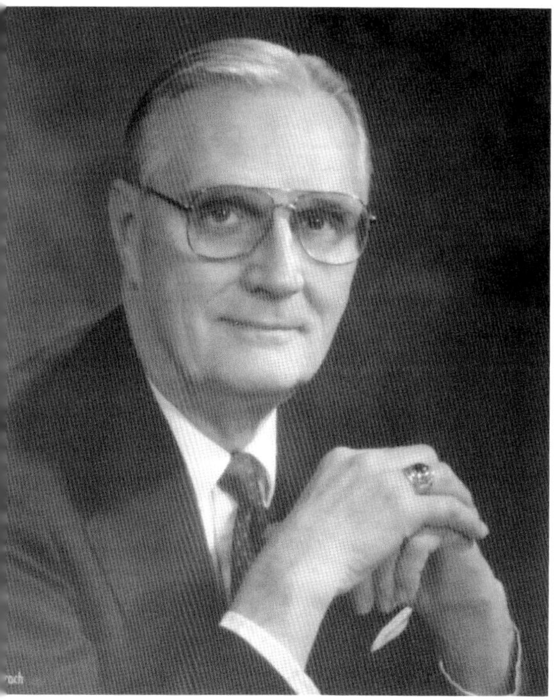

Marshall Strenger (c. 1918–1994)

Strenger counted among his ancestors Nelson Pratt (1825–1903), who had worked on construction of the 1858 Lake Forest Hotel, the first building in town, located in what now is Triangle Park. Pratt opened a store in 1868. Marshall Strenger, a decorated World War II pilot and, later, a colonel in the US Air Force Reserve, served as mayor from 1987 to 1990. He ran H.T. Strenger, Inc., a local plumbing business started by his father. (City.)

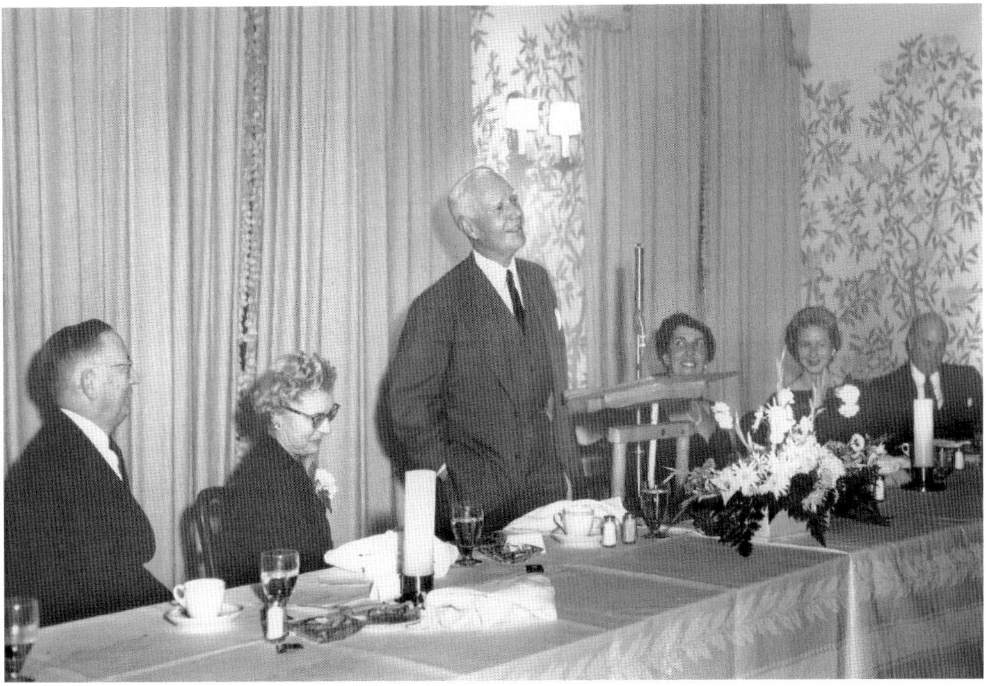

R. Douglas Stuart (1886–1975)
Quaker Oats vice president and, later, chair, and Chicago, Burlington & Quincy Railroad board member R. Douglas Stuart served as ambassador to Canada (1953–1956). He was the husband of Harriet McClure Stuart and father of Robert D. Stuart (1916–2014) and Margaret Stuart Hart. He is shown here, standing, at the 50th anniversary of the local First National Bank in 1957. Lake Forest College president Ernest Johnson is seated at far left. (Louis E. Laflin Jr. Collection, LFCLASC.)

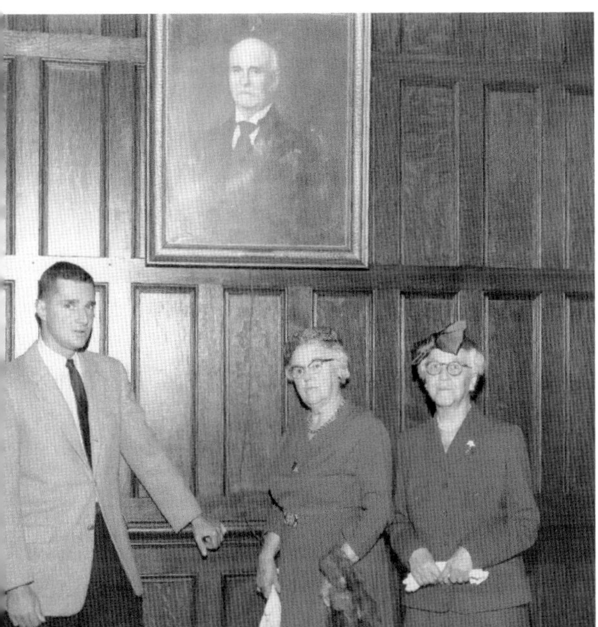

Francis C. Farwell II (1922–2010)
During his term as mayor (1984–1987), Frank Farwell oversaw the beach redevelopment in 1986–1987 and acceptance of the gift of the Ragdale property. Here, he stands below a portrait of Calvin Durand, a former mayor (1891–1895), with two of Durand's daughters in Calvin Durand Hall, Lake Forest College, around 1960. Farwell, the son of Albert Farwell and a great-grandson of J.V. Farwell, was a partner with William Blair & Co. (LFCLASC.)

Adlai Stevenson II (1900–1965) and Jane Warner Dick (1906–1997)

Stevenson was an Illinois governor (1949–1953), two-time Democratic nominee for president (1952 and 1956), and ambassador to the United Nations (1961–1965). During summers, he and his family rented houses in Lake Forest near Onwentsia, including 383 North Washington Road, later the home of local historians Katherine (Trowbridge) and Edward Arpee. By 1938, he had built his farmhouse west of Lake Forest in what is now Mettawa. The property is now a historic site owned by the Lake County Forest Preserve district. In the 1960s, he participated in some college symposia for his friend Ruth Winter. Many notable locals supported his Democratic political campaigns, even though they were staunch Republicans. The sketch below shows Adlai Stevenson's sister, India Edwards, left, Jane Warner Dick (Mrs. Edison Dick), center, and the 1952 presidential candidate Stevenson on the campaign trail leading up to the November 1952 election. It is entitled "A Very Congenial Triumvirate." The image comes from Mrs. Dick's Christmas 1952 book, *Whistle-Stopping with Adlai*. The book was printed by Chicago's October House, apparently pretty quickly; the identity of the sketch artist, "B.," is not provided. See also page 79. Jane Warner Dick is pictured in the inset. (Sketch, Edison W. Dick; inset, LFCLASC.)

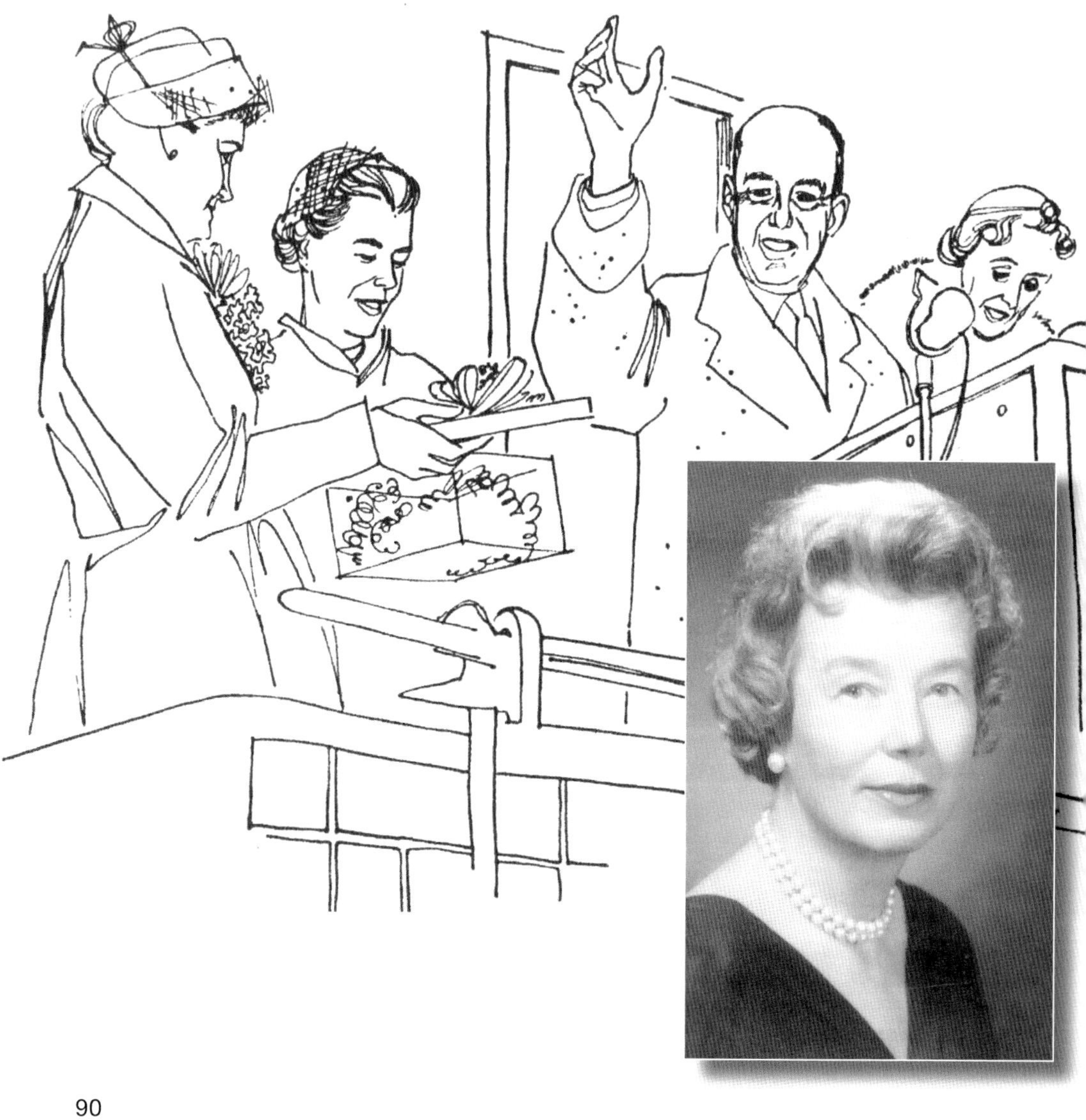

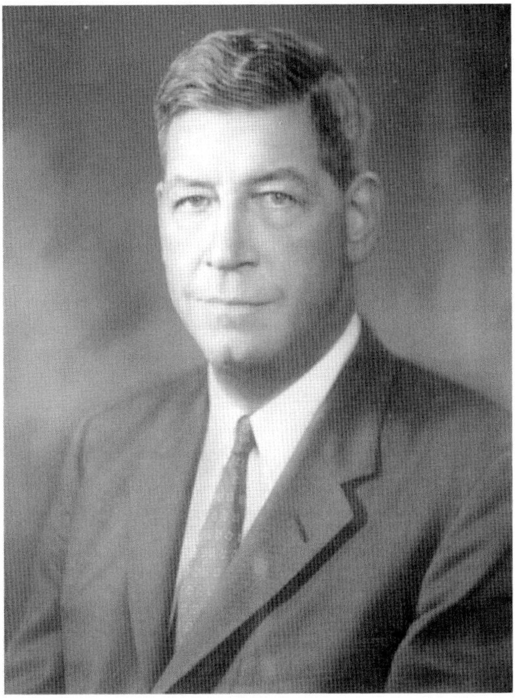

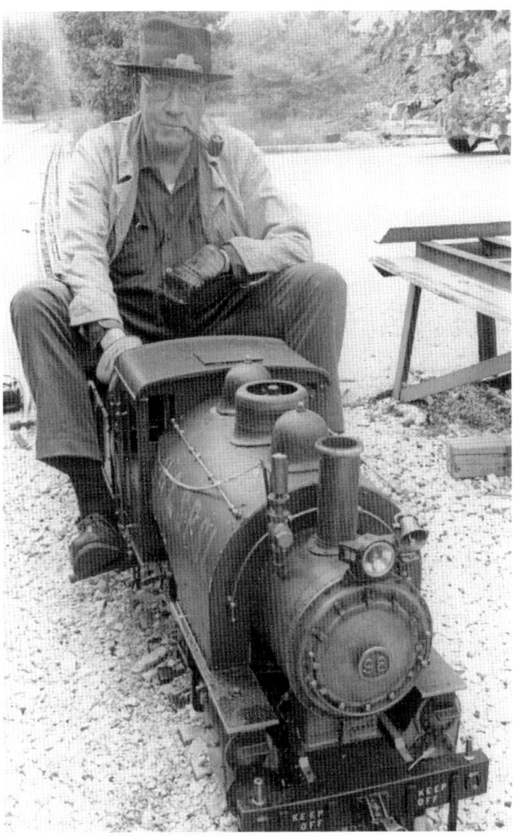

Elliott Donnelley (1903–1975)
Donnelley, mayor from 1954 to 1957, when Deerpath and Sheridan Schools were opened, grew up in town on Green Bay Road, near West Park. He built on Ridge Lane in 1934 and for his family of four boys off of Waukegan Road in 1955. He loved trains and ran a scale-model railroad-kit business, Scale Craft, from the mid-1930s to the 1950s. He also entered the family printing business, later serving as vice chairman, due to his ability to communicate effectively with the workers at the plant. In the same era, he was drawn into philanthropy. Donnelley was on the Lake Forest College board by 1942 and, by the 1960s, was the board chair. He donated for the library at the college (named for him and his family, 1964). Elliott was a nationally known steam locomotive preservationist. His live-steam, garden-scaled train outfit ran on his Waukegan Road estate. (Above, City; below, LF-LBHS.)

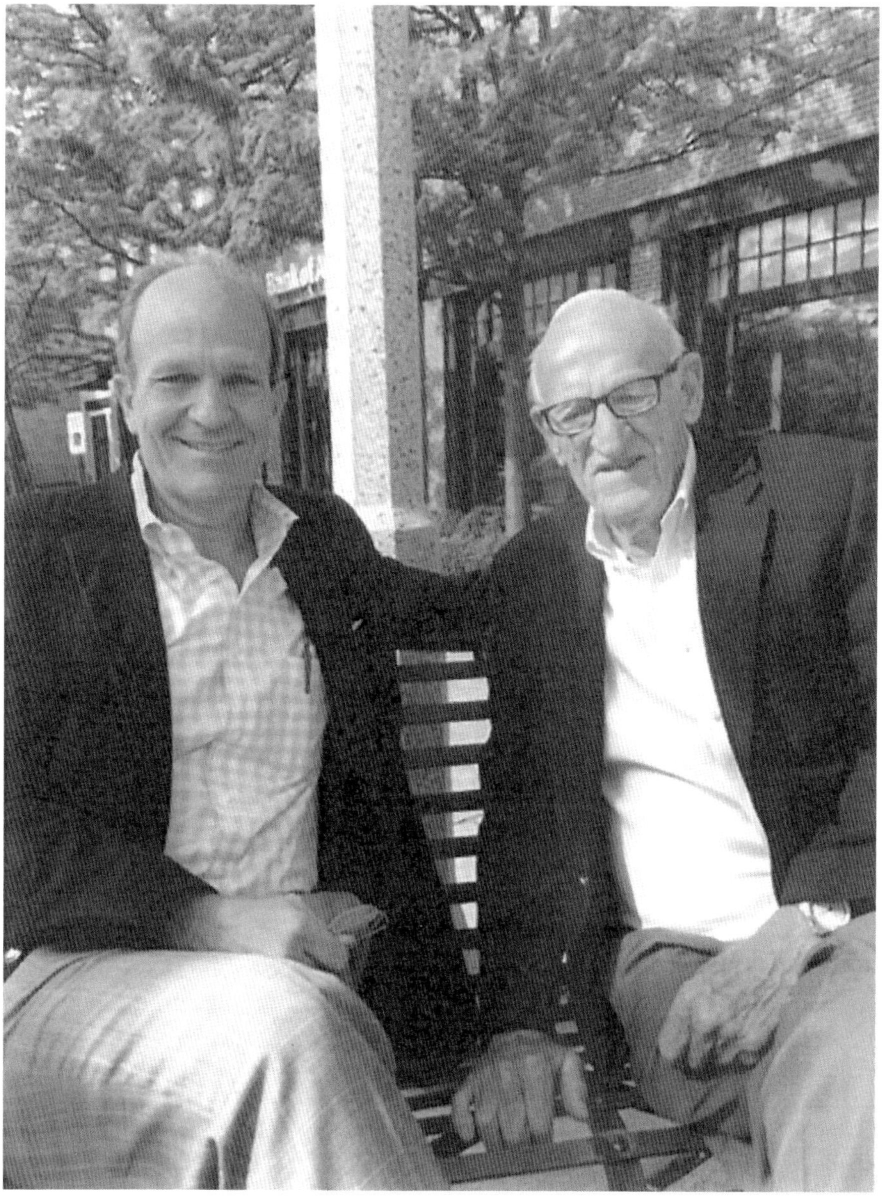

Thomas E. Swarthout and James E. Swarthout

The city has benefited from the contributions of four generations of Swarthouts. Thomas Swarthout (left) held positions as alderman in Lake Forest for six years and as chair of the Lake Forest Hospital board; he served on the Forest Park Board; and he is a trustee of the North Shore Water Reclamation District. His father, James Swarthout (right), served as mayor of Lake Forest (1975–1979), as a trustee of the Water Reclamation District for 34 years, and contributed 25 years as a volunteer fireman. Both Tom and Jim have served as chairmen of the parks and recreation board.

In business and real estate, James Swarthout ran a Ford dealership on the former Knauz-Boutin garage and gas station site on Western Avenue, north of Westminster Avenue. This later housed Lake Forest Sports Cars and, by the early 2000s, the Swarthouts replaced all this with the two-story office building housing the Bank of America, Caputo's, and other local businesses. (Swarthout family.)

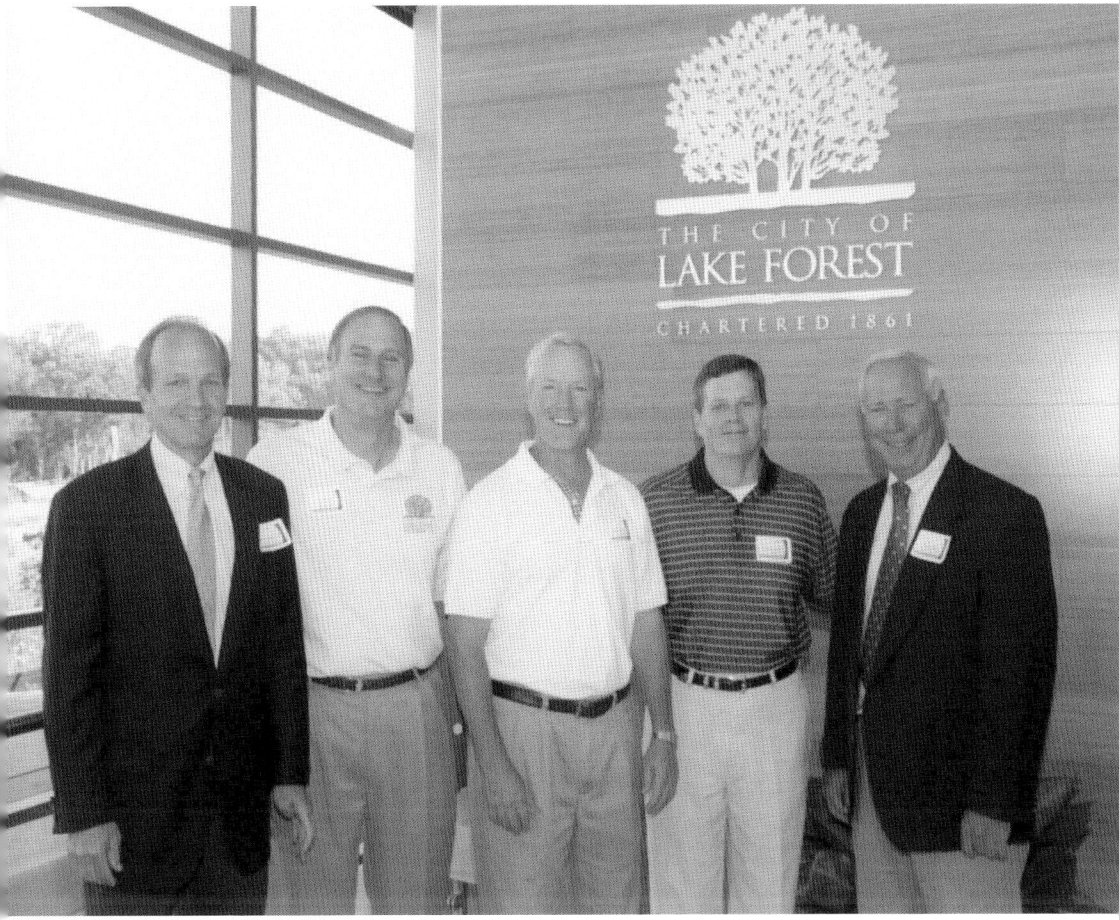

Robert R. Kiely Jr. and S. Michael Rummel

Bob Kiely (center) has served as the city manager of the City of Lake Forest since 1990, appointed by the mayor and city council. He is shown here with the following: former alderman Tom Swarthout (far left); Mike Rummel (second from left), mayor (2005–2009); James J. Cowhey Jr. (second from right), mayor (2009–2013); and former public works director Tom Naatz.

Through a quarter of a century of economic booms and busts, Bob Kiely has guided the city through its major westside building boom, constructing a new municipal services building (2009) and overseeing the expansion and renovation of the 1899 city hall (1998). He earned his bachelor of arts degree from Lake Forest College in 1979 and got his master's in public administration from the University of Kansas in 1981. He began as assistant city manager from 1980 to 1982, held the same position in Wilmette (1982–1986), then served as city manager in Prospect Heights (1986–1990). Kiely has taught as an adjunct at Northwestern University and has served leadership roles in state and midwestern professional municipal organizations. He lives and has raised his family locally.

Mike Rummel earned his bachelor of science degree from Northwestern in 1973. After serving on the city council from 2001 to 2005, he served as mayor the next four years. Today, he is serving a second four-year term on the Lake County and Forest Preserve Boards, representing Lake Forest, and he is treasurer of the Forest Preserves. Rummel is president since 1978 of his Rummel Associates insurance agency and lives in Lake Forest with his wife, attorney Melanie Rummel. She is an active leader in LFOLA, a former board president of Lake Forest K-8 School District 67, and president of the Lake County Bar Association. (City.)

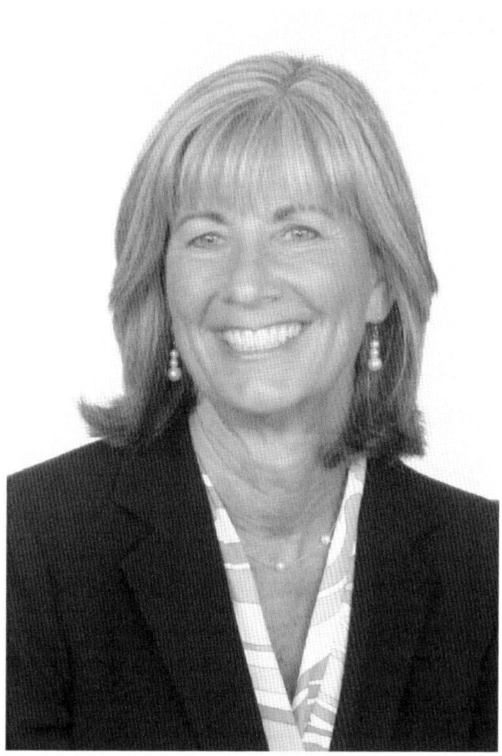

Susan Garrett

Susan Garrett earned her bachelor of arts degree from Lake Forest College in 1994 and received an honorary doctorate of laws from the same school in 2012. From 1997 to 2013, she served in the state legislature (general assembly, 1997–2003; senate, 2003–2013). A Democrat, she also represented the diverse communities north of Lake Forest and Lake Bluff. From 2009 to 2013, Garrett served in the leadership as majority whip. She appears below in 2013 with Mayor Don Schoenheider receiving an honor for her service in state government. She chairs the nonpartisan, nonprofit Illinois Campaign for Political Reform (ICPR), formed in 1997 by former senator Paul Simon. (Right, Susan Garrett; below, City.)

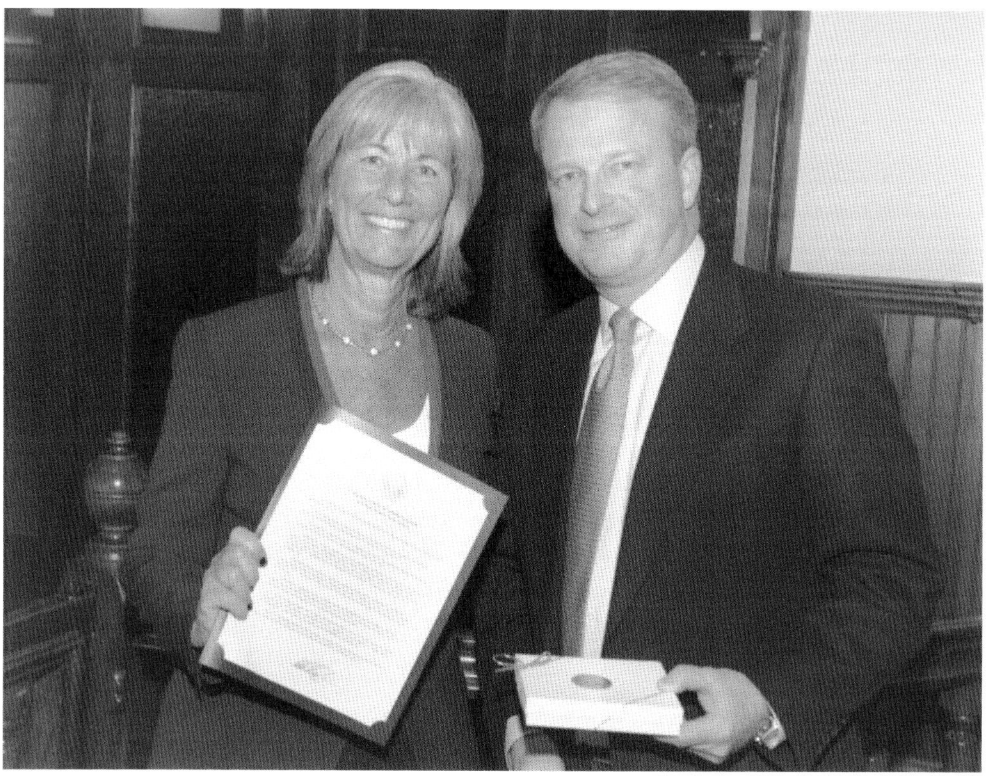

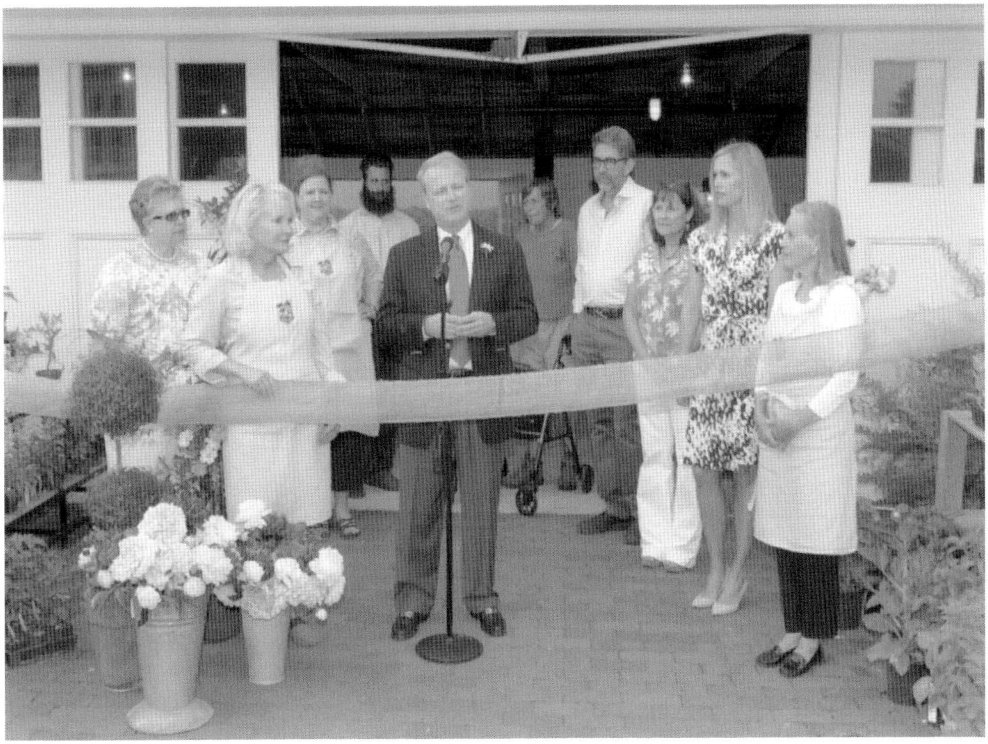

Donald Schoenheider

Mayor Schoenheider was elected in April 2013. He had been Third Ward alderman and served for five years on the city's Building Review Board. With almost 30 years of experience in commercial real estate development brokerage, he brought strong experience in state and local government and community development. Mayor Schoenheider (center) is shown here at the ribbon-cutting ceremony for the Elawa Garden Market with Maddie Dugan, far left, and Craig Bergmann, fourth from the right (page 44). (City.)

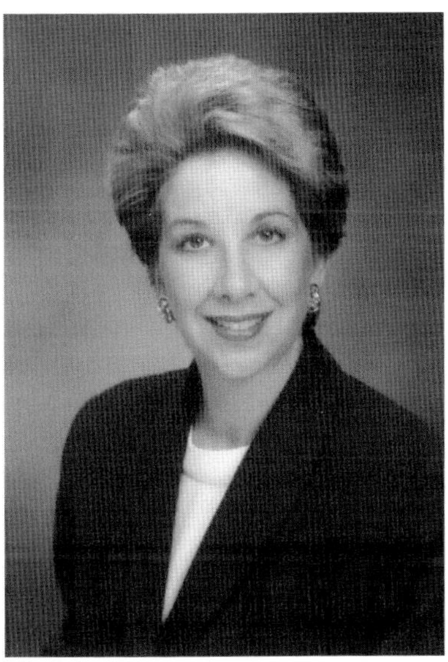

Corrine Wood

Wood served as the first woman lieutenant governor of Illinois (1999–2003). In office, she focused on issues of economic development, the environment, and women's health. She launched a statewide campaign to increase funding for breast cancer research through "A Check for the Cure," which became the top tax-return check-off and raised more than $2 million during her term. (Corrine Wood.)

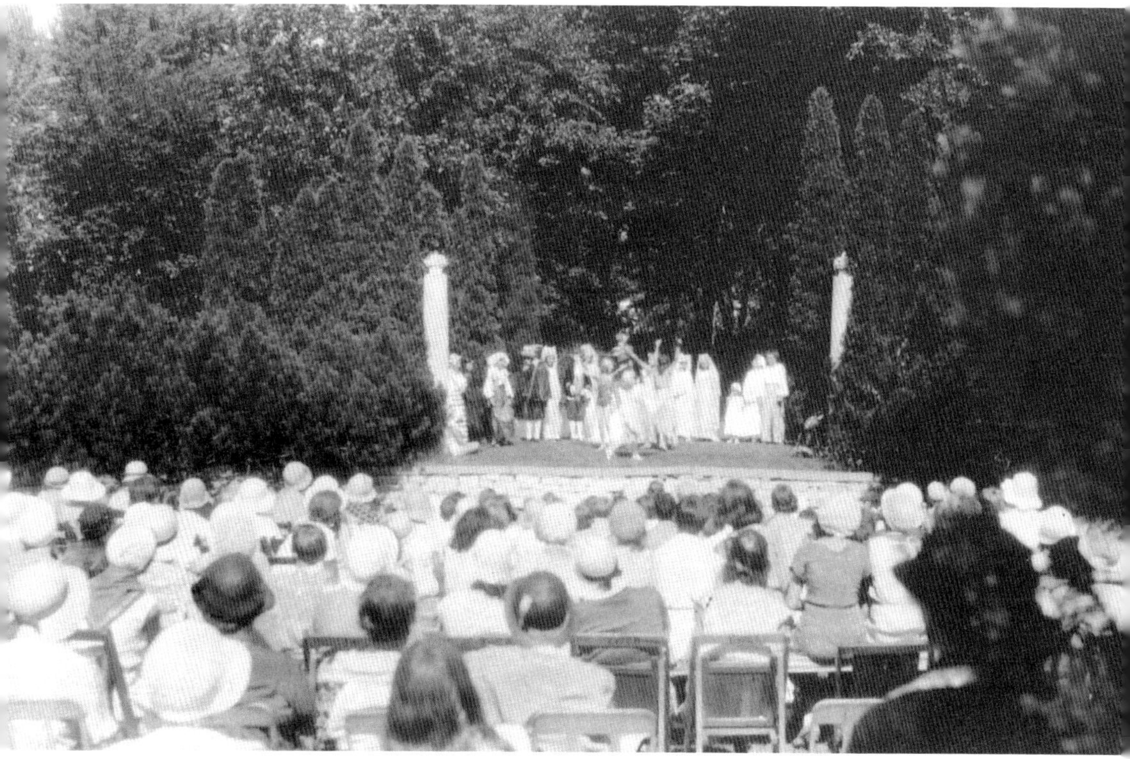

Ragdale Ring

Architect Howard Shaw (page 37) had designed the Ragdale Ring garden theater on the north portion of his country place around 1912. This feature drew on Renaissance Italian gardens for its stage and on the council ring conception of Shaw's frequent collaborator, landscape designer Jens Jensen, for its audience area. The low limestone wall of the ring, at seating height, is derived from Native American precedents and employs regional stone, following Jensen's idea of restoration of native features. Shaw designed and built the theater for his wife, Frances Wells Shaw, who wrote plays and poetry. Seen here in 1914 is a troupe of costumed children putting on *The Pipes of Pan*, written by Frances Shaw, for a daytime audience seated on folding chairs within the ring and looking east. (LFCLASC.)

CHAPTER SEVEN

Artists and Literary, Musical, Theater, and Media Personalities

Flowing from and around local educational institutions since the early days have been art, literature, theater, and—by around 1910, when the first nickelodeons appeared in town—the media. There were amateur artists, including those in the Deerpath Art League, active since the 1950s with its annual Labor Day Art Fair. Professional artists included the notable illustrator Milo Winter, the McMahon family, Sylvia Shaw Judson (*LFEPC*, page 123), and teachers and professors, such as Franz Schulze and Michael Croydon at Lake Forest College and Al Pounian at Barat College. Many successful artists have emerged from amateur efforts, including Grace McGann, Fay Peck, and Lorna Marsh, the last using painter Grace McGann's Fairlawn studio.

Music dates to the early days, with Charles Holt playing the organ for the new 1887 Presbyterian church. By 1891, Siegfried E. Gruenstein, who started at the academy that year at age 14 and later attended the college, took over, and he continued in the post until 1939. He was the dean of Illinois organists and edited the journal *Diapason*. Lessons in voice and instrumental music were based in Ferry Hall after 1869, and musical recitals and performances were a favorite form of community entertainment. In the 1890s, the African American Jubilee Singers of Fiske University, Tennessee, performed at the Presbyterian church. Lake Foresters supported the Chicago Symphony, and Reginald De Koven, husband of Anna Farwell De Koven, had written articles promoting its founding in the Farwells' weekly *America* in 1890–1891. De Koven was a composer whose 1890 hit operetta *Robin Hood* included his memorable wedding favorite, "Oh, Promise Me." The De Kovens were married in 1884 in town; after 1890, they only summered at Fairlawn, living variously in Washington, DC, where De Koven founded the Washington Philharmonic, and in New York, with their own 1912-completed Park Avenue townhouse.

Lake Foresters also supported the Chicago Symphony at Ravinia. The Lake Forest Symphony was founded in 1957 as an amateur chamber orchestra. It grew to 60 players by 1965, and by 1991, it was a fully professional orchestra under Victor Aitay, concertmaster of the Chicago Symphony. The amateurs formed a new orchestra, the North Shore Symphony. The Camerata Singers, a 16-member vocal group, began in 1980 and continued to 2008. They sang their Sunday afternoon concerts in more commodious Lake Forest homes, lending a distinctive feature and draw to their three decades of existence. Lake Forest High School's choral program in the period reached new levels of achievement with Tim Haskett, and the choral and the instrumental groups, the orchestra and band, flourished with trips to Europe and in the Metcalf Auditorium, built in 1959 and remodeled around 2000.

The Old Town School of Folk Music, Chicago, was founded by a 1931 Lake Forest College alumnus, Win Stracke; songwriter Steve Goodman attended the college briefly in the mid-1960s. Many informal musical groups have thrived, including the Buckthorns, the Clumsy Mumsies, and the Samuel Dent Memorial Jazz Band, the last with Scott Meland and Brookes Smith, an Atteridge family descendant and proprietor of Smith's Men's Store (*DLF*, page 84).

Writers here have included poets, novelists, playwrights, and journalists. Some of the earliest writing about Lake Forest was for the *Chicago Tribune*, apparently by William Bross, an early supporter, institutional trustee, and visitor. Athlete Fred Hayner, later a local resident, was sports editor for the *Chicago Evening Post* in the 1910s when he wrote about the first drive of a golf ball going off the bluff at Forest Park into the lake in 1892, hit by golf legend Charles Macdonald. Novelists have included both men and women, from Anna Farwell De Koven, writing from the 1890s to the 1940s, to the notable Ward Just, writing since the 1960s. A summer guest of Arthur and Mary Aldis around 1911 was Harriet Monroe, the founder of *Poetry: A Magazine of Verse*; by the 1970s, poet Alice Ryerson founded the Ragdale Foundation to accommodate residencies like Monroe's more formally.

Mary Aldis herself was a playwright with her own small playhouse for giving one-acts by amateurs—her friends and neighbors. This pioneering amateur troupe traveled to Boston, where Countess Cissy Patterson Gizycki won acting acclaim. Mary Aldis also nurtured Chicago's Little Theatre director, Maurice Browne, providing him with an apartment on the Aldis compound.

These amateur one-acts were a reaction against a new media innovation: the nickelodeon. Later in the century, Lake Foresters on the silver and small screens would include Richard Widmark, Joan Taylor (Rose Marie Emma), Jack Benny, Robin Williams, Cathy Joosten (*The West Wing* and *Desperate Housewives*) and Vince Vaughn. John Hughes (1950–2009) was a truly legendary film writer and producer. His work includes the iconic North Shore–set *Ferris Bueller's Day Off* (1986).

The age of computers, the Internet, and social media, beginning in the 1980s, also has transformed the distribution of art, photographic and other images, writing, performance, and communication. Lake Forest–raised John Vignocchi, one of many who have migrated to Los Angles, serves as an executive producer in computer gaming for Disney in California. On another scale, harkening back to amateur efforts a century ago, Lake Forest–raised Vero Beach, Florida, resident Bob Craig a few years ago launched a Facebook page, "I Remember Lake Forest When." It has some 2,700 participants.

In sum, creative expression, both amateur and professional, has been an integral part of the local lifestyle since the 1880s.

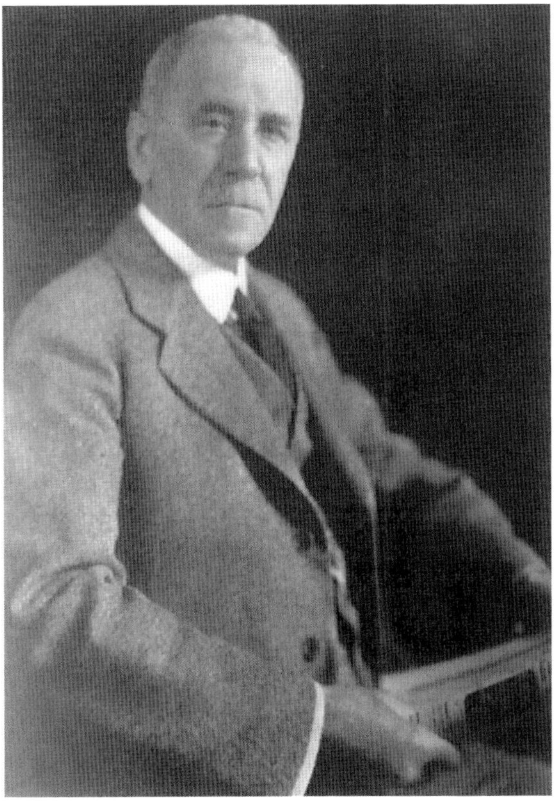

Slason Thompson (1849–1935)
Arriving in Chicago in the 1880s, Canadian journalist, literary editor, and memoirist Thompson moved from the *Chicago Herald* in the early 1880s to the C.B. Farwell–sponsored *America* weekly, working there from 1887 to 1892—the period of Farwell's senate stint. Thompson then worked as a data gatherer, publicist, and book author for the Association of American Railroads. His lakefront house, Seven Cedars (below), was built in 1905, designed by Arthur Heun. Thompson was an active golfer at Onwentsia and Old Elm. When Onwentsia threatened to redesign the 1896 course, Thompson wrote a 1911 polemic against the change, *The Rape of the Links*, a play on Alexander Pope's 1712 mock-heroic poem *The Rape of the Lock*. In 1929, as the new Lindeberg-designed Onwentsia clubhouse opened, he gave a history of the club, *The Annals of Onwentsia*. His 1930 memoir, *Way Back When*, is invaluable Chicago and Lake Forest history. (Both, LFCLASC.)

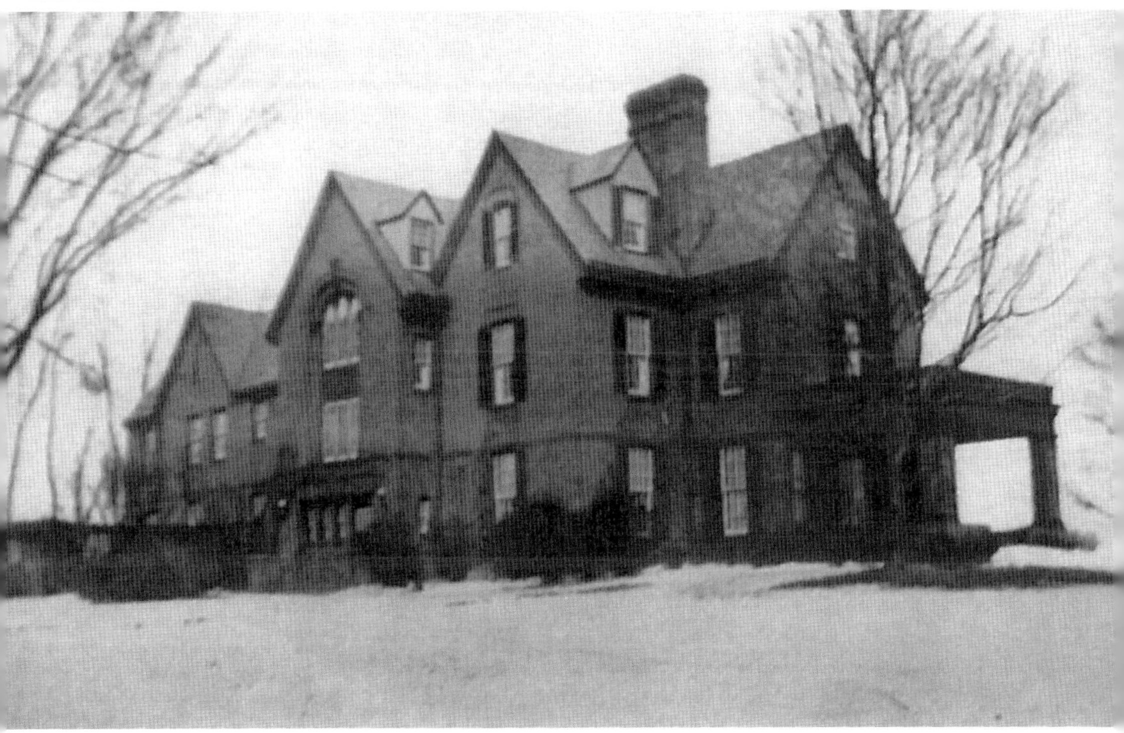

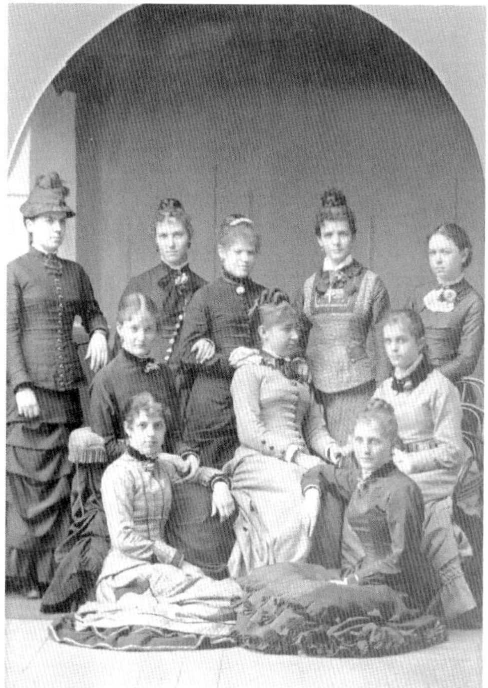

Anna Farwell De Koven (1860–1953)

Eldest daughter of US senator Charles Farwell and the wife of composer Reginald De Koven, Anna Farwell De Koven wrote novels, biographies, a translation from the French, and essays. She earned her bachelor of arts degree from Lake Forest University in 1880. Her published books include a translation of Pierre Loti's *Iceland Fisherman* (1889), the romance *A Sawdust Doll* (1895), and *Women in Cycles of Culture* (1940). Here, she stands second from right with Lake Forest University women in 1877. (LF-LBHS.)

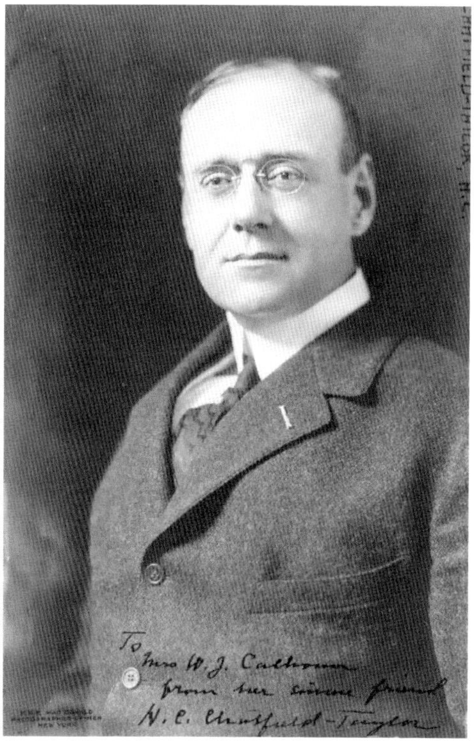

Hobart C. Chatfield-Taylor (1865–1945)

Hobart's long name came from a legacy that led to his adopting the Chatfield heritage. He married Rose Farwell, daughter of Senator Farwell, in 1890. An author, he wrote novels and two memoirs, *Cities of Many Men* (1925) and *Charmed Circles* (1935), with much about Lake Forest. An 1886 graduate of Cornell University, Chatfield-Taylor played key social roles in the 1893 World's Columbian Exposition and in founding Onwentsia (1895) after bringing golf to Lake Forest in 1892. (LFCLASC.)

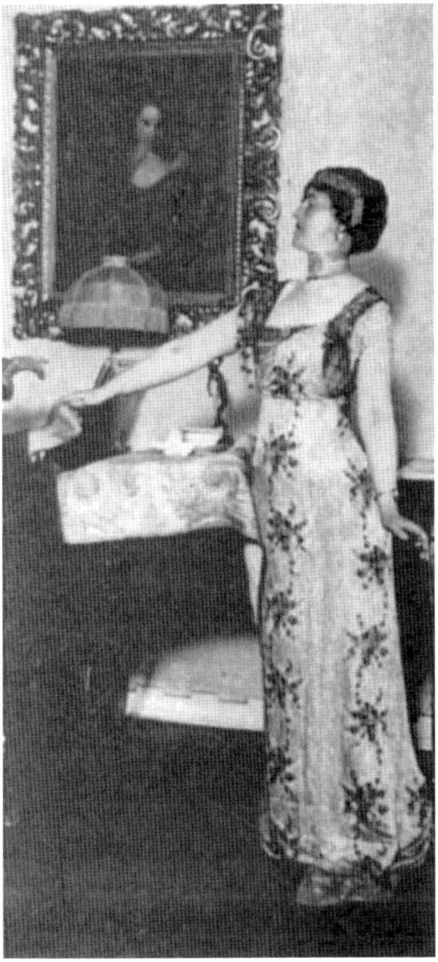

Mary Reynolds Aldis (1872–1949)
Mary Reynolds Aldis, married to Arthur Aldis, summered at her Lake Forest compound in the first half of the 20th century. She was a writer and a patron of the arts at her Lake Forest cottage-turned-playhouse. Her works include *Plays for Small Stages* (1915) and a novel, *Drift* (1918). Her Lake Forest Players, active from about 1910 to 1916, were nationally known pioneers of amateur theatricals. (LFCLASC.)

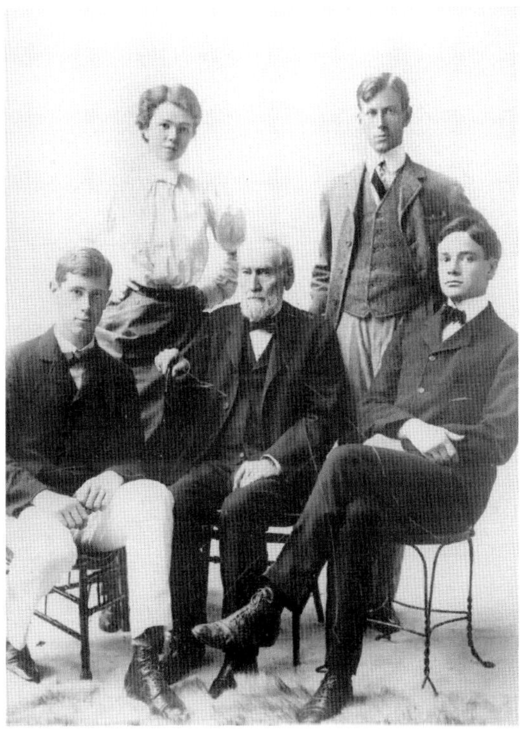

Eleanor Medill Patterson (1881–1948)
Pioneer newspaper publisher Cissy Patterson passed a significant interval in Lake Forest from about 1908 to 1913. The Countess Gizycki's complicated life and marriages are best explained in Amanda Smith's excellent 2012 biography of Cissy, *Newspaper Titan*. Shown here around 1900 are, from left to right, (seated) Robert R. McCormick, *Tribune* publisher Joseph Medill, and Joseph Medill Patterson; (standing) Cissy Patterson and Medill McCormick. Joseph Patterson, Cissy's brother, was soon living west of Lake Forest. (LFCLASC.)

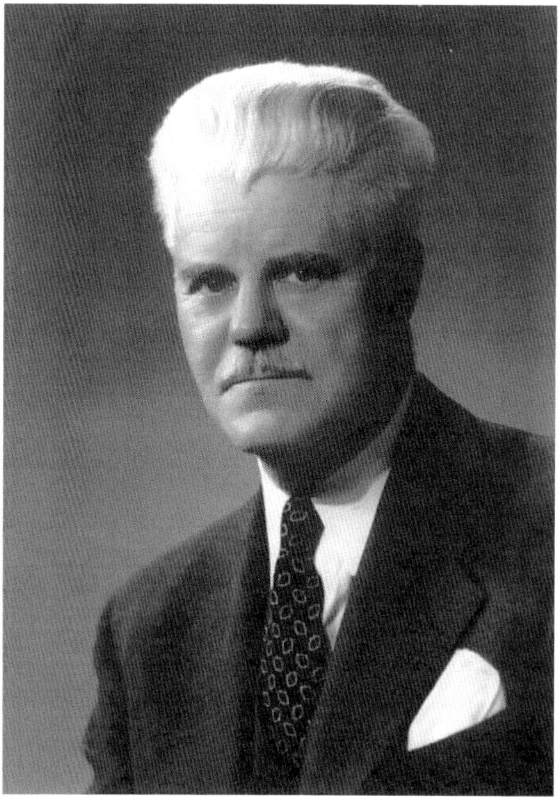

Milo Kendall Winter (1888–1956)

Artist and local resident Milo Winter specialized in color-plate-illustrated children's books from the heyday of that genre, the 1890s to the mid-1920s. From Dickens's *Christmas Carol* (1912) through *The Three Musketeers* (1923), Winter created vivid color windows into 20 such classics for Chicago publisher Rand McNally, challenging East Coast publishers' offerings by artists Howard Pyle and N.C. Wyeth. By 1925, radio had eclipsed reading aloud. (LF-LBHS.)

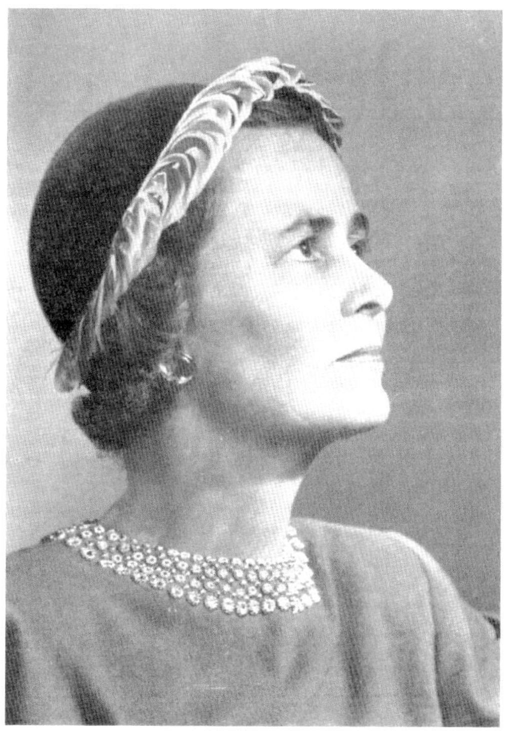

Dorothy Keeley Aldis (1896–1966)

Author Dorothy Keeley Aldis was the daughter-in-law of Mary Aldis and, like her, an author of novels and children's books. Her novels include *Their Own Apartment* (1935), *Time at Her Heels* (1937), and *All the Year Round* (1938). *Favorite Poems of Dorothy Aldis* (1970) makes available the best of her verse for children. Upon her 1966 death, *Elementary English* dubbed her "The Poet Laureate of Children." (LFCASC.)

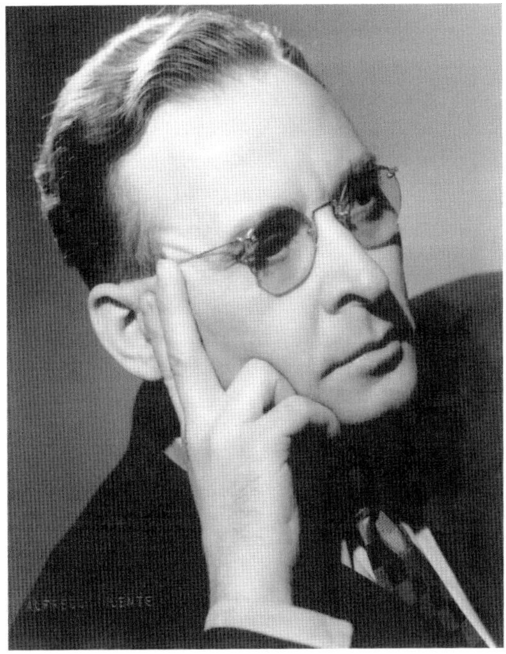

Garrett Leverton (1896–1949)

Leverton, a professor of theater and a theatrical agent with Samuel French, headed up the Lake Forest College drama program in the 1920s and willed to the institution his papers and collections. As an agent, he worked tirelessly in the 1930s and 1940s to advance the work of writers he respected—notably Lynn Riggs, whose 1931 play *Green Grow the Lilacs* became in 1943 the first great hit musical, *Oklahoma!* His papers are at Lake Forest College's Donnelley and Lee Library. (LFCLASC.)

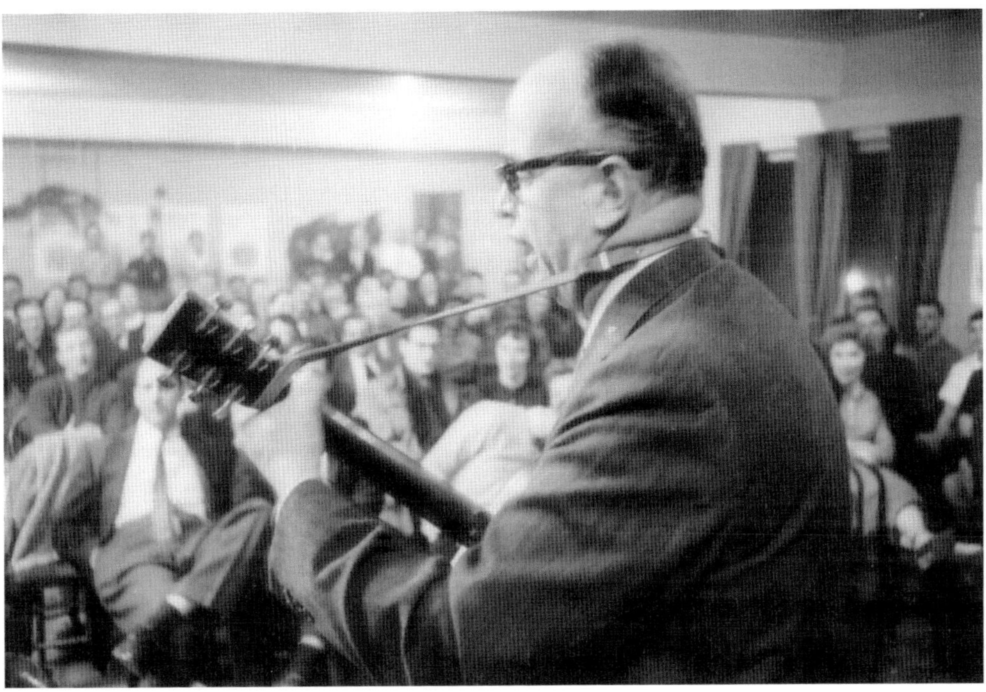

Win Stracke (1908–1991)

Folksinger, musician, composer, stage actor, television personality, and 1957 founder of Chicago's Old Town School of Folk Music, Win Stracke graduated from Lake Forest College in 1931. He was a friend of and collaborator with Studs Terkel. With Pete Seeger and others, Stracke believed that music could help promote the cause of working people. He composed the state's 150th-anniversary celebration song, "Illinois, Illinois." (Photograph by Kiko Konagamitsu; courtesy of the Old Town School.)

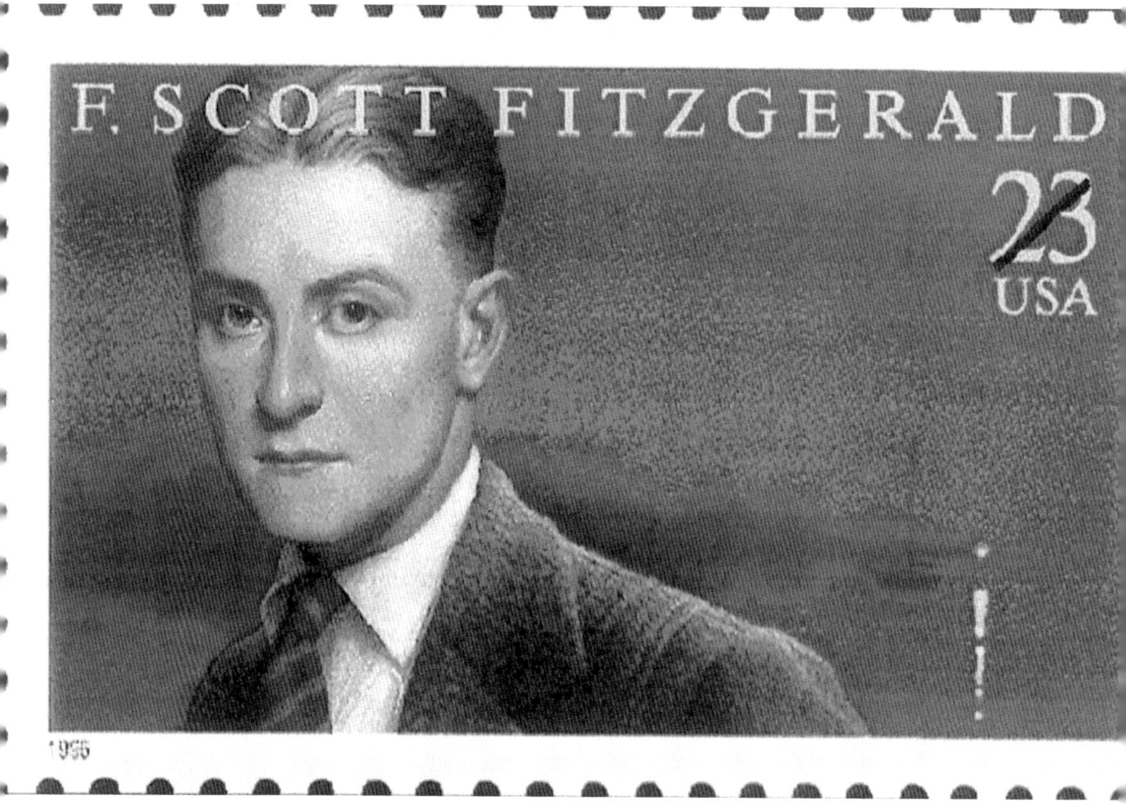

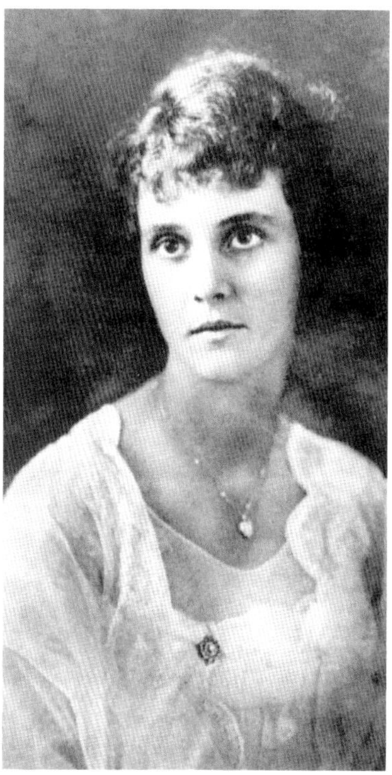

Francis Scott Fitzgerald (1896–1940)
Well-documented in James L. West III's *A Perfect Hour* (2005) is Fitzgerald's flirtation, mostly in letters, with Ginevra King (left) and his brief visit to her in Lake Forest. On this episode hinged the coverage of Lake Forest in the author's 1925 novel *The Great Gatsby*.

But, according to a February 23, 2015, Facebook post by Scots local historian David Forlow, Fitzgerald stayed with James H. Douglas Sr. at 910 North Green Bay Road in the summer of 1919, in the period when he was revising his novel *The Romantic Egoist*, rejected in 1917. He later gave Douglas a signed copy of his 1920 novel *This Side of Paradise*, the result of his work that summer. Fitzgerald had tried an advertising career in New York after the Armistice, but before long, he turned to reworking his prewar project to resubmit to Scribner's, his future publisher. That summer, he may also have worked on his story "May Day," about the sad postwar circumstances and mood in New York. It appeared in the July 1920 issue of the *Smart Set*. David Forlow's new information about Fitzgerald's only real extended stay locally casts light on the would-be author seeking more elite social experience in Lake Forest, following up on his introduction from Ginevra King. (Both, LFCASC.)

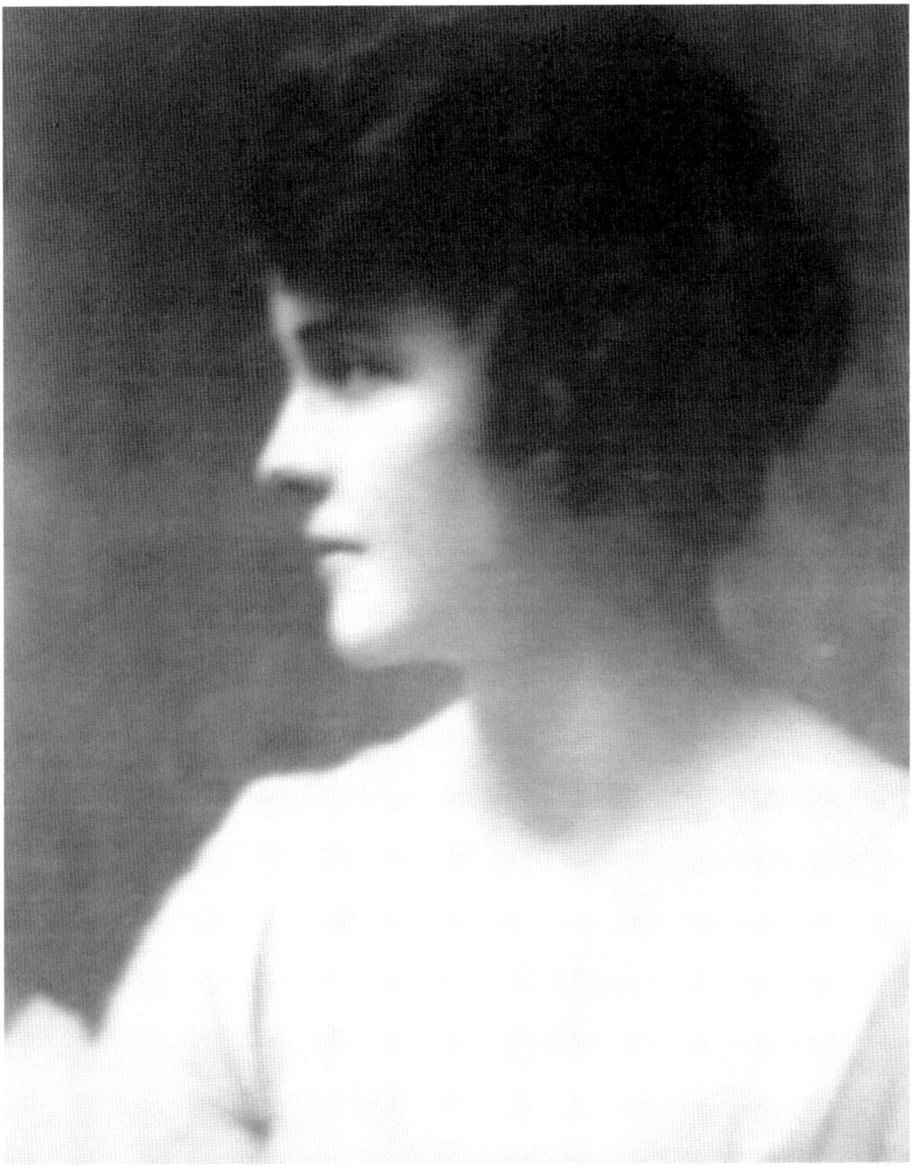

Ginevra King (Mitchell) Pirie (1898–1980)
A teenaged Ginevra King was the enchanting daughter of Lake Forest's Onwentsia-set Charles Garfield King family. She had a brief, mostly correspondence-centered friendship with young Princeton student F. Scott Fitzgerald of St. Paul. As James L. West III, in his 2006 book on their shared experience, describes, they perhaps only had a "perfect hour" once or twice, and under chaperoned circumstances. But their writing back and forth was full of energy, with the unobtainable, very wealthy Ginevra writing a prescient story, included in its handwritten entirety by West, about their meeting up years in the future. It provides a kernel of the storyline involving Ginevra in Scott's writing, most memorably as Daisy Buchanan in *The Great Gatsby* (1925).

Ginevra married twice, first to William Mitchell in 1918; the couple had three children. In 1937, she married John T. Pirie Jr. For a perfect couple of meetings and some intense brief correspondence, she and Scott, like a meteor, lit up the American literary sky of the 1920s and 1930s. (LFCASC.)

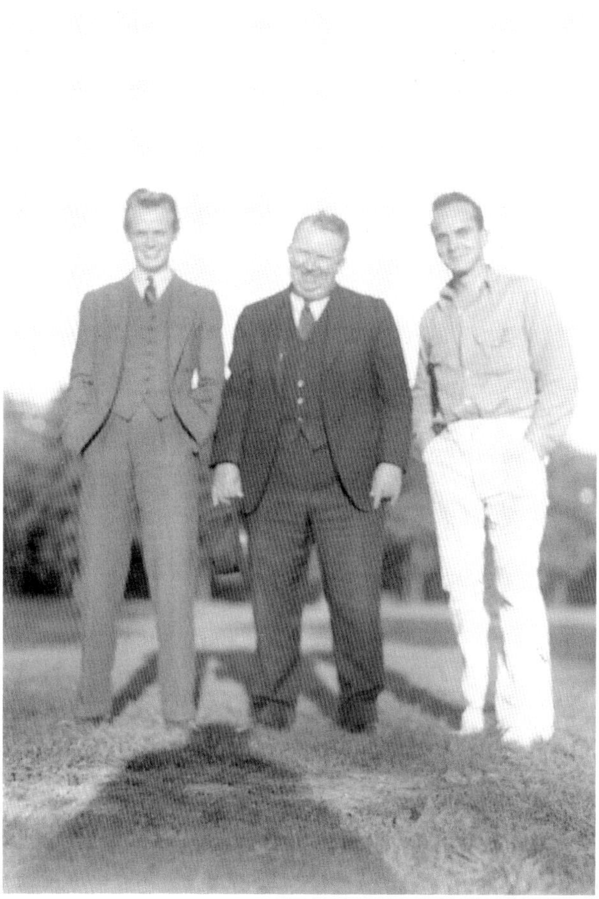

Richard Widmark (1914–2008)

Widmark (left) earned a bachelor of arts degree from Lake Forest College in 1936. He began his career teaching drama for two years under the college's theater director, Tommy Tomlinson (center). Widmark went to New York and, by 1943, was appearing on Broadway. He rose to stardom as a tough guy in the noir film *Kiss of Death* (1947). He moved to Hollywood, where his image was cleaned up, and he starred in Westerns, historical and detective films, and, later, television. (LFCLASC.)

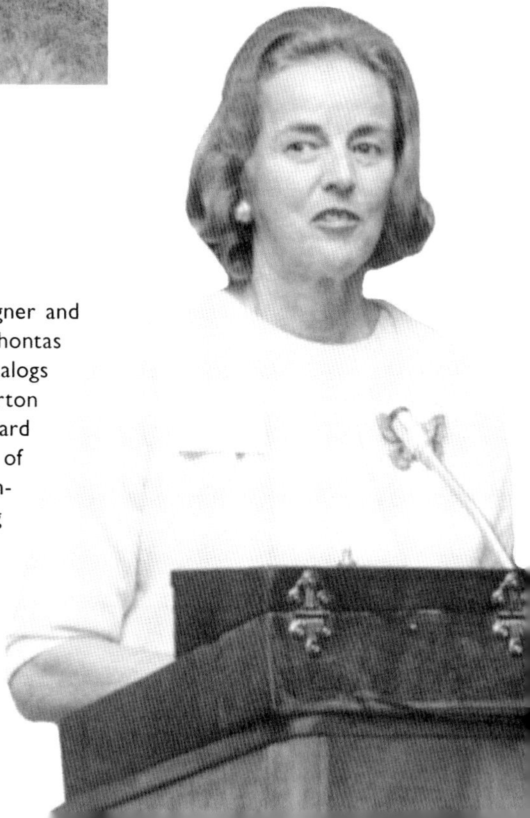

Suzette Morton Davidson (1912–1996)

Resident Suzette Morton Davidson, a book designer and publisher, operated her own limited-edition Pocahontas Press. She also designed books and exhibition catalogs for the Art Institute and publications for the Morton Arboretum, where, by the 1960s, she was board chair. She was a niece of Jean Cudahy and daughter of Sterling Morton. Davidson was briefly a daughter-in-law of Alfred and Clarice Hamill, the three sharing many projects. (Morton Arboretum.)

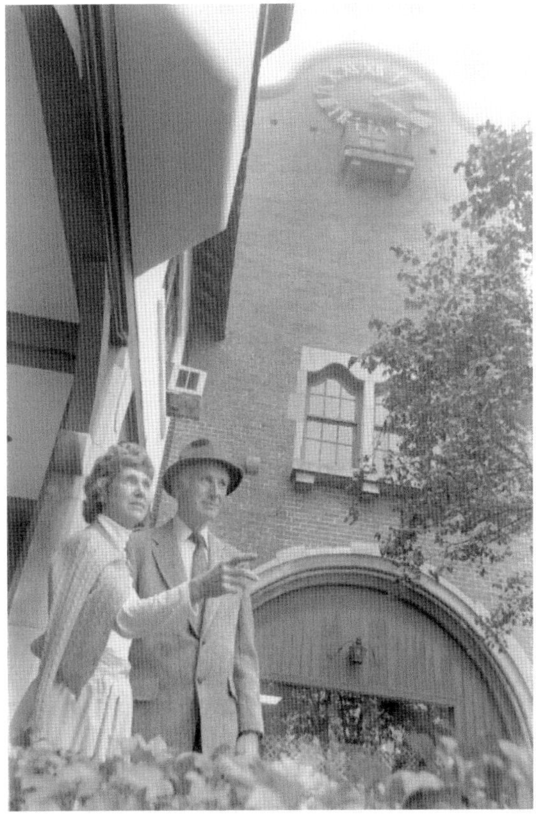

Susan Dart McCutcheon (1920–2007)

New Orleans–born Susan Dart was the spouse of John T. McCutcheon Jr., *Chicago Tribune* editorial page editor. She wrote a pioneering natural-foods and cooking syndicated column for the *Tribune* from 1976 to 1981, wrote a "Forest Ranger" column for the *Lake Forester*, and authored several historical books in the 1980s and 1990s. Here, the couple is unveiling the Market Square fountain sculpture on August 12, 1982. It was created by John McCutcheon's aunt Sylvia (Judson) Haskins. (City.)

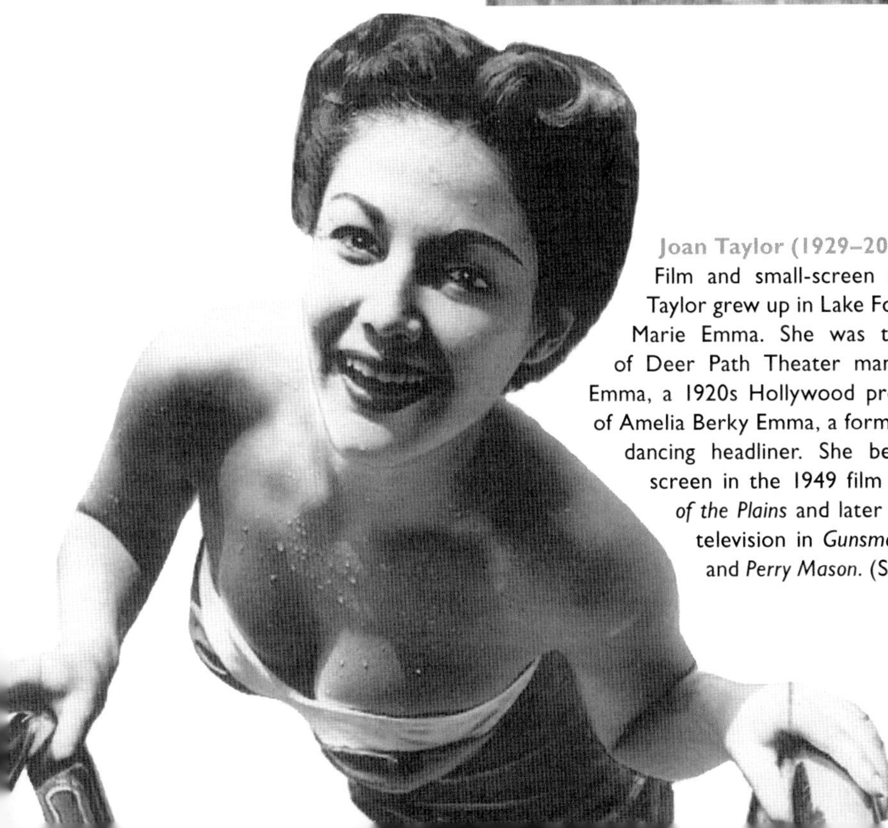

Joan Taylor (1929–2012)

Film and small-screen actress Joan Taylor grew up in Lake Forest as Rose Marie Emma. She was the daughter of Deer Path Theater manager Joseph Emma, a 1920s Hollywood prop man, and of Amelia Berky Emma, a former vaudeville dancing headliner. She began on the screen in the 1949 film *Fighting Man of the Plains* and later appeared on television in *Gunsmoke*, *Rawhide*, and *Perry Mason*. (SMP.)

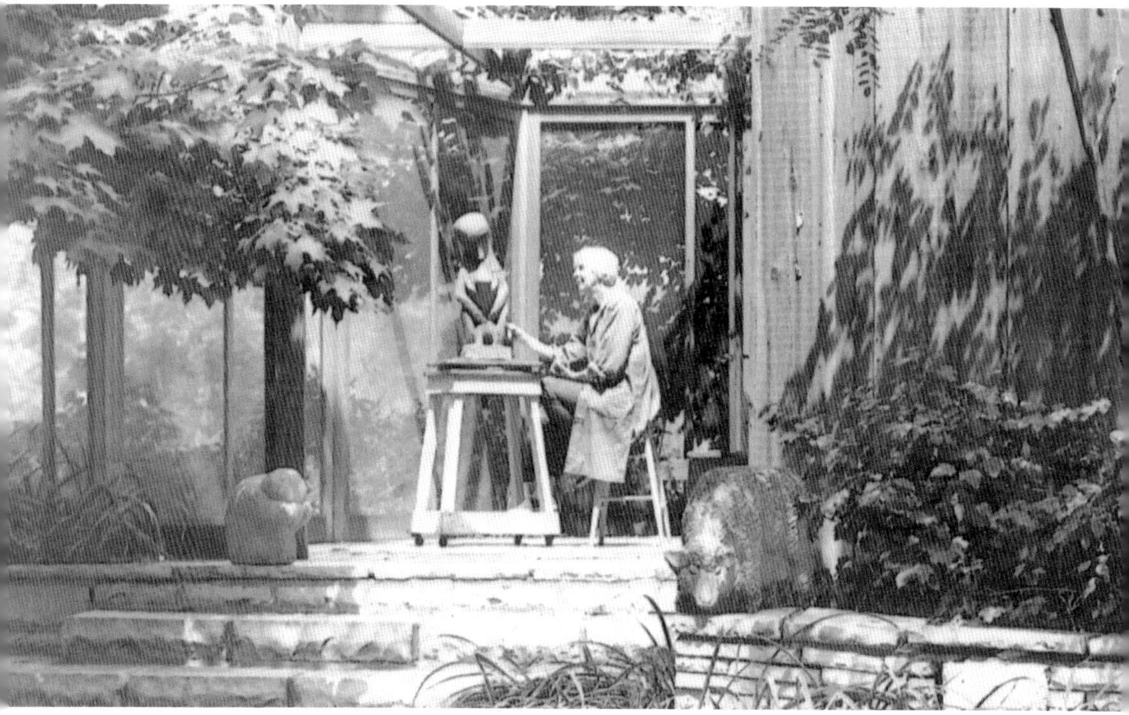

Sylvia Shaw Judson Haskins (1897–1978)
The daughter of architect Howard Shaw, Sylvia Haskins (School of the Art Institute of Chicago; Atelier Bourdelle, Paris) was encouraged by her father to sculpt. After her marriage, she continued to create; by 1936, she had work in Brookgreen Gardens in South Carolina, among other collections. She was productive into the 1960s, publishing *For Gardens and Other Places* in 1967. Her works include *Bird Girl*, located in Savannah, and a sculpture of a Quaker martyr, *Mary Dyer*, in Boston, Philadelphia, and Richmond, Indiana. (LFCLASC.)

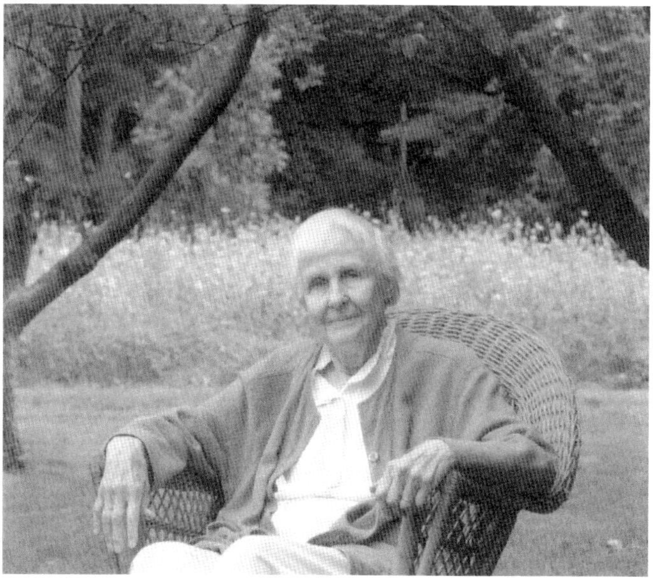

Alice Judson Hayes (1922–2005)
The daughter of sculptor Sylvia Shaw Judson Haskins and the granddaughter of Howard Van Doren Shaw, Alice Judson (Ryerson) Hayes launched the Ragdale Foundation artists' community in 1976. In 1986, she gave the seven-acre Ragdale estate to the city, which then leased it back to the foundation. The mother of four, educator, patron, and administrator was a fine poet, with a strong but small body of work, notably *New and Selected Poems* (1987). (LFCLASC.)

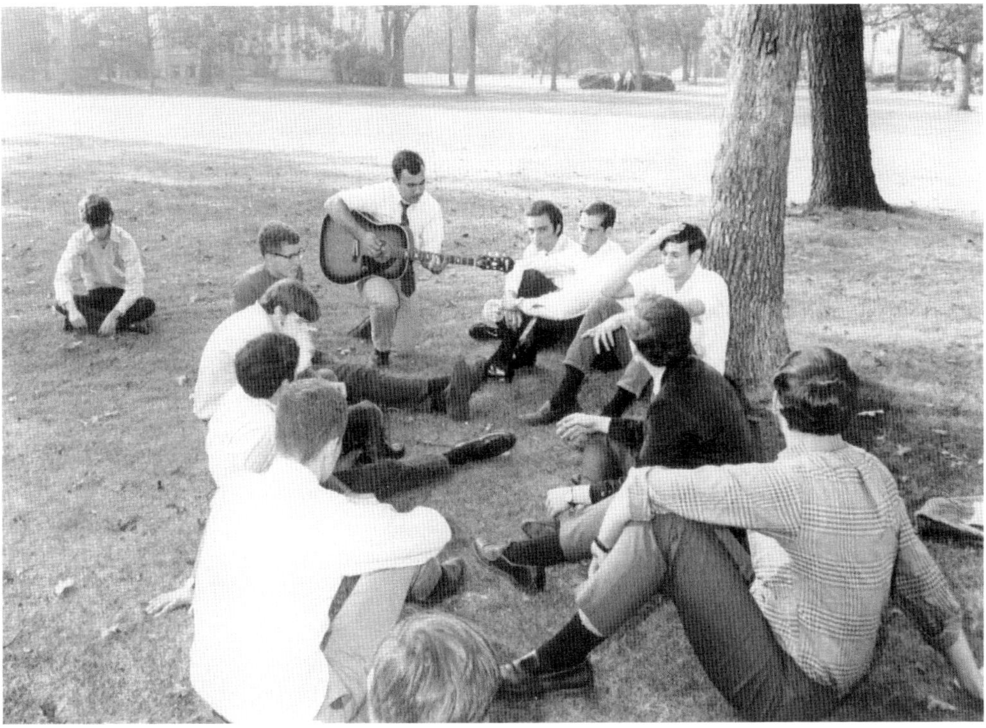

Steve Goodman (1948–1984)

Guitar-strumming folksinger and songwriter Steve Goodman, shown here with his guitar on campus, briefly attended Lake Forest College in the 1960s, while also performing in Chicago. Diagnosed with leukemia and leaving school, Goodman was a prominent Chicagoan of the 1960s, 1970s, and early 1980s, writing such songs as "The City of New Orleans," "The Dying Cub Fan's Lament," and the 1984 song "Go, Cubs, Go." Goodman biographer Clay Eals covers the Lake Forest period. (LFCLASC.)

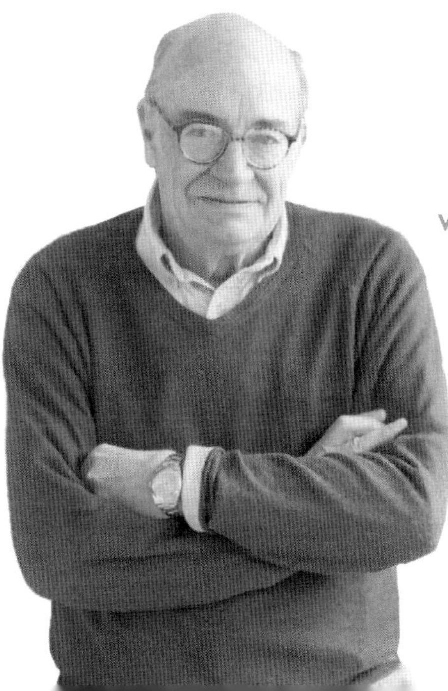

Ward Just

Nantucket resident and National Book Award–nominated novelist Ward Just has included his childhood and young-adult versions of Lake Forest, Waukegan, and the North Shore in many of his stories and novels. These include *A Family Trust* (1978), *An Unfinished Season* (2004), and *Rodin's Debutant* (2011). He grew up at the Knollwood Club, the son of the publisher of the *Waukegan News-Sun* and of a Swift family scion. He attended Lake Forest Academy. (Houghton Mifflin Harcourt.)

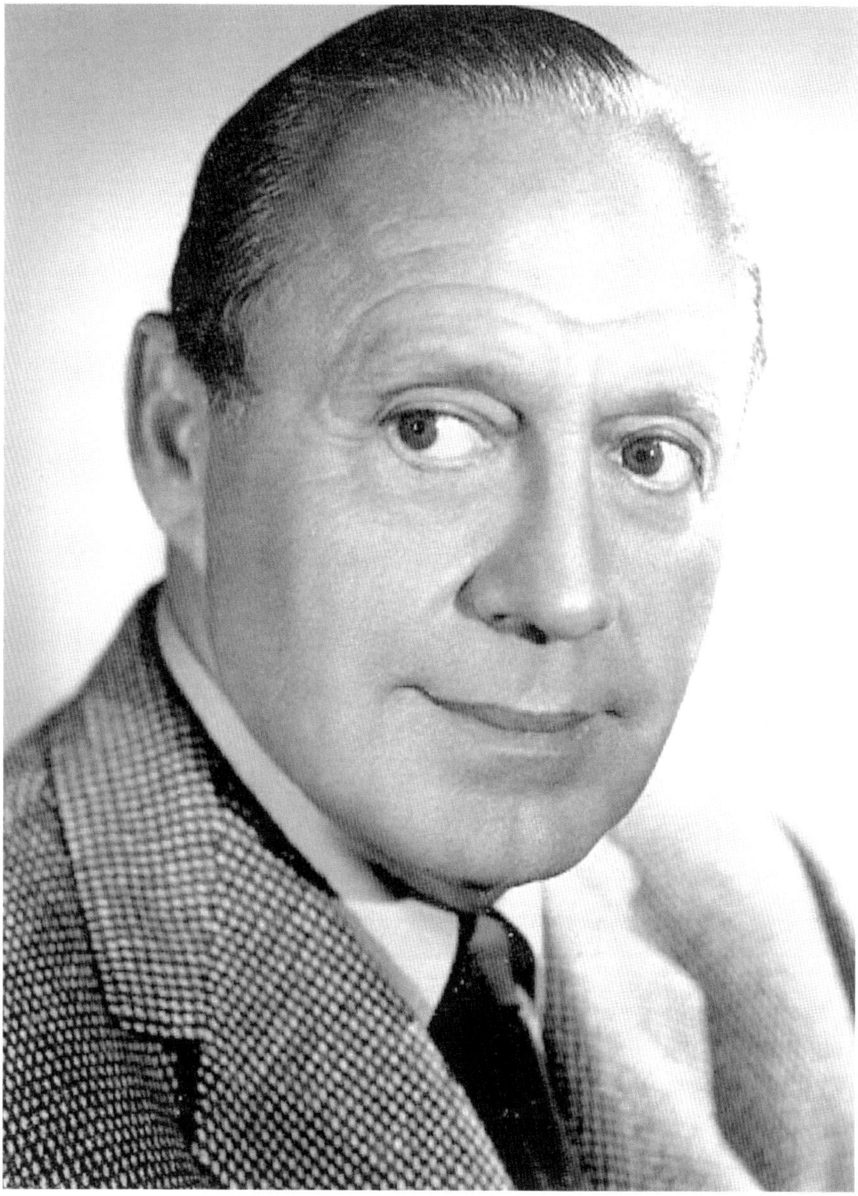

Jack Benny (1894–1974)

Born Benjamin Kabulsky in Chicago to Eastern European immigrants, Jack Benny grew up in Waukegan. His father was Meyer Kabulsky, who ran a clothing store in Lake Forest, on the northeast corner of Market Square, in the 1930s and 1940s, with an apartment above. When Benny became a comedic film and radio star, he visited his parents in Lake Forest when he could. He had not thrived at Waukegan High School and dropped out to play the violin in vaudeville by the age of 17. There, he met the young Marx Brothers, leading to a lifelong friendship with Zeppo and a successful career that spanned the middle of the 20th century. He was a very successful Hollywood film actor between 1929 and 1945, including the first Benny–Fred Allen feud movie, *Love Thy Neighbor* (1940). One of his last films, *The Horn Blows at Midnight* (1944), became the butt of many jokes on later Benny radio and television programs, along with his violin playing. (LFCLASC.)

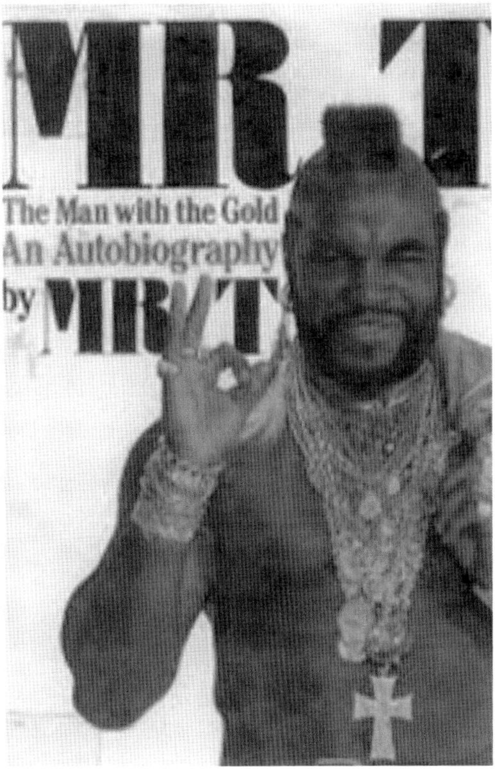

Mr. T. (Laurence Tureaud)
Upset about 1980s city interference on his property, Tureaud cut down more than 100 oaks there, an action that led to a new ordinance disallowing such actions. His persona, with his Mandinka warrior hairstyle, won him a leading role in the 1982 film *Rocky III*, followed by a role on the 1980s television series *The A-Team.* In 1984, he published *Mr. T: The Man with the Gold: An Autobiography.* (LFCLASC.)

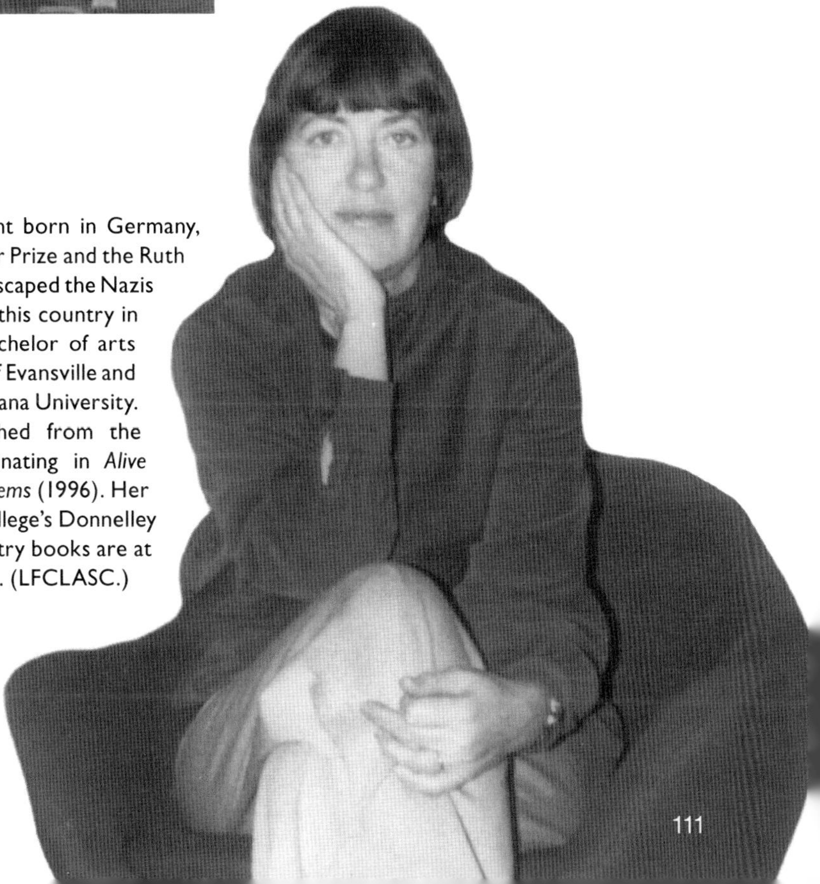

Lisel Mueller
A longtime Mettawa resident born in Germany, Lisel Mueller won the Pulitzer Prize and the Ruth Lilly Prize for her work. She escaped the Nazis with her family and came to this country in the 1930s. She earned a bachelor of arts degree from the University of Evansville and did her graduate study at Indiana University. Her poetry career flourished from the 1970s to the 1990s, culminating in *Alive Together: New and Selected Poems* (1996). Her papers are at Lake Forest College's Donnelley and Lee Library, and her poetry books are at Chicago's Poetry Foundation. (LFCLASC.)

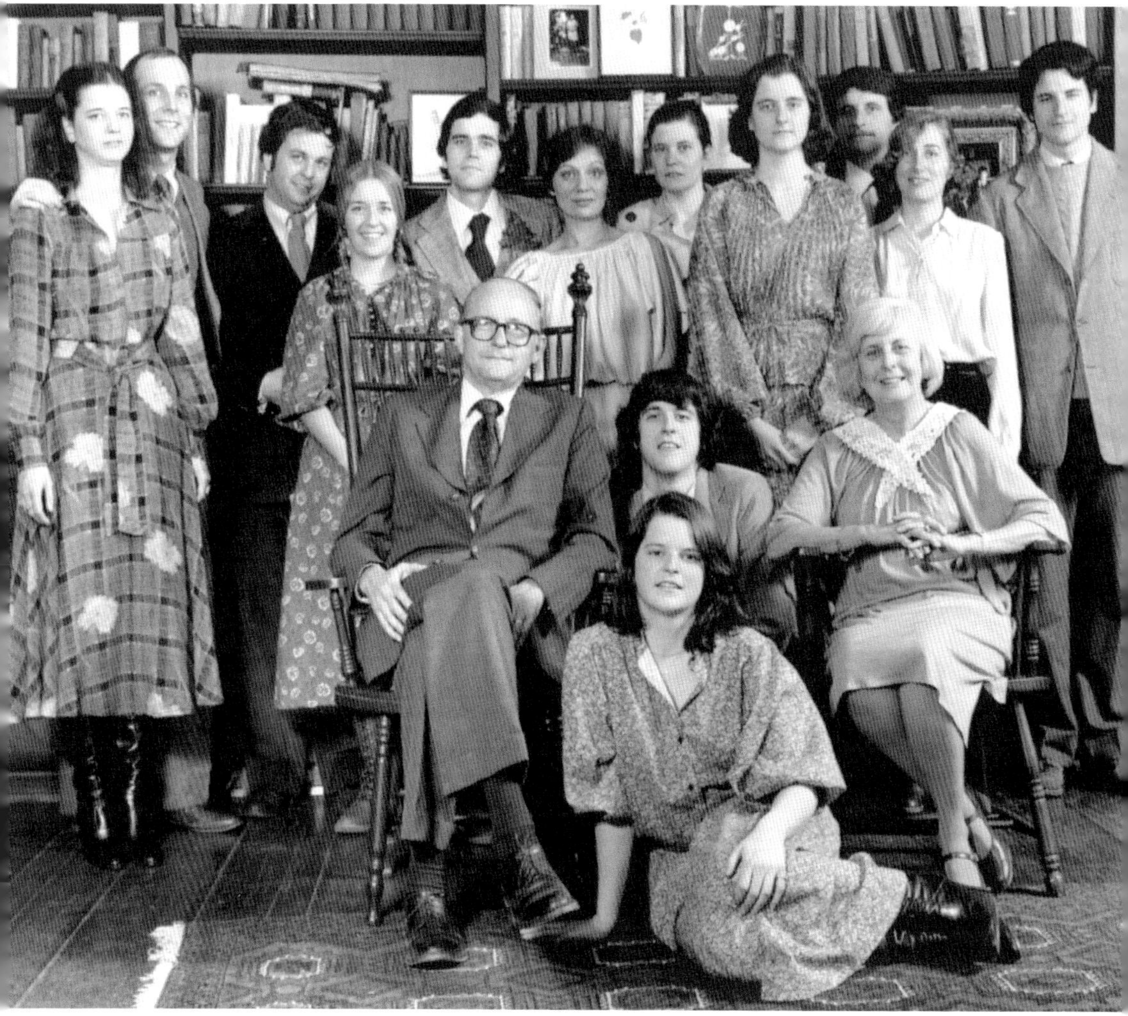

(William) Franklin McMahon (1921–2012)

Award-winning artist and reporter Franklin McMahon lived in various, always interesting houses in Lake Forest with his travel reporter/author wife and collaborator, Irene (Leahy) McMahon (1921–1997), and his large family, from around 1950 into the 2000s. After World War II and art school for Franklin, he and Irene hoped for a Wright-designed home but could not afford it. Instead, they had the gifted Edward Humrich design them a modern, Wright-ian house on South Waukegan Road. As their brood expanded, they moved into the former David Dangler Tudor place on Mayflower Road, and then they downsized to the Keck & Keck–designed Fagan house off West Old Mill Road, south of the Lasker estate. In the new millennium, Franklin moved to nearby Lincolnshire, at the Sedgewick retirement home there, still close to much of his family.

Franklin was a prolific, varied artist, with between 8,000 and 9,000 drawings, illustrations of several books, and eight art-filled films for television. His projects ranged from 1950s Lake Forest College publicity photographs to *Life* magazine spreads on high-interest social topics, such as the 1955 Emmett Till trial in Mississippi, a nationally significant civil rights piece. That stunning sequence of drawings set a direction for his career beyond book illustration to a more involved, political, and social justice level of coverage of major events, from space launches to the "conspiracy" trial of Bobby Seals and others in the wake of the 1968 Democratic Convention. Political figures were frequent subjects, and one of his drawings of Adlai Stevenson in the setting of his Mettawa country house just west of Lake Forest is now on exhibit at that place—in 2015, a house museum. McMahon's work, widely exhibited and with many awards, is owned by major institutions and museums. Lake Forest College gave him an honorary degree in 1979; today, one of his drawings of a Chicago Symphony trip hangs outside the college president's office in North Hall.

Every year at holiday time, the McMahons sent out photo cards of their growing family. Shown here is one of the later ones, including the artist and Irene and their young adult children. Seated in front is Michelle, and between Franklin and Irene is Michael. Those standing are, from left to right, Mary; third from left, William Franklin; fifth from left, Patrick; and then seventh from the left and following to toward the right, Debbie, Margot, Mark (page 20), Carolyn McGregor McMahon, and Hugh. (LFCLASC and Mark McMahon.)

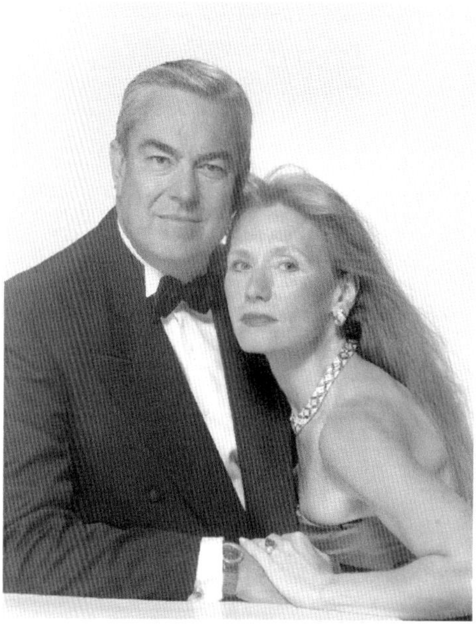

Bill Kurtis and Donna LaPietra
Also shown with Susan Wright on page 76, Bill and his longtime producer and life partner Donna LaPietra have a summer and weekend place in Mettawa and share work lives at Kurtis Productions in Chicago. A well-known television journalist, producer, narrator, announcer, news anchor, and conservationist, Kurtis has interviewed Local Legends for the Lake Forest–Lake Bluff Historical Society beginning in 2010. In 2014, he and Donna interviewed each other as they received the historical society's Local Legends honor. (Kurtis Productions.)

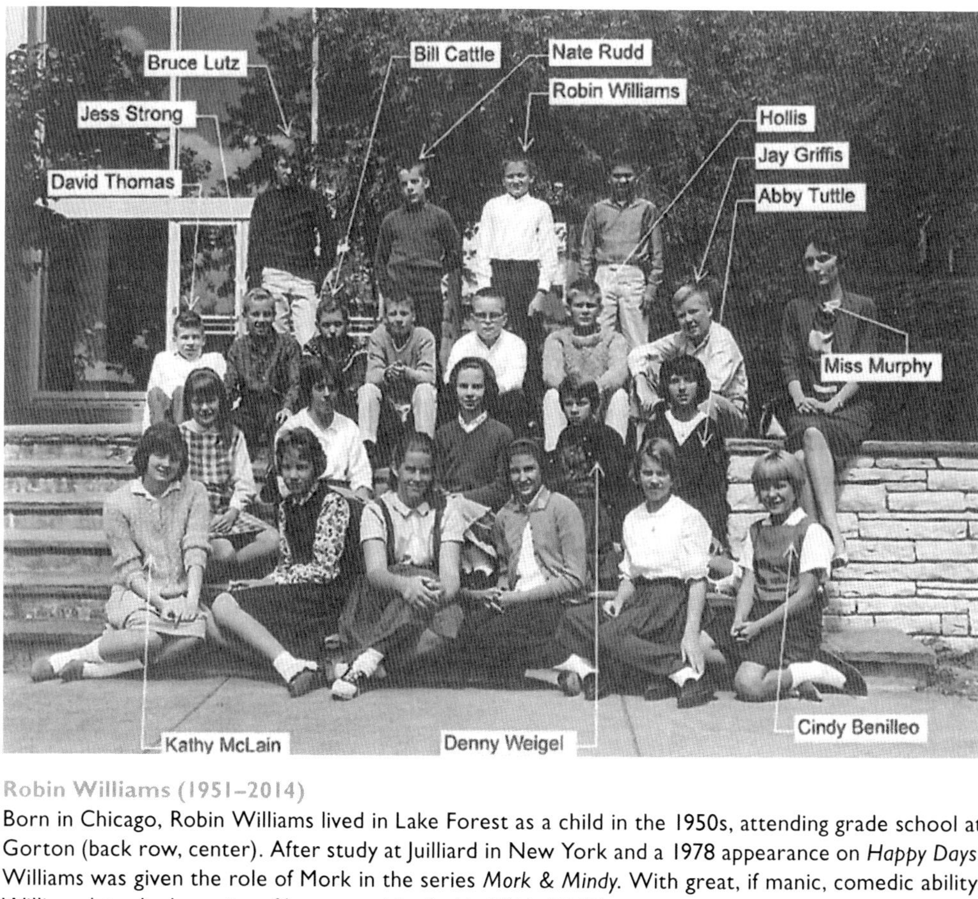

Robin Williams (1951–2014)
Born in Chicago, Robin Williams lived in Lake Forest as a child in the 1950s, attending grade school at Gorton (back row, center). After study at Juilliard in New York and a 1978 appearance on *Happy Days*, Williams was given the role of Mork in the series *Mork & Mindy*. With great, if manic, comedic ability, Williams later had a serious film career. He died in 2014. (SMP.)

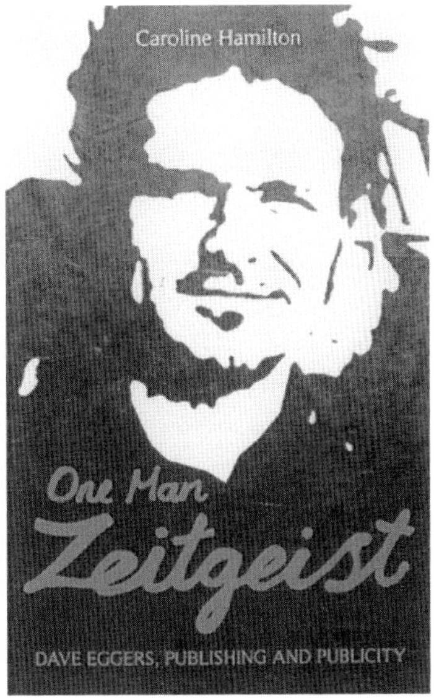

Dave Eggers

Eggers achieved national attention with his 2000 memoir, *A Heartbreaking Work of Staggering Genius*, which was nominated for a nonfiction Pulitzer Prize. He graduated from Lake Forest High School, a classmate of actor Vince Vaughn. Living in San Francisco since 2000, Eggers has carved out for himself a unique, new-style career as a journalist, entrepreneur, publisher (*McSweeney's*), novelist, and philanthropist. (Simon & Schuster.)

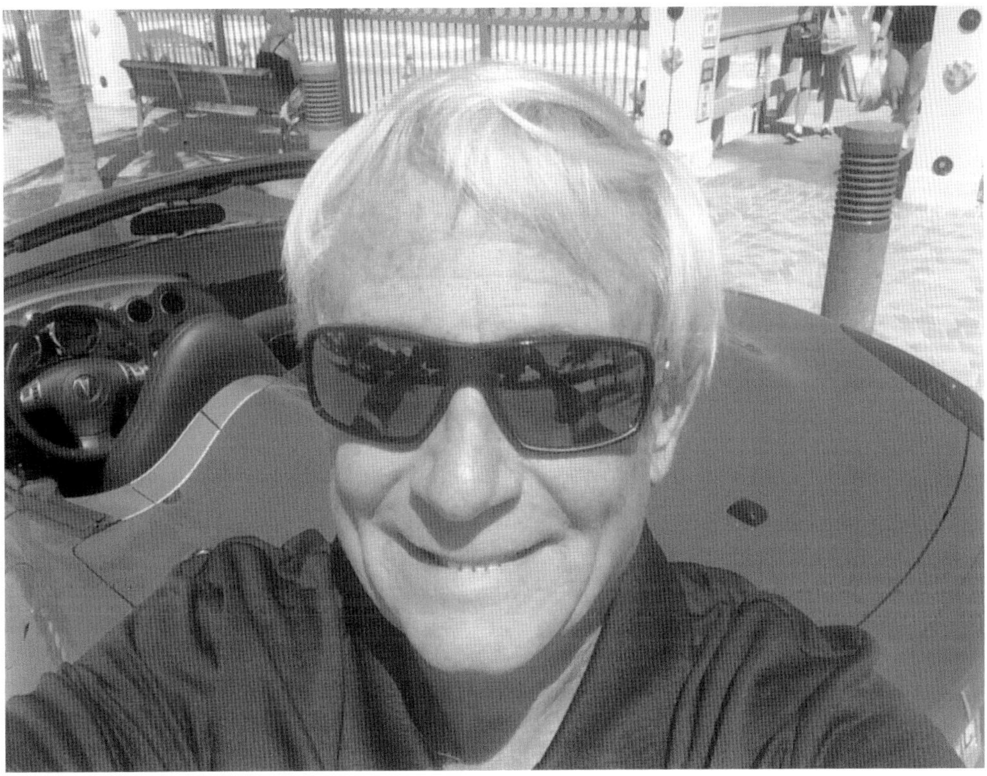

Bob Craig

Bob Craig grew up in Lake Forest's midcentury Meadowood neighborhood, graduating from Lake Forest High School in 1972. He went to the University of Florida and later relocated to Vero Beach, with a career as a builder, developer, and realtor. In 2011, he launched the Facebook group "I Remember Lake Forest When," which has grown to over 2,700 participants by mid-2015. He has another group, "I Remember Vero Beach When." (Bob Craig.)

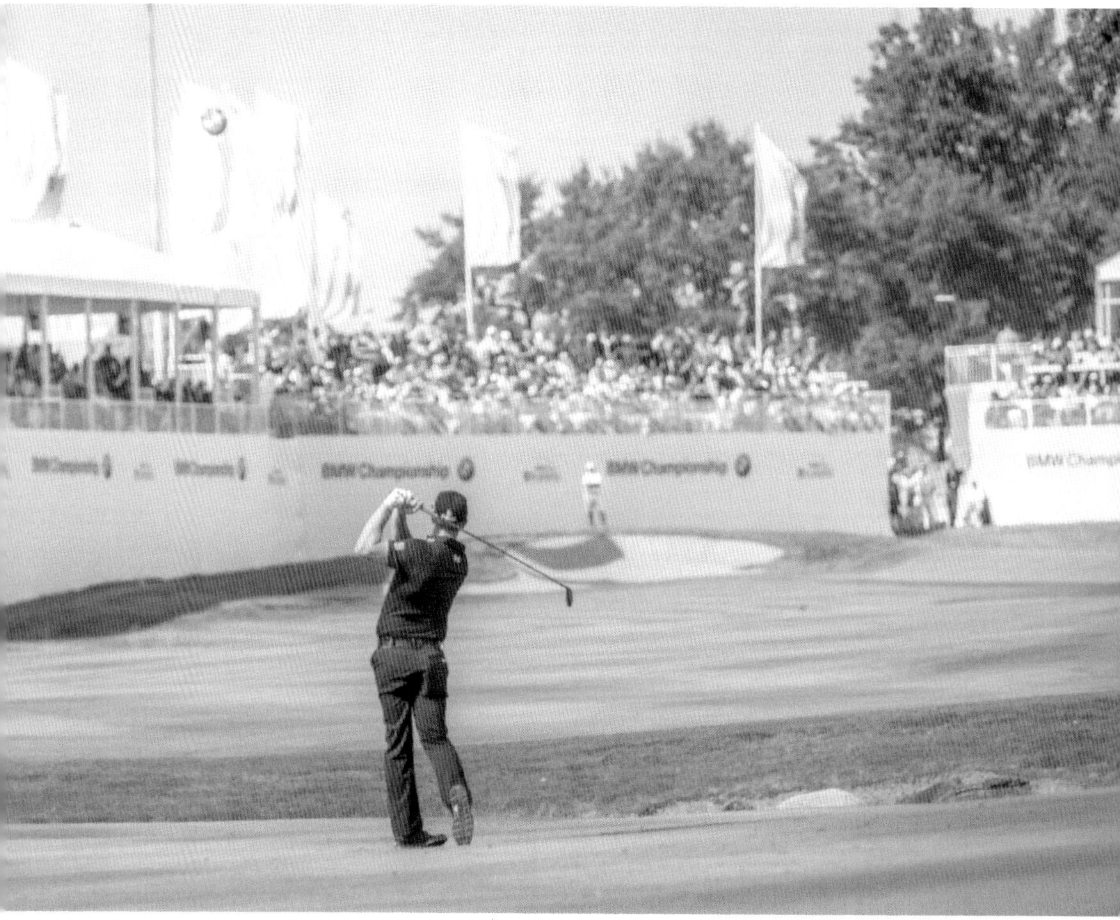

Zach Johnson at the 2013 Conway Farms BMW Championship

Tournament winner Zach Johnson takes a swing for a long drive at the September 2013 BMW Golf Championship. This event took place at the stellar Conway Farms Golf Club in west Lake Forest. Long known as the Western Open, since 2007, this annual tournament has been played under its current name. It alternates between the Chicago area and elsewhere in the Midwest. It continues as a benefit for the Evans Scholars program, which provides college scholarships for caddies. The 2015 Conway Farms event enlisted 2,000 volunteers, and, as always, was played under the aegis of the Western Golf Association. After many years of play at Cog Hill in the southwest suburbs, the tournament was scheduled again at Conway Farms for September 14–20, 2015. This fairly young, award-winning course, designed by Tom Fazio "around the traditions of Scottish links golf," opened in 1991.

The 2015 event was won by Australian Jason Day, one of a new, 20-something generation cluster of pro golfers revolutionizing the game with their unheard-of low scores.

Prior to the 2013 BMW event, the Conway Farms course already was a well-known tournament site, beginning in 1997 with the men's NCAA Division I tournament. It hosted the Western Amateur tournament in 2009, and, in 2012, the US Mid-Amateur Championship. Lake Forest has a century-old tradition of hosting major golf events, including the 1906 US Open and the 1915 Women's Amateur, both at Onwentsia. In 1956, the Knollwood Club course hosted the USGA Amateur Championship. But it is unlikely that any area sporting event has drawn more than the 2013 BMW tournament, racking up total attendance of around 140,000.

The BMW Championship is scheduled to return to Lake Forest in 2017. (City.)

CHAPTER EIGHT

Sports Figures and Athletes

Last and certainly not least among legendary Lake Foresters is sports. The first fitness or physical training for Lake Forest Academy boys took place in the fall of 1859, with drill instruction by Elmer Ellsworth of the Zouaves, in anticipation of war breaking out.

Sports was a presence in the early town, with academy students in the 1860s playing baseball in good weather and, by 1864, according to Arpee (1944), using a wooden, barnlike gym for calisthenics in bad weather. Physical activity also came from days off, working on clearing local streets in the pre–Civil War days. Exercise often then came with a useful purpose.

Sports became a key factor in the development of the town beyond the schools beginning in the 1890s. Golf began in 1892 here, informally on the lakefront Forest Park and on the C.B. Farwell estate across Lake Road. This activity was organized as the Lake Forest Golf Club in 1894, moving to the Leander McCormick farm around 1895. The first links at Onwentsia opened in mid-1896. Onwentsia soon added polo, tennis, and fox-hunting. Horse shows brought as many as 15,000 spectators by the 1910s.

Fox-hunting was an arcane English blood sport, a vestigial aristocratic and royal sport from feudal times. Here, it took root west of Onwentsia around 1900. Moreover, it shaped the future terrain of Lake Forest—ranging west across the prairie and farmland toward the Des Plaines River. Arthur Aldis was the master of the Onwentsia Hunt. When farmers objected to the riders rampaging through their fields, the Chicagoans bought up their agricultural acres to create gentlemen's farms in emulation of English precedents. This expansive territory, with its close ties to the old eastside club grounds and Green Bay Road, led the municipality's growth rapidly west, by 1925 to the Everett community south on Waukegan Road. By 1928, the hunt relocated north to open country west of Waukegan, in the Millburn area. There, many Lake Foresters built barns with accommodations for daytime living and occasional sleeping. But the hunt, from 1900 to 1928, had informally delineated the reach of Lake Forest as a social demarcation, and the municipality followed as far as the tollway. Thus, Lake Forest's reach westward, unusual for a lakefront Chicago suburb, was dictated by this aristocratic leisure pursuit a century ago.

The Alcott, later Bell, School on Sheridan Road near Deerpath Road did not have athletic facilities; by 1902, the Winter Club had been set up farther north on Sheridan Road. In winter during the early 1900s, there was a toboggan slide from the westside club grounds, over the road, to the property east. Ice hockey, too, was popular at the Winter Club, and Lake Forest College students played there, as well. The professional Chicago Blackhawks hockey team was begun by Lake Forest's McLaughlin family.

A group of local gardeners came from Cornwall, and they played cricket in the 1930s. But locals mostly played baseball, basketball, and bowled. The recreation department of the city managed the townspeople's pastimes; after World War II, George Ekdahl and Fred Jackson were the directors. South Park, developed between the wars, had baseball and tennis areas. Tennis courts, too, were at West Park. The college's Farwell Field (1902) housed a summer program for neighborhood youngsters.

At the schools of Lake Forest University, the shared gymnasium opened in 1891 with indoor baseball and football, keeping the infirmary busy until basketball was invented soon after. By 1895, a first women's intercollegiate basketball game took place there between the college's women and the women of Ferry College, the latter then a single-gender, four-year program at Ferry Hall on Mayflower Road. The college's sports included, from early on, track and field, baseball, basketball, and football. The 1888 football squad was the 16th team organized in the nation. Swimming, hockey, and soccer were added in the 1960s, and new women's sports came after the early 1970s, including basketball, hockey, soccer, and volleyball.

In 1916, the townspeople's Young Men's Club Gym opened at the west end of Market Square. It was later a recreation department facility before the Hastings Road building was erected around 1980. The high school by 1935 had football and basketball, and track and field notably, but also field hockey for women, swimming, and lacrosse. Lake Forest College also used the high school's gym and pool, the 1891 gym floor being too small for regulation basketball and the 1891 pool too primitive. After World War II, the Lake Forest College Alumni Memorial Fieldhouse opened, with a large space that could be set up for many sports. After the Sports Center was built in 1968, this became a hockey rink. The center had courts for racquetball and handball, the latter becoming, under coach Mike Dau, a niche sport in which the small institution would achieve national dominance.

Sports locally were for all by the 1890s, mild exercise for the Chicago office and ladies-club bound, with some going for even more risk with polo. And a full range has been available for young people of all levels. Since the 1970s, AYSO soccer has been a widely shared youth activity, using the highly visible West Campus fields of Lake Forest High School. A big change in this period has been the increase in athletic opportunities for girls and young women under Title IX. At the college level, under athletic director Jackie Slaats, Lake Forest women's teams in basketball and softball became Division III conference perennial contenders and winners, as were volleyball and hockey teams. Men's sports at the college lost baseball and track and field in the 1970s due to gender rebalancing, but they has recently regained the sport of golf. Various club sports like rugby make for lively competition around the Chicago area, as well. The 2010 Sports Center addition reflects the 21st-century emphasis on active lifestyles for all.

Improbably, perhaps, Lake Forest edged into being a locale for some professional-level activity, starting after World War II with the Chicago Cardinals holding summer practices at Lake Forest College. Later, the Chicago Bears replaced the St. Louis–relocated Cardinals. By the late 1970s, Bears coach George Halas entered an agreement to build a small facility adjacent to Farwell Field on the college campus, with a 20-year lease—after which the building would become college property. Thus, this was the epicenter of excitement during the Bears' Super Bowl season of 1985–1986. Soon after, the crowds of preseason camp visitors became so large that the team had to move to Platteville, Wisconsin. Near the end of the Bears' lease period, the organization built a new, larger facility complex in what was west Lake Forest by that time, adjacent to the tollway north of Route 60. This remains the team's headquarters in 2015.

Spectator participation for sports remains at a high level, if no more for the equestrian events that drew 15,000 here a century ago. Recent big draws have been the BMW golf matches of 2013 and 2015. Lake Foresters, including the late movie mogul John Hughes, have been avid fans of the Cubs and the Bulls. Residents also root for the Blackhawks, recent winners of multiple Stanley Cups. The mystique of the chronically losing Chicago Cubs has been studied by Lake Forest College professor of sociology and anthropology Holly Swyers in her 2010 book *Wrigley Regulars: Finding Community in the Bleachers.*

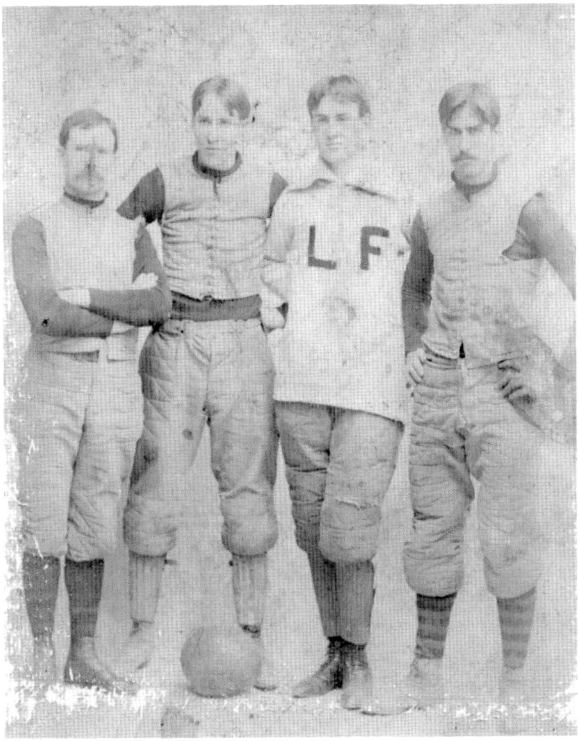

Fred Hayner (1871–1929)
Resident Fred Hayner, far right, played football while earning his bachelor of arts degree at Lake Forest University (1891–1895). He is credited with inventing the flying tackle. He wrote for campus publications and went on to a career in sports journalism at the *Chicago Evening Post*. He credited Lake Forest with being the birthplace of Chicago golf, with Charles Macdonald hitting the first drive off the Forest Park bluff in 1892. Hayner campaigned for the public golf course. (LFCLASC.)

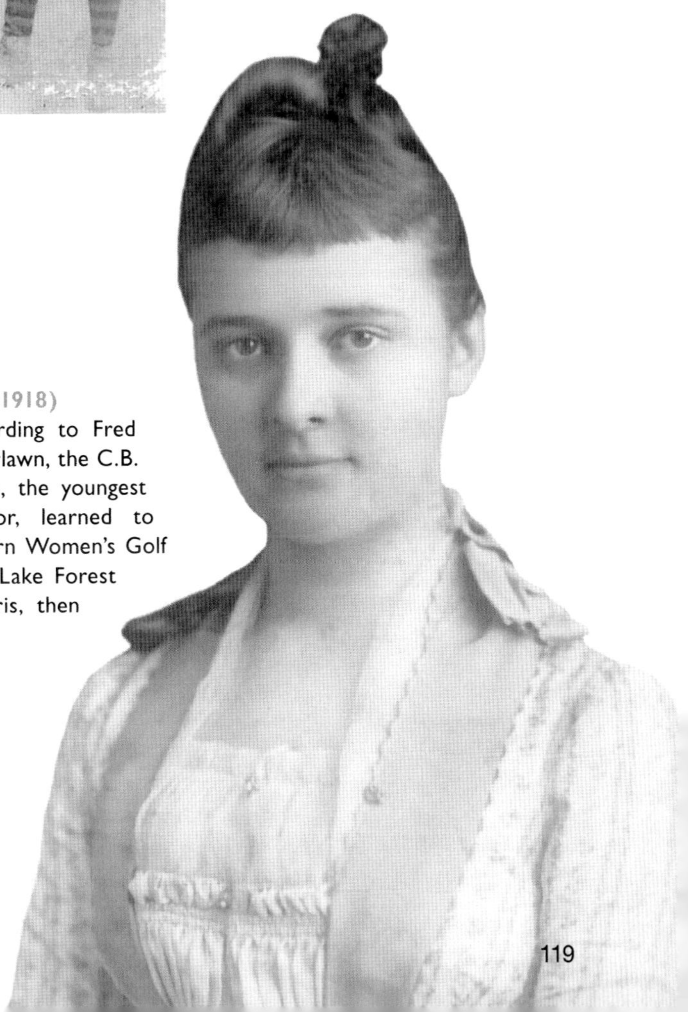

Rose Farwell Chatfield-Taylor (1870–1918)
Golf was first played in Chicago, according to Fred Hayner, in 1892 at Forest Park and at Fairlawn, the C.B. Farwell estate across Lake Road. There, the youngest Farwell daughter, Rose Chatfield-Taylor, learned to play; six years later, she won the Western Women's Golf Championship. She had graduated from Lake Forest College and studied bookbinding in Paris, then opened a Chicago atelier. (LFCLASC.)

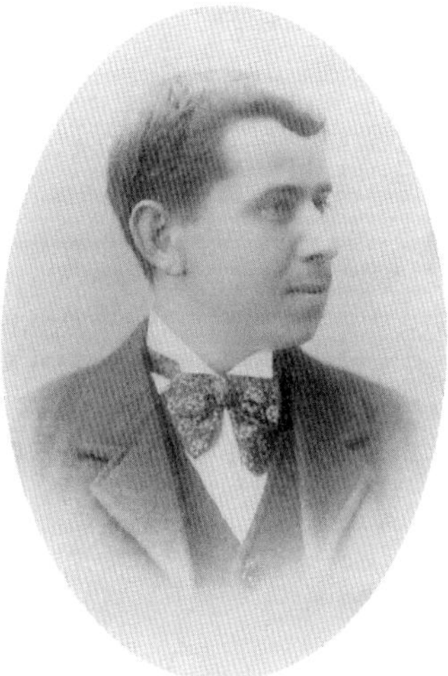

Robert Foulis (1873–1945)

Scottish-born Robert Foulis was Onwentsia's first golf professional by 1895–1896, and he went on to promote golf in St. Louis. He was the first of a series of Onwentsia pros trained in Old Tom Morris's shop at St. Andrews, the birthplace of modern golf. He was succeeded by George Marshall, some of whose bespoke clubs are still in town. (Gary Kern.)

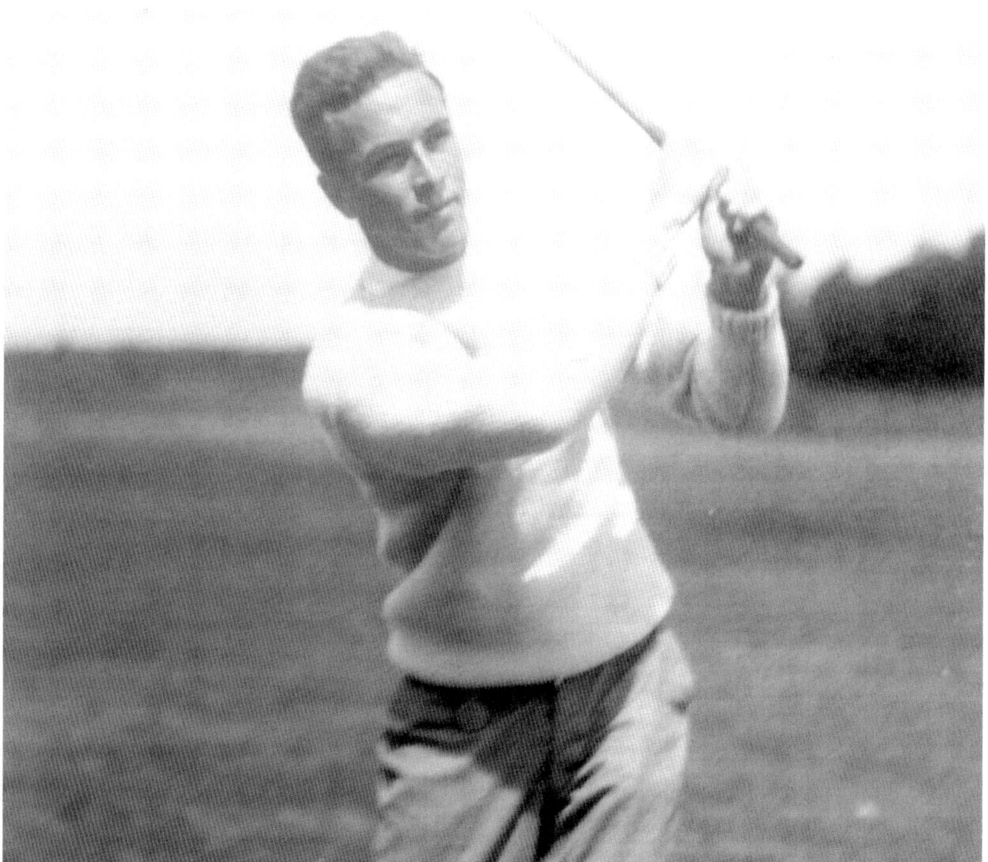

Robert Gardner (1890–1956)

Robert Abbe Gardner twice won golf's US amateur title, first while a student at Yale in 1909 at age 19. No one repeated the feat at a younger age until Tiger Woods, 18, in 1994. Gardner won again in 1915. He also excelled in college as a pole-vaulter and was a national champion at racquets, a sport related to squash. (LFCLASC.)

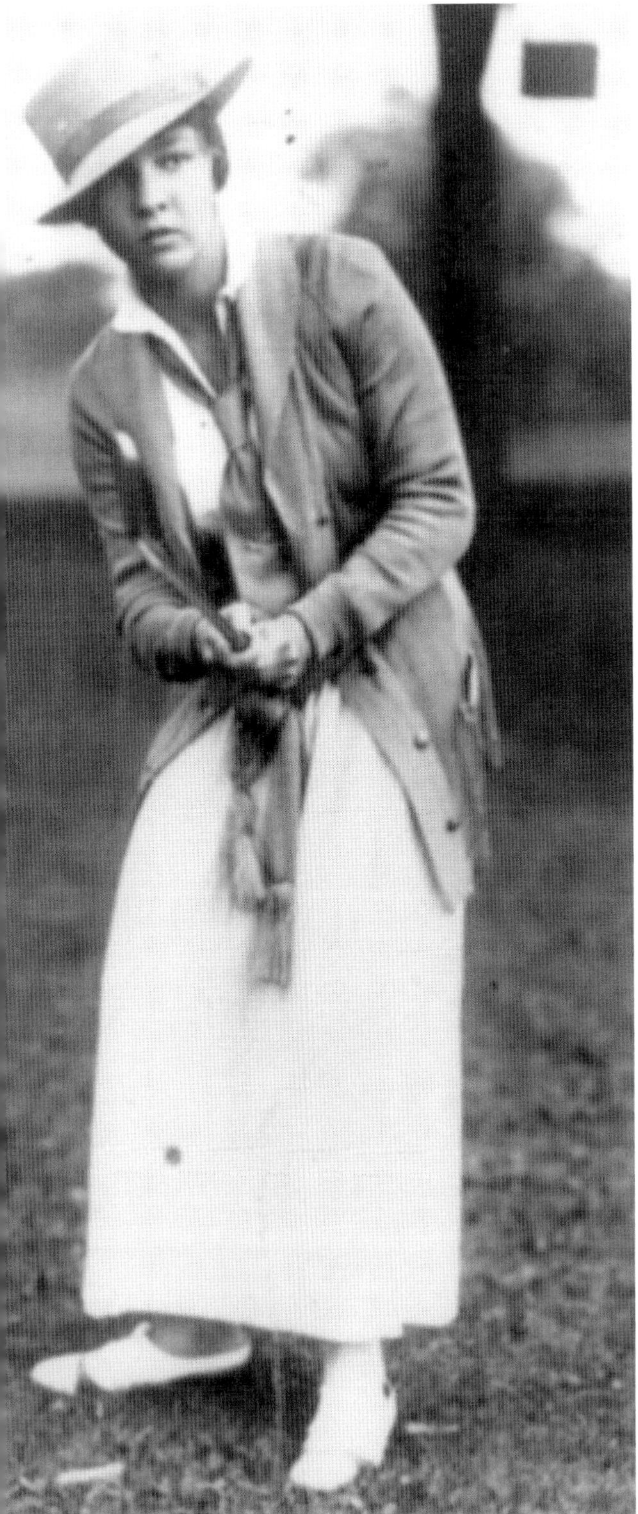

Edith Cummings Munson (1899–1984)
Certainly legendary, larger than life in her early years, Edith Cummings later married Curtis Munson. She was the daughter of Chicago capitalist David Mark Cummings, with an estate just south of the cemetery on Lake Road. Her brother Dexter's house remains across from his father's land on upper Lake Road. Edith Cummings was the 1923 US Women's Amateur golf champion, and her photograph appeared on the cover of *Time*. Through her association with her childhood and Westover School friend Ginevra King, she knew the young F. Scott Fitzgerald. As a result, and perhaps overshadowing her importance in golf, she was the model for golfer Jordan Baker in *The Great Gatsby*, a supporting role for Ginevra's modeling for Daisy Buchanan in the world-famous 1925 novel. As Mrs. Munson, she led a quiet life in Detroit with her husband, Curtis. (LF-LBHS.)

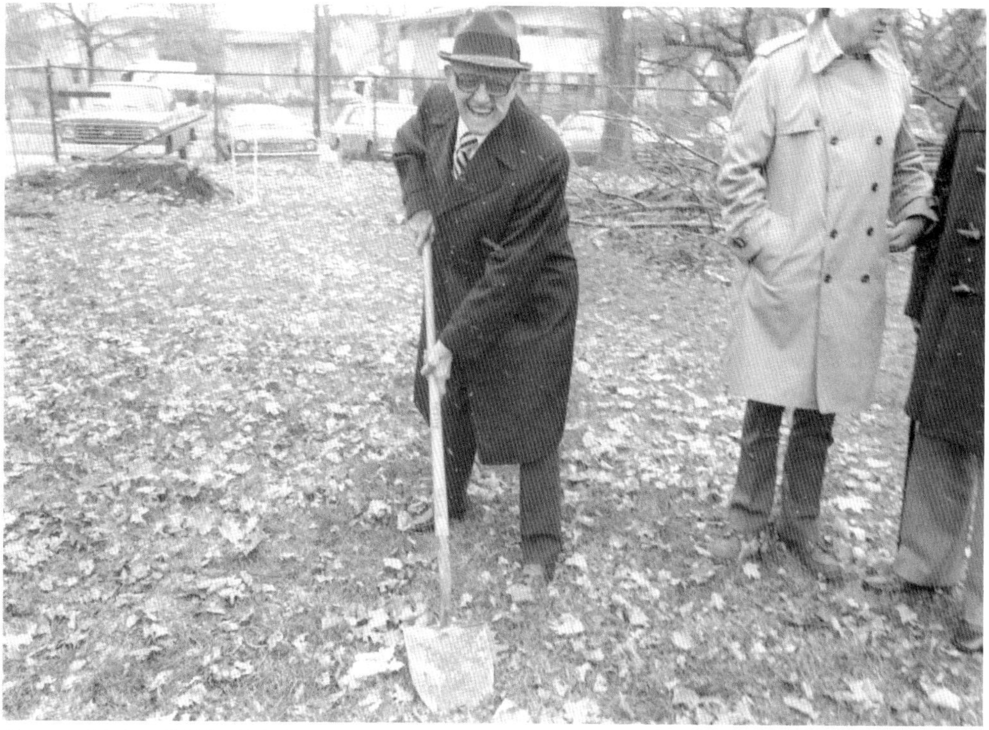

George Halas (1895–1983)

Halas was a founder of post-college football with the Decatur Staleys. He moved the Staleys (later, Bears) to Chicago, and they won the first NFL title in 1921, the first of six for Halas during his 40-season career. He brought the team's facilities to Lake Forest in 1979 at Halas Hall at Farwell Field. The Bears moved around 1998 to a larger facility near the tollway on the west side of town. (LFCLASC.)

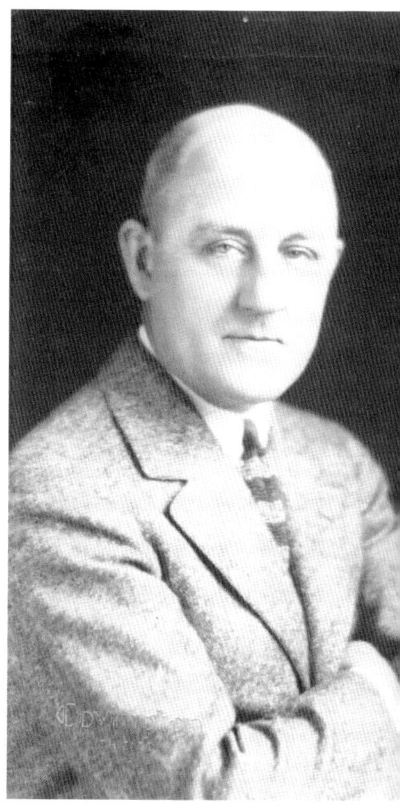

Ralph Jones (1880–1951)

Jones coached the Chicago Bears from 1930 to 1933, when Halas returned as coach. Jones won the NFL championship in 1932. He had coached at Lake Forest Academy and was hired as the college men's coach for football, basketball, and baseball, staying on until 1949. He led undefeated football teams around 1940 and experimented with protective gear in the 1940s, including helmets and shoulder pads. (LFCLASC.)

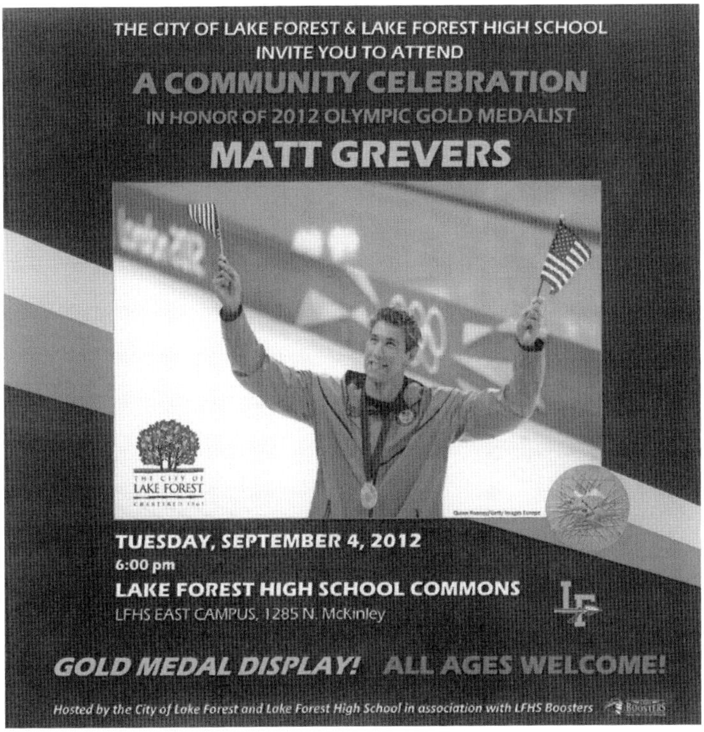

Matt Grevers
Born in Lake Forest in 1985, Matt Grevers, known as "Dutch" and the "Gentle Giant," is a six-time Olympic medalist swimmer. He won gold medals in 2008 and 2012. Grevers graduated from Lake Forest High School before venturing south to Northwestern. He was married in 2013. In August 2014, Grevers won the 100-meter backstroke at the US Championships. He tweeted "Go Scouts!" to the Lake Forest High School girls' varsity swimmers, including his sister, last November. (City.)

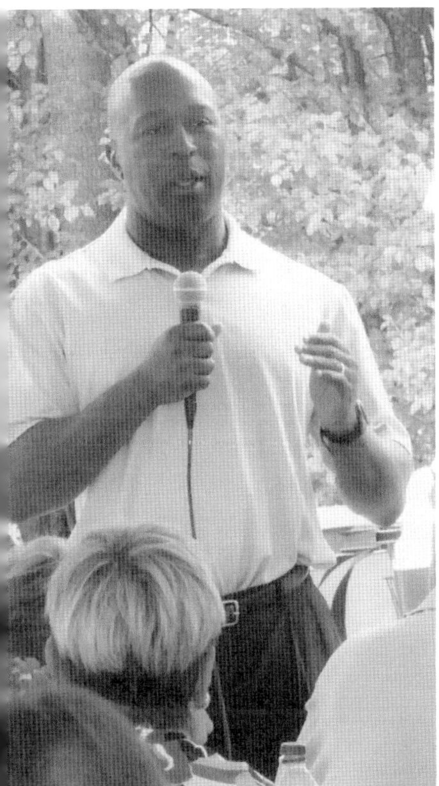

Lovie Smith
Resident Lovie Smith coached the Chicago Bears from 2004 to 2012 and moved to Florida to coach the Tampa Bay Buccaneers in 2014. Named for an aunt, he grew up in Big Sandy, Texas, where he was a star defensive end, linebacker, and safety in high school. He continued his excellence in college. He then coached at Tampa Bay and St. Louis before coming to Chicago, leading the Bears to the Super Bowl in 2007, losing to the Indianapolis Colts. (Joanna Rolek, Chamber of Commerce.)

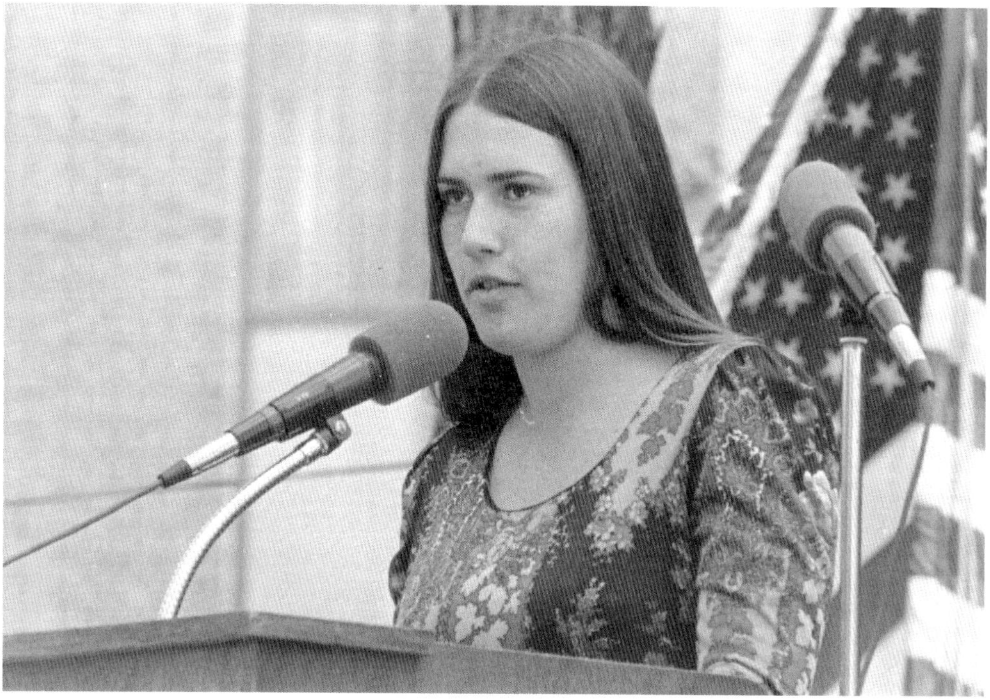

Diana Nyad

"Never, ever give up," and "Find a way," exhorted 60-something Diana Nyad in early September 2013, when she finally completed her goal of swimming from Cuba to Florida, after previous failed attempts—beginning in 1978 at the age of 28. She earned her bachelor of arts degree from Lake Forest College in 1973. A recording-breaking swimmer, an author, and a broadcast journalist, Nyad achieved her feat at an age when many are thinking about retirement. She spoke at the 2015 Lake Forest College commencement. (LFCLASC.)

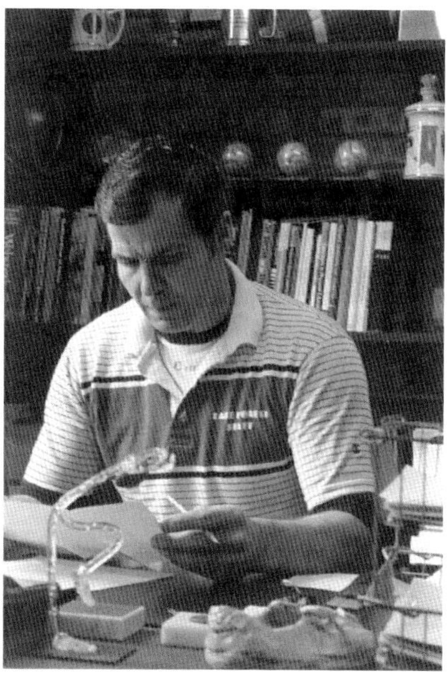

Michael Dau

Dau earned his bachelor of arts degree from Lake Forest College in 1958 and is currently studying for his master of liberal studies degree at the college. He has been a leading figure on campus since the mid-1950s. A star in football then, he and his future wife, Paula, were chosen "Ordinary" couple—an accolade in that conformist era. Dau returned to coach football and, in 2015, continues to head up the college's nationally dominant handball teams. He also has led in maintaining athletics archives and an athletics hall of fame. (LFCLASC.)

BIBLIOGRAPHY

Alderman, Merle N. *Lake Forest.* Art and History Edition. Chicago: American Communities Company, 1916.

Arpee, Edward. *The History of Lake Forest Academy.* Chicago: Ralph Fletcher Seymour, 1944.

———. *Lake Forest, Illinois: History and Reminiscences, 1861–1961.* Enlarged ed. with supplement by Susan Dart. Lake Forest, IL: Lake Forest–Lake Bluff Historical Society, 1991.

Chakoian, Christine. *Worship, Fellowship, and the Work of the Kingdom: The First Presbyterian Church of Lake Forest, Established 1859.* Lake Forest, IL: First Presbyterian Church of Lake Forest, 2013.

Cohen, Stuart. *Inventing the Modern American House: Howard Van Doren Shaw, Architect.* New York: Monacelli Press, 2015.

Coventry, Kim. *From Cairo to Chicago: The Courtship and Marriage of Harold Cornelius Smith & Emily Birnie Smith.* Chicago: 2014.

Coventry, Kim, and Arthur H. Miller. *Walter Frazier: Frazier, Raftery, Orr & Fairbank Architects: Houses of Chicago's North Shore, 1924–1970.* Lake Forest, IL: Lake Forest–Lake Bluff Historical Society, 2009.

Coventry, Kim, Daniel Meyer, and Arthur H. Miller. *Classic Country Estates of Lake Forest: Architecture and Landscape Design 1856–1940.* New York: W.W. Norton, 2003.

Curry, Martha, RSCJ. *Barat College: A Legacy, a Spirit, and a Name.* Chicago: Loyola Press, 2012.

Ebner, Michael H. *Creating Chicago's North Shore: A Suburban History.* Chicago: University of Chicago Press, 1988.

Halsey, John J., ed. *History of Lake County, Illinois.* Chicago: Roy S. Bates, 1912.

Kelsey, Susan L., Arthur H. Miller, and Shirley M. Paddock. *West Lake Forest.* Charleston, SC: Arcadia Publishing, 2012.

Kelsey, Susan L., and Shirley M. Paddock. *Downtown Lake Forest.* Charleston, SC: Arcadia, 2009.

Lake Forest–Lake Bluff Historical Society. *Lake Forest Day: 100 Years of Celebration.* Charleston, SC: Arcadia Publishing, 2008.

Maloney, Cathy Jean. *Chicago and Its Botanic Garden: The Chicago Horticultural Society at 125.* Evanston, IL: Northwestern University Press, 2015.

McCormick, Harriet Hammond. *Landscape Art: Past and Present.* New York: Charles Scribner's Sons, 1924.

Miller, Arthur H., and Shirley M. Paddock. *Lake Forest: Estates, People and Culture.* Charleston, SC: Arcadia Publishing, 2000.

Schulze, Franz, Rosemary Cowler, and Arthur H. Miller. *30 Miles North: A History of Lake Forest College, Its Town, and Its City of Chicago.* Lake Forest: The College, 2000.

Thorne, Martha, ed. *David Adler, Architect: The Elements of Style.* New Haven, CT: Yale University Press, 2002.

Wolner, Edward W. *Henry Ives Cobb's Chicago: Architecture, Institutions, and the Making of the Modern Metropolis.* Chicago: University of Chicago Press, 2011.

INDEX

INDEX

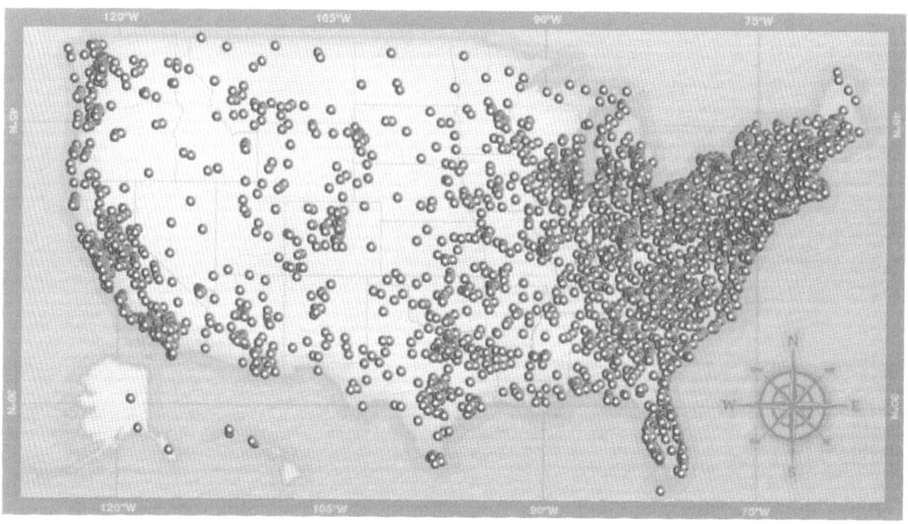